UNDERSTANDING PRINCIPLES OF POLITICS AND THE STATE

Revised Edition

John Schrems

University Press of America,® Inc.
Lanham · Boulder · New York · Toronto · Plymouth, UK

University Press of America,® Inc.
4501 Forbes Boulevard
Suite 200
Lanham, Maryland 20706
UPA Acquisitions Department (301) 459-3366

Estover Road
Plymouth PL6 7PY
United Kingdom

Printed in the United States of America
British Library Cataloging in Publication Information Available

Library of Congress Control Number: 2007929170
ISBN-13: 978-0-7618-3825-8 (paperback : alk. paper)
ISBN-10: 0-7618-3825-2 (paperback : alk. paper)

™ The paper used in this publication meets the minimum requirements of American National Standard for Information Sciences—Permanence of Paper for Printed Library Materials, ANSI Z39.48—1984

Contents

Preface

Understanding Principles of Politics and the State is a work in applied political theory using current political society and politics as its backdrop. It is a revised and updated version of my *Principle of Politics: An Introduction* (Prentice Hall, 1986). There is a danger in such an undertaking because timely illustrations can be quickly outstripped by events. Nonetheless it is hoped that the reader will see the points for what they are and be able to make their own application of the principles to changed circumstances.

The title change is meant to convey the degree to which the work has been updated. In addition to the title and content changes endnotes for each chapter have been replaced with context references, a bibliography listing works cited appears at the end of the book. Furthermore, tables, graphs, and illustrations have been moved to the back of the book as single-page appendices. Cross-references to the appendices are found at the beginning of the index, in the table of contents, and within the text.

In the earlier book I asked for comments from all readers and I extend that invitation again. Comments of any kind are welcome. They can be substantive comments about the contents and the argument or editing corrections. To facilitate your contribution please write to me at: john.schrems@villanova.edu.

Acknowledgements

I have been sustained by in all my efforts by my wife, Mellie Ledesma Tirador Schrems. Steven M Krason of Franciscan University and Edward Lynch of Hollins College have supported and encouraged me over the years. Villanova University staff members Joan Prendergast and Diane Mozzone assisted in manuscript preparation. Rachel Schaller, of Villanova's Information Technologies, provided invaluable assistance on the format specifications of University Press of America. She also set in electronic format the materials in the appendices and helped in the preparation of the table of contents and the index. Margaret King provided copy editing and general editing help. Copy editing assistance and general comments were provided by: Amando S. Dalisay, Gregory C. Gallagher, Richard Michael Lamothe, Kathleen Maloney, Emily A. Martin, John A. Marty, Agatha C. Mingos, Marlee E. Morden, Lauren B. Tacoma, and Montez R. Tyson. Because of their assistance the reader should be able to get to the ideas without working though misspellings, clumsy sentences and other writing problems, although any problems that are left are my responsibility and not theirs. My colleague Hafeez Malik was always available for helpful advice and encouragement. My friend Ernie Giglio, Professor Emeritus at Lycoming College, gave words of encouragement that made a difference in getting this revised edition finalized. Kail C. Ellis, O.S.A., Dean of the College of Arts and Sciences, likewise provided encouragement and assistance.

Judith L. Rothman, Vice President and Director, University Press of America, has been unusually helpful in making it possible for the publication of this revised edition. Page presentation and editing errors in the 2006 edition have been remediated to make this cleaner and slightly slimmer version more acceptable to the reader.

An earlier version was published privately so that those who had been using the first Prentice-Hall edition, even through photocopies, could have an early draft of the update. The loyalty of these users and their support over the years is much appreciated. I hope this University Press of America edition continues to be satisfactory for years to come.

Introduction

For more than five hundred years science has convincingly demonstrated that the sun does not so much set as the earth rotates giving the appearance of sunset as well as sunrise. Still, there are few of us who have not admired, especially while on vacation, a beautiful "sunset." Sunrise and sunset are poetic terms of everyday usage that substitute for what science has told us is real. Even astronauts use the poetic language of sunrise and sunset while in a position better than most to see the actual rotation of the earth. The poetic language of sunsets does not interfere with scientific activity, and science has not changed the poetry of sunsets.

In the political world there is an aversion to the suggestion of discrepancies between common understanding and scientific understanding of social and political life. In non-democratic countries there may be an attempt to portray a superiority of the government's understanding to that of the masses, but that contention is not accepted in democracies. While it may be agreed that there are complexities which are beyond public discernment, democracy nonetheless holds to a position of the people as singular. This role of the people is a challenge for political science since it delves into the political world much as the physical scientist does the physical world. Can there be the same equanimity between scientific and poetic (or public) understanding in matters of political life as that enjoyed in the world of physical science?

There is a myriad of understandings that compete for public hegemony and the public is not even aware that the competition exists. In addition, political science propounds theories and explanations of sharp disagreement and of which the public has sparse knowledge. This is not to say that the public is uninformed. Owing to the widespread growth of communications and literacy, the general level of education and awareness is ever increasing. Though there is a frequent cynicism about the public interest in politics, it is false to say that the public is unaware since lack of interest can as easily follow from awareness as from lack of awareness. Whether previously uninterested, whether aware of theories of politics or not, the sorting through of the variety of topics and theories to be found below can enlighten and bring a reader to a more active interest in an area more fascinating than the ocean or the stars.

A personal experience of the stuff of politics occurs, whether recognized as such or not, in the constant bombardment with elections, security issues, reminders of history, the need for order, engaging in or avoiding law suits, the raising and lowering of taxes, employment concerns, and avoiding poverty or increasing wealth. In these experiences the individual encounters democracy, the state, authority, the legal and logical origin and purpose of the state, constitutionalism, justice, rights, private property, group competition, bureaucracy, and various forms of government. A dramatic difference between the physical world and the political world is that the physical cannot be other than it is while the political is always changing. Because of this difference, science can tolerate and even enjoy the poetic language of sunsets without interference with space exploration. That is not as easy when it comes to political things.

The fixed principles in politics that make possible an ordered understanding, similar to that found in science, to the seeming confusion of the observed world is the focus of this book. Descriptions of political facts swirl endlessly. Newspapers, almanacs, autobiographies, television, and textbooks catalog political facts. An encyclopedic collection of facts is useless without meaningful ways to organize them. Organizing principles to understand politics can be found in considering the goals, purposes, and values of ordinary life as well as the depictions of the political world developed over time from philosophers in the ancient world to contemporary political scientists. Examining these fundamentals gives clarity to facts, events, and theories previously lurking in shadows.

Three different ways to understand the fundamental topics of the state and politics will be presented in this book. Each is a distinct way of looking at the same basic phenomenon. The view reflected in each depiction comes from ancient and modern thought, philosophical and scientific attempts at generalizations, and from the summary conventions of centuries. Each view has consequences affecting ordinary political life today. Emphasis is on principles that underlie and explain. Some topics and discussions initially will be unfamiliar. Some will be old topics treated in a new way. Discernment will come slowly and will give insight to a realm of reality previously unknown. This discernment is necessary since a difference between political science and science is that the outsider knows the limits of personal knowledge in science while in the political world the limits of knowledge are often not recognized and this has personal and public consequence.

The best way to understand politics is to examine competing views and principles. The principles will be examined without forcing a point of view. As the premises and assumptions are examined, the reader can weigh the arguments and come to a personal choice of preference, or come to no preference. Different views of the political world make a difference in how people behave. By this examination, the reader will grasp that politics is important and that the importance flows not from the facts but from the choices in how facts are understood.

The world of political life can change without warning and in no discernible pattern. This means that political science must adjust to the nonstatic political reality instead of the other way around. It is upside down to expect the political world to fit neat scientific requirements of academic categories and concepts. In addition, those who study the political world must contend with the conventional explanations held by the public. Though the public explanations may or may not be correct, they are formidable in their ability to ignore the most perfect of scientifically discovered truths. Political science must know the poetic, the "sunrises" of the language of political life, as well as the competing theories and the still unproven explanations. Unlike the natural sciences that can ignore the poetic versions of reality, political science must be ever mindful of truth as well as the public's perception of it.

What Follows

The chapters of this book are grouped into three. Chapters One, Two and Three get immediately involved with the political world of democracy, the work of political scientists, and then a description of the discipline of political science itself. Chapters Four through Eight examine the state under a number of aspects, from the abstract to the practical. Chapters Nine through Fifteen deal with multiple aspects of governing, from principles of operation to forms of government.

A "plunge in" or immersion approach is used in the discussion of democracy in the first chapter and the description of the political system that follows. Democracy is looked at in terms of three differing views. The reality of politics is experienced in these conflicting views.

In the second chapter the discussion of the political system shows the predominant organization schema used by political scientists in describing the vastness of political reality. Following this immersion with democracy and the political system, the third chapter consists of a discussion of the scope and methods of political science.

It may be argued that the sequence of the first three chapters should be reversed. According to this expectation formal introductions and formal definitions should precede all else on the fear that without starting definitions the discipline will constitute a mountain of data surrounding a vacuum. Such an approach gives more prominence to the discipline than to political reality. Here instead the experiencing of the political world, if merely democracy, and to the depiction of the political world in the political system will engender an appreciation of the variety within the discipline and within real political life. The scope and methods of the discipline described in the third chapter will expose the various understandings of the real world that come about through differing efforts.

The next four chapters deal with four different aspects of the state: its nature, authority, origin, and purpose. Some of the critically important principles for the organization and justification of government are found here. Principles and theories establish parameters and bases for a consideration of the range and limit of governmental activity. Questioning whether government can or should engage in certain activities is no less relevant today than 200 or 2500 years ago. The four aspects of the state and the competing principles by which they can be understood will be viewed as discrete topics. The different purposes of the state, known as collectivism, individualism, and the common good are best appreciated by seeing their roots in the origin and nature of the state and authority. In chapter nine, on "Ideologies," the linking of the four topics and the differing principles will be carried out in more familiar language.

All the elements of ideologies are contained within the principles and the four aspects of the state. Ideologies use information for practical gain and that gain often comes at the expense of accuracy. In the desire for advantage persuasive rhetoric is used. While some attention will be given to the various ideological attempts to explain reality a focus on the fundamental principles will be primary. Rational or logical linkages of one aspect of the state to another are always tentative. Ideologies give the appearance of certainty to topics that are only tenuous. Such appearances are the appeal and the weakness of ideology.

The first goal of this book is the understanding of applied political theory. The nature, authority, origin, and purpose of the state involve the principles upon which political attitudes, policies, and practices are based. Applications and ideologies that are far removed from principles should be approached with caution. From the focus on principles an appreciation is gained for the roots of divergent views in politics. Also gained is an insight into the dynamics and contradictions of the political world. If principles lead to understanding, then that knowledge has been successful. Success in this goal is measured by the logic of what is said.

The different views of the purpose of the state and the different ideologies are theoretical expressions of range and limit of governmental activity. More practical expressions of range and limit are found in the treatment of individuals, groups, and intragovernmental relationships. These more practical concerns take up the rest of the book. While theoretical principles will not be totally discarded, it is important to investigate concrete events separately.

The different views of the purpose of the state affect how governments regard their responsibilities. All rulers claim to be concerned with the common good. What a specific government means by that good, how it is defined, who defines it, and what price must be paid to achieve it are critical in determining good government. These concrete examples require understanding the principles of justice, rights, constitutionalism, the treatment of groups within society, and intragovernmental relationships experienced in presidential or parliamentary forms or federal or unitary forms.

Of interest will be the examination of citizenship and personal rights. Also examined are the relationships between the state and various groupings within the state. Particular attention is given to the relation of religion and politics, church and state. Along the same lines will be a discussion of world government as an expression of interstate relations.

The principle of subsidiarity provides an organizing schema throughout these considerations. Although the term subsidiarity may at first appear unfamiliar, it will be shown to be of common experience. It will ultimately be seen as little more than a way to summarize and describe how the political world of our immediate experience works. The principle is both empirical and normative. It is empirical in the sense that it describes the actual practice of the relationship of the individual and of groups to the state. It also describes major aspects of justice, constitutionalism, and federalism. Subsidiarity is normative in the sense that it can be used as a canon as well as a guide for future understanding. It will be seen that this role as norm and guide applies to undeveloped rights, such as privacy, and to other relationships between the individual and the state. Its presence or absence will serve as a guide for understanding relationships in the political community and as a test for good regimes. It is the ultimate applied political theory.

Justice, rights, constitutionalism, the relationship between a political regime and its cultural setting, the forms of governments and the structural permutations of forms will be described to gain an appreciation of who does what in the political world. They will serve as principles or bases by which to judge acceptable and unacceptable regimes. This practical concern does not mean that the earlier theoretical dimensions are forgotten. The thread of the theoretical will continually appear. Overall politics and the state are approached in terms of both fundamental theoretical and practical principles.

The first chapter starts with the poetic understanding of democracy as "popular control of political leaders." Isn't that the correct understanding? That is precisely the point with which this introduction started, the sorting out of the poetic and the scientific. As the discussion of democracy and the succeeding chapters develop a clearer understanding will unfold of the mixture of everyday poetic language of politics and more careful scientific views. The interrelationship of these views and the inability of one to do without the other will reveal the problematic difference between the political world and that of the natural sciences.

Chapter 1 Democracy: Three Views

Democracy is one of the most common and most fundamental political concepts. This book begins by examining three views of democracy. Since the time of Plato, and before, the relationship between ruler and ruled was questioned. For some, democracy is the entitlement of each citizen to participate in ruling and being ruled. For others it is a device for exploiting the rich by the incompetent masses. Since those ancient times the discussion still resolves itself into variations on those themes.

Though most of the ancient and contemporary discussions dichotomize democracy between rich and poor, elite and mass, informed and uninformed, anti and pro, it is more complicated than that. Few admit to being anti-democratic. Even its most severe critics claim that they represent the true sense of the doctrine. Some totalitarian regimes have claimed to represent its true intention more so than the United States.

The first of the three views of democracy is the one that is most familiar. It is referred to here, as in much of the literature, as the "traditional," "conventional," or "consensus" view. The second view challenges the traditional. It claims to be a rational criticism and finds the traditional view as myth. This challenge agrees with the definition and terms of the traditional view while disagreeing with its conclusions. The third view reexamines the first two to produce a distinct, though not radical, alternative.

Traditional View: Popular Control By The People

The basic terms of the conventional or traditional view of democracy are simple and uncomplicated. It is the democracy of daily conversation, of elections, of editorials and sermons. It has democracy as popular control or rule by the people. Despite its simplicity it is necessary to know what "rule" or "control" means, who the people are, and to what effect they govern. Exploring such concepts leads to a fuller understanding.

Government makes decisions of public consequence and enforces them. Whether democratic, totalitarian, authoritarian, monarchical, or whatever, all governments make decisions and all governments enforce them. Democracy's uniqueness is in the role that the people have. It must be explained since the business of enforcing and administering public policy cannot rest in a day-to-day sense with the public in general. Some fixed government personnel must exist for enforcement responsibilities, foreign policy objectives, economic objectives, or health and welfare programs. These personnel are the police, the diplomatic corps and military services, or, more generally, "the bureaucracy."

Small town democracies and earlier, less complicated eras are thought to be different. In these simpler conditions it is thought that government is or can be closer to the people. In the United States there is a widely held view that the simpler form of democracy existed in earlier times and that we should ever strive to stick close to it. A brief examination of "Jacksonian democracy" and of the New England town meeting will help clarify the terms of democracy. After that the expectations of representation will further elucidate traditional democracy. Along with this will go a consideration of the proper role of the people.

Jacksonian Democracy

The concept of "Jacksonian democracy" (named after Andrew Jackson, seventh president of the United States) maintained that any ordinary person, the so-called "common man," could hold any ordinary governmental office. This common-man rule was to combine with frequent turnover of officeholders in order to bring government closer to the people. This Jacksonian theme of simpler government performed by the average citizen can be discerned in populist campaign material of the recent past and even in the sophisticated political literature of contemporary political parties. Historical evidence reveals, however, that beginning with Jackson himself and lasting for many years this language was a camouflage for a voracious spoils system that replaced government workers in the previous administration with the supporters of the successful challenger. Jackson's effective political rhetoric had labeled these supporters as the "common man."

When many job applicants who flooded Washington after Jackson's victory did not get a job they were not told to return in six months to replace those originally selected. There is no evidence of an attempt to institutionalize "Jacksonian democracy" during the Jackson years (1829-1837) by legislating strict limits on the terms of all governmental offices. Such a limit would have mandated a system of rotation and would have legally expanded the number of people who directly participate in government. Jacksonian practice, as opposed to the "theory" of Jacksonian democracy, is consonant with the fact that the business of administering and enforcing government obligations cannot rest with the public in general.

The recognition of the reality of practical job effectiveness over the Jacksonian theory of frequent turnover found expression later in the professionalization of government employment in merit selection civil service. It took until 1883 for this to be accomplished but eventually civil service replaced the earlier spoils system. The professionalized civil service is what is referred to, in common terminology, as the "bureaucracy." It is through these civil servants that the administrative and enforcement functions of government are accomplished today. The bureaucracy may be either the small town clerk or the nearly three million national civil servants. In both instances individuals of experience continue to hold their position while they remain effective, are forced out by elections, or until they choose to leave government.

Town Meeting Democracy

The democracy of the small town is sometimes viewed as an idyllic exception to the hard practicality of the representative democracy. Ancient Greek city-states, Swiss cantons, and New England towns are offered as examples of the simpler and more personal sovereignty. Here the people are said to rule "directly." Because of the smaller size of the jurisdiction the people are said to be able to run themselves directly without the need of elected officials. Still, a town clerk oversees the day-to-day running of local affairs. Every community must have a clerk who carries on daily functions and who, not incidentally, is largely responsible for preparing the agenda of the annual meeting. Furthermore, the very town meetings are representative rather than truly direct. No matter what the composition of the meeting in terms of age, sex, or property holding it represents all the members of the community. Those present represent themselves as well as those not present and those below the age limit for attendance.

Despite the occasional news story, usually in the spring of the year, about the convening of an almost idyllic town meeting, the reality of it is otherwise. No one can maintain that this claimed direct democracy has no administrative or executive function. All governments must delegate implementing functions. Ancient Athens, another idealized version of direct democracy, had its popular assembly. It also had a policy-making council as well as a special institution of independent and influential generals. The New England town had, and has, its clerk and, as always, its town fathers. The reality of town leaders, clerks, generals, and councils contradicts the imagined self-management of direct democracy. Despite the claims to the contrary, direct democracies are not an exception to either the representative or administrative roles found in all governments.

Public's Role in Democracy

Since enforcement responsibilities cannot be the public's claim, democracy's distinguishing characteristic must be found elsewhere. The legislative function is more important. The public's concern is whether a program should be undertaken, not how it is to be administered. The preservation of natural resources is policy. The implementation of environmental protection law is the administrative issue. Administrators or experts may point out the wisdom of the law; the final decision as to whether government should assume the task rests with the people.

To this democratic imperative the question follows about how the popular decision-making is to be carried out? What are the procedures and machinery through which the policy framing, legislative, function is accomplished? The answer is found in the system of elected representatives. Democracy is more specifically "representative democracy."

In the history of local government in the United States, town meetings were gradually replaced by what are called "representative town meetings." What most American towns have today in their city council, town board of commissioners, or whatever, is still technically and legally a "representative town meeting." The procedures and machinery through which citizen involvement takes place is generally referred to as representative government. Individual representatives are periodically elected for some limited and fixed term. Many variations of length of terms, number and responsibilities of offices and qualifications occur. The feature of the many electing the few is essential. It is this characteristic of elected representatives making the legally binding decisions for the community that distinguishes democracy from all other forms of government.

The Role of the Elected Representative

Important questions arise about the role of the representative. By what process should the representative make decisions? What relationship should exist with the constituents who elect the representative? Once elected, must the representative keep in close contact with the district, not just for the practical matter of being reelected, in order to know the views of the constituents on the topics of the next legislative vote? Is the representative bound to vote according to the preference of the district if that preference is known? What is the obligation of the representative if he or she holds a view that is opposed to the preference of the district?

Factually, there is a close correlation between voting records of representatives and the attitudes of constituents. The lack of immediate knowledge on specific issues is offset by the close correlation between the voting record of the elected representative and the characteristics of the constituency. Coming from similar social, economic, and organizational groups, conflicts seldom occur between the elected representative and the district.

The crucial question about the role of the representative surfaces when there is a known disagreement between the district and the representative and all sides are fully aware of the disagreement. The answer can be put in terms of two theories: virtual representation, and actual representation.

Virtual Representation

The word "virtual" means that physical characteristics are present but substance or essence is missing. Computer games use "virtual reality." Sporting events or find-and-attack competitive games are created for purposes of entertainment far removed from actual physical combat. In virtual representation the elected official, not the district itself, determines the district's interests. Policy decisions are made in terms of the representative's own judgment of what is in the best interest for the constituents. It is not the constituents' actually stated preference that determines the vote. In this way the representative acts as a trustee for the district. This theory is sometimes called the "trustee" representation.

The classical argument for this theory of representation was stated by Edmund Burke, a member of Parliament from 1765 to 1795, in his "Speech to the Electors of Bristol." Burke argued that the member owes to the constituents his or her best judgment, whether it agrees with theirs or not. The representative should give great weight to the views of the constituent, but in final analysis the studied judgment of the representative must be the basis of his or her vote.

Such a view is not just abstract political theory or history. It is still part of political life. In the 1978 debates in the U.S. Senate over ratification of the Panama Canal Treaties, Senate Majority Leader (at the time) Robert C. Byrd (D., W. Va.), in supporting the treaties, invoked Burke saying, as quoted in *The New York Times* on February 10 of that year, "I'm not going to betray my responsibility to my constituents. I owe them not only my industry but my judgment. That's why they sent me here." Byrd added, "If I were to make a judgment based on the names on a petition or on the mail, what we'd need is a computer or a set of scales to represent the people of West Virginia." Numerous instances of Byrd's argument could be found at any time if there were politicians bold enough (and secure enough in their concern for reelection) to so reveal what they do. That there are few who make such public statements does not obviate the argument that they must frequently act as Byrd did.

Actual Representation

Actual representation, the counterpoint to the position of Burke and Byrd, is present also in all legislative debates. In the Canal debates a senator from a neighboring state who was opposed to Byrd's position argued that senators must vote as their constituents would vote. He maintained that they have a responsibility to listen to the voice of the people and that when the overwhelming majority of the people are opposed, it should be persuasive. In actual representation the representative must vote as the constituents would *actually* vote. Hilaire Belloc and Cecil Chesterton gave classical articulation to the actual representation argument when they argued that if the representative is in the habit of voting "Yes" when the people would say "No" then the representative is but an oligarch. For Belloc and Chesterton the representative is merely a mouthpiece deriving authority from the constituents.

The classical language of the debate between virtual and actual representation come to the surface only rarely. However, the essential ingredients are present in all major political issues. To understand democracy the question of the proper role of the representative must be resolved.

The answer to the question of the role of the representative must not be distracted by speciously practical concerns like the need or desire of incumbents to be reelected. Nor should attention be diverted by the knowledge or, more likely, lack of knowledge on the part of the public of what the representative is doing on most issues. The question of virtual representation versus actual representation should be answered in context of the vote itself. Is it right or wrong to vote contrary to the wishes of the constituents? This is especially critical in situations where the action taken is irrevocable, as in starting or ending a war, disposing of lands held in public trust, ending a life, or changing constitutional or institutional structures. In more relaxed situations the issue is merely academic.

Common democratic theory, the view of Belloc and Chesterton, holds that actual representation is "the only democratic theory of representation." For the conventional, traditional, consensus view of democracy when there is a conflict between the representative and the constituents, "the verdict of the majority ought to prevail." This is popular control.

Popular Control

Popular control is not naive, nor is it a rhetorical construct, a strawman, to be later rejected. Furthermore, it does not ignore the possibility that the public may be wrong and the system thereby weakened. The traditional view has optimism to it based upon a profound faith in mankind. Expressed by long recognized thinkers and leaders such as Locke, Rousseau, Jefferson, Madison, Jackson, and Lincoln, modern democratic theory is understood to maintain that the people are a better judge of their interests than a ruler who claims to make judgments for them.

The contention is that the individual and the community ought to make judgments on matters affecting their own lives and that the experience of making such judgments will improve over time. Letting surrogates of the public, whether the representative or the dictator, make the decisions "until the individual or the community matures," as is so often the rationale of authoritarian decision makers, only delays maturity.

There was a clamor for "participatory democracy" in the United States and elsewhere during the 1960s and 1970s. It continues today although not in the publicly disruptive manner of the earlier period. Public memory of the 1960s is often limited to the protests about the Vietnam War. In reality the political movement that surrounded those protests was broader in content and time. An expression of the principles of participatory democracy is found in the organization called Students for a Democratic Society, known as the *SDS*. Their goals and principles were set forth in a document called the "Port Huron Statement," written by Tom Hayden in 1962. The SDS was an amalgam of students and others of "the New Left" who gained notoriety in anti-Vietnam war protests and in riots at the Democratic National Party convention in Chicago in 1968. The date of the Port Huron Statement indicates, however, that the SDS's founding preceded the Vietnam War as an immediate issue.

The Port Huron Statement voiced concern with many particular issues: the seniority system of selecting congressional committee chairpersons, which had led to Southern conservative domination in Congress; the localized nature of the political party system; racial discrimination and gerrymandering in voter registration and districting procedures; an enormous lobby force selfishly distorting national interests for business interests; and political campaigns of personality and image instead of campaigns of issues and options. These issues were legitimate democratic concerns irrespective of immediate partisan consequences.

It is fascinating to note that all the areas mentioned have been changed since 1962 and most of the changes have been in the direction advocated by the SDS. The fundamental point about participatory democracy is an enduring quality that links it to traditional democratic values. The SDS spoke of a basic "faith" in the worth of the individual, similar to the faith expressed by Rousseau, by the authors of the Declaration of Independence, and by Lincoln in his belief that not all of the people can be fooled all of the time. The SDS's call for participatory democracy started with a regard for men "as infinitely precious and possessed of unfulfilled capacities for reason, freedom, and love." They see men as having potential for creativity rather than violence and unreason.

A disclaimer follows the claim of man's worth that to so view man is not to "deify" him. Instead it is to have faith in his potential on the basis of which can be established a democracy of individual participation. Thus they see "participatory democracy" as one in which individuals share in those social decisions determining the quality and direction of their lives.

The SDS was not widely applauded at the time because of accompanying rhetoric and disruptiveness in their behavior, which stirred, and often rightly so, negative reactions. As a result the common reaction was to classify the group as radical. Since many years have passed and the passions of the 1960s have waned, the statement of the SDS can be looked at with less emotion; their positions can be seen as a version of the ancient academic distinction between elite guidance and popular control.

Sentiments of faith in the individual, human potential, and collective good sense are constants in the literature on democracy. It is a simply stated view that in matters that vitally concern the community the consensus of common opinion is a wiser and safer guide to decisions than the dominating leadership of one person or of a select class. In the words of Schmandt and Steinbicker (*Fundamentals of Government*, 218), this view flows from an act of faith in the abiding good sense of the average human and in the view that in a society of rational beings, the judgment and experience of the many will, in most instances, be superior to the judgment and experience of the few. Hence they hold, the verdict of the majority ought to prevail in case of conflict. Expressed in their textbook from the early 1950s, those sentiments were followed by the intriguing acknowledgment that the device of the majority, which ought to prevail, is a "practicable rule of law" that is, like other human instrumentalities, "subject to weaknesses and imperfections."

Schmandt and Steinbicker's view stands in contrast to the decade later Port Huron Statement, that acknowledges no weaknesses and imperfections, save for the "potential" of violence. The former work stated that "the people" are subject to error "through ignorance, shortsightedness, prejudice, passion, and hysteria." This litany of error did not dissuade their democratic faith and instead they maintained that in the long run self-interest and happiness keep humans on the right course. The judgments of the few are faulted by the continuing temptations of power, position, and wealth. The 1960s proponents of participatory democracy did not mention these fallibilities and instead focused on the positive democratic values.

The values of individual worth and collective wisdom are found in Aristotle's *Politics,* (III, 1281b-1281a, 25), one of the earliest full treatises on democratic government. In an analogy to music he commented, the many are better judges than a single man of music and poetry, some understand one part, and some another, and among them they understand the whole. And, he added, in the application to democracy, the many, of whom each individual is an ordinary person, when they meet together may very likely be better judges than the few good. "May" and "very likely" are important qualifiers, showing a hesitancy that acknowledged the error and imperfect judgment common to humankind. Aristotle points to a danger in allowing the mass of people to share the offices of state since their folly will lead them into error, and their dishonesty into crime, yet, he also warns that there is danger in excluding large numbers of people from these duties since a state in which many poor men are excluded from office will necessarily be full of enemies.

The latter concern about creating potential enemies is a weak endorsement for democracy. Nonetheless his support is strong when he comments, that if the people are not utterly degraded, although individually they may be worse judges than those who have special knowledge, as a body they are as good or better. He comments that the artists themselves judge not all arts solely or best, that the resident of a house is as good a judge as the builder and the guest will judge better of a feast than the cook. In other words, politics is always judged by the recipients of policy and is not to be judged just by the policy planners. Practitioners and students of politics would do well to remember this.

There are many contemporary mechanisms for the role of the people, for the majority to prevail. Regular and periodic elections are obvious examples. Another is the "initiatives" where the public can in some jurisdictions get policy issues placed on the ballot through petition. Through the latter process the legislature is bypassed and "the people's will" is expressed directly in law. Examples are found in every election. The referendum is another illustration of direct majority preference. Here the legislative body, in some jurisdictions, chooses to or is forced to present some issues for public ballot approval. The most obvious exercise is in state constitution and local charter amendments. It also comes in some school districts, where local property tax increases are restricted unless approved by referendum. Some jurisdictions limit liquor sales in the same way.

Majority assertions are also found in petitions, polls, and constituent surveys. Citizenry interest and advocacy groups conduct surveys claiming to reflect majority preference. Such efforts are prominent today in the area of environmental policies. Though the effectiveness and accuracy of these mechanisms may be challenged on several grounds, they are incontestably expressions of popular feelings about policy. The extent to which legislators are influenced by surveys sponsored by advocacy groups or by other manifestations of public opinion is open to debate. Elected officials see the public relations merit in soliciting the views of the constituents and then publicizing the results. The findings, not surprisingly, correspond with the official's inclinations.

Public citizen lobbying organizations are founded to promote particular political and social interests. These organizations such as environmental groups, anti-smoking, mothers against drunk driving, handgun control, defense of owning firearms, promoting the interests of retired persons seek to influence policy makers as well as the public. They contact officials, place advertisements in the print media, radio, television, and on the Internet. These groups see themselves as filling a vital public need, as linchpins in the democratic process. They view the accomplishment of their particular objectives as fulfilling the promise of democracy. They practice a quasi-democracy within their own organizations by referenda of their members about preferences. Members are asked their preference for emphasis among preselected issues. The central staff of the organization does the selecting. It could hardly be done otherwise. Such a process is reminiscent of the earlier observation about the town clerk preparing the agenda for the annual meeting in the claimed directly democratic New England town.

These public interest organizations as practical manifestations of the theory of participatory democracy advocate that decision-making of basic social consequence be carried on by public groupings and that the economy should be open to democratic participation and subject to democratic social regulation. These words echo SDS founder Tom Hayden's organization, Campaign for Economic Democracy. CED sought more democratic control of the economy. Hayden's position and the activities of the other groups clearly reflect the fundamental understanding that (1) the common and universal dimension to the democratic formula is popular control, (2) that "popular" is used in the sense of widespread, and (3) that "control" means that the verdict of the majority should prevail.

THE SECOND VIEW: CHALLENGE TO POPULAR CONTROL

Some scholars describe democracy as a myth or an illusion. One even suggests that popular control over political leaders is the sustaining myth of democracy. That is the view of Gabriel Almond (*Comparative Politics*, 186), past president of the American Political Science Association, no frantic revolutionary, instead the quintessence of the academic establishment. Similarly, Robert Dahl, another past president of the Association, found that the ancient myth about the concern of citizens with the life of the democratic city was false in the case of New Haven, as it may have been, he said, in Athens. A French political theorist and analyst of bureaucracy, Jacques Ellul, referred to the "illusion" that the citizen can master or control or change the state through political channels. Discussion of these challenges will come shortly.

There have always been challenges to the concept of democracy. Plato, Aristotle's teacher, operated from the perspective that philosophy ought to prevail and he derisively referred to the incompetence of public opinion. The philosophy of democracy must be examined as well as external challenges to it such as Nazism, Fascism, Marxism, and Communism. Other "ideologies" and even some religions seem to challenge democracy. Some use democracy for their own purposes. Fascism, for example, directly challenges democracy and the competence of the people but it uses democracy to gain office. Marxism, where it has arisen in the past and even in some contemporary versions, claims to be the epitome of democracy though in many instances it refuses to use democracy once it comes to power. It claims that the Western forms of government are really anti-democratic and that only with the demise of these pretenders will true democracy prevail.

The questions raised by the external challenges cannot be settled until after many other topics are discussed. Views on the state, the treatment of citizens, constitutions, and forms of government give perspective for judgment. It will take the rest of this book to gain that perspective.

Proponents of the conventional view of democracy hold that in the long run the judgment of the people is a sounder basis for decisions than the judgment of the few. The preference for the majority rests on a basic faith in the average person and a basic distrust in position or office holding. It is precisely to the competence of the average person for decision-making and judgment that the challenge to democracy is raised. The very faith in the people and the capability of the democratic system as well as the ability of the system to register its will are challenged as myth. In coldly logical terms the challenge appears irrefutable. The solid case for popular control made previously will be used against it.

Argument against Popular Control

The argument is simple: The people lack sufficient information and knowledge. Instead, those who are informed should control. Three reasons why the people are not informed are given by Gabriel Almond, in his *Comparative Politics*: the technological complexity of most matters of importance, the difficulty of assessing responsibility because of the inability to establish definite cause-and-effect relationships, and the remoteness of the public from most political issues except those that affect them personally.

Technological complexity: Issues such as American foreign policy, international and domestic economics, long term energy policy, environment problems, urban bankruptcy, state budget deficits, Medicaid, health care and prescriptions-drug concerns, social security's stability, continuing concern with crime, or concern to balance fighting terrorism and protecting civil liberties are challenges to popular control. Experts in one field have difficulty enough assessing responsibility, or understanding technical problems, or keeping abreast of issues in fields of other experts. To claim that "technical" matters are "the people's" responsibility reveals its impossibility by definition. Such complexity prevails that it can be stated syllogistically:

> In democracy the people should decide everything except what is technically complex,
>
> But everything is technically complex,
>
> Therefore the people should decide nothing.

It is unreasonable to expect the people to be adequately informed on technical issues. This is the dilemma of democracy in its claim of popular control.

Assessing responsibility: Complexity in all things political makes it impossible for the average citizen to sort out the parties involved in any particular policy area and to ascertain who is primarily responsible for things going wrong or right. We know that elections are frequently influenced by how the public feels about the conditions of the economy and how it seems to be affecting them, but who can the public hold responsible for the conditions of the economy? The President and his fiscal recommendations? The Congress with its budgetary procedures? The Federal Reserve Board with its independent monetary policies? The Democratic Party with its spending proposals? The Republican Party with its tax attitudes? The international economy? The capitalist system? The "business cycle"? Before some "rascal" currently holding office can be kicked out, it ought to be necessary to establish some semblance of a cause-and-effect relationship between that rascal and the condition of concern.

Although everyone claims responsibility when things are going well, everyone can disclaim responsibility, and correctly so, when things are going poorly.

Wars are a primary example. Presidents, generals, and congressional leaders take credit when things go well. When things go poorly each leader and each institution has many fingers of blame pointed in different directions. The Vietnam experience, now of mostly unhappy memory, is still a compelling example of the inability of fixing responsibility. The arrow of responsibility can be pushed back from the "military industrial complex," to Congress's original hawkish reception of the administration's initiatives, to a "cold warrior" Secretary of State, to a "macho" President Johnson, who did not want to be the first in American history to suffer defeat. That arrow of responsibility, according to exponents of psycho-history, might be pushed to the president's mother who planted those feelings in her childrearing practices. Though that string of responsibility seems far-fetched, some follow its full length, while others for no more obvious reasons stop earlier in the path to fix responsibility.

The string of whom to hold responsible for the Vietnam policy is more than curious because most of the blame has been centered within the boundaries of the United States. Ironically this focus was encouraged at the time by the practice in testimony before congressional hearings of constantly referring to "the other side" without specifically identifying the other side. The American public knew there was an "other side" but they were never helped by their government in identifying exactly who that was. Thus with the opponent identified as an abstraction, it was easier to fix responsibility on more concrete officials within the United States. In the more recent conflict of terrorism, al-Qaeda, and Iraq, some of the information is sufficiently nebulous and the central figures are shrouded in mystery that it becomes easier once again to focus attention on American mistakes.

Only years after the Vietnam conflict ended was information forthcoming about the amount of assistance provided by the Soviet Union or China to the North Vietnamese and the Vietcong. There was no general public awareness of the rivalry between the two suppliers. Having this information would give precision to the "other side." In 1979 the American public learned that Peking, from 1964 to 1971, sent 300,000 soldiers to Vietnam, including antiaircraft crews. Interestingly it was China and not the United States that supplied this information and did so not as a service to the American public but as a diplomatic tactic in its own border conflict with Vietnam. Furthermore, even these numbers are no basis for establishing that China was the principal supplier since the Soviet figures have never been given. By the time this information became known the public had more immediate interests and found Vietnam once again an abstract historical topic. Only diehards in various parts of America would continue to focus on the issue and they had little chance of arousing public interest.

A credible explanation as to why the United States did not attempt to fix blame by specifying who the other side was during the days of the conflict is that to do so could have resulted in an undesirable escalation of the conflict. Three decades after the end of the war it is still legitimate to ask if anything useful, or (more likely) harmful, would follow a full disclosure of the respective degree of involvement of the other powers. A disclosure could kindle resentments and adversely affect current foreign policy efforts. Today both Russia and

China are important in areas of United States foreign policy in ways unimaginable a decade or two ago. To "set the record straight" has an abstract appeal that is more likely to be practically foolish.

The problem of information in the Vietnam example or with Iraq at the present constitutes a double dilemma for the open democracy. Maintaining limits on information given to the public and being taken advantage of by the enemy, or supplying the information and escalating the conflict is the first dilemma. The second is the propensity of inevitably finding someone to blame at home if a clearly recognizable and identified foreign adversary cannot be found versus the possibility of irresponsibly blaming someone abroad to distract attention at home. Vietnam, Iraq, or any area of foreign policy dramatically demonstrates the complexity of the issues the public is supposed to assess and the dependence of the public on information supplied by the government.

Even if accurate information on foreign policy is available the public still is incapable of deciphering it since the issue goes beyond the immediate country of concern. Strategic choices of allies, former allies, former enemies, conflicts in and between developing countries, traditional rivalries, the need for strategic materials, and economic competition are involved in almost all foreign policy issues. On such choices even the experts disagree. A further dimension is the advantage on the part of enemies that do not have to pay attention to public displeasure because their media and public opinion are largely controlled or stifled. For the United States to have its policies freely debated can handicap it in comparison with its foes.

A new phase of the concern about information began with the war in Iraq. There, though the openness of debate was as confusing as or more confusing than ever prior to the war, public saturation with information during the war became the order of the day. Initiating a practice of embedded reporters, where members of the media were attached to military field units, the public had news from the military front twenty-four hours a day. Newspaper and radio reporting on the war increased to unprecedented degrees. Live television pictures from the battlefields and cities of Iraq were available as the bombs exploded. Though some of the television reporting seemed repetitive the public appeared unsated. How the public could translate their knowledge into practical policy terms remains far from clear and once the opening phase of the war ended the dearth of manageable information returned. What the American public can discern in Iraq's domestic situation is as much a mystery as any other part of the world.

Public Remoteness: The third reason why people are not informed, according to Almond, is remoteness. Issues of war and peace arouse the public even though intellectually the cause-and-effect relationships and the facts are unmanageable. Even with massive news coverage there is remoteness because of the lack of personal experience. Emotional closeness of war when family and friends are involved makes the issues no less remote in analytical terms. Though the public knows more they remain distant from contextual justifications. They are even more remote from the ultimate dimension of paying for the sizeable and complex undertaking.

There are many other issues about which the public is similarly remote. The general public is usually uninformed about issues of farm policy unless they live on a farm or unless the price of beef rises inordinately. With more than seventy-five percent of the population in urban areas and no major food supply crises issues of farm subsidies, though still real to suppliers, receive little public attention. Likewise the public is uninterested in dam and water projects unless they live in an unpredictable flood area or until they suffer from drought. In time of flood or drought the general public's concern is too late and that concern will abate when the immediate situation passes. Few people make the connection to the rise of the requirement to carry flood insurance, after floods hit distant regions, to government regulations intended to help insurance companies. Consumers passively go along with such regulations that are in effect a tax without discussion. While business scandals are additional areas that affect the public and individuals as they lose jobs or pensions the public remains remote because of an inability to perceive what can be done even when it affects their own family. Additionally, for the public the whole area of business, finance, trade, and the economy in general are all remote in the sense that while everyone is affected very few can grasp what is going on.

The remoteness factor reinforces technical complexity and assessment of responsibility. Together they argue the inability of the public to control leaders and policy. If the public cannot know and understand the issues it is neither possible nor reasonable for them to control the political leaders who decide policy.

Popular control is further exacerbated by the inability to know exactly what decisions the political leaders have made. Thousands of decisions are made and the public might be aware of ten. And, those ten are the ones that the politician or that politician's opponent chooses to bring to the public's attention. An additional consideration is that the public does not know when it will receive information or whether the information it receives is correct. A barrage of information comes at election time from candidate and opponent, an unreliable time for assessment of facts and responsibilities.

The Election Myth

It may appear cynical but there is an element of truth in the observation that what takes place in an election is less the dissemination of information than the reversing of roles as in the Caribbean carnival. In carnival the world is symbolically turned upside down for a day, royalty parade as peasants and peasants parade as royalty. In elections voters become rulers for a day and the rulers become simple voters. Even as elections are portrayed as serious business, they take on a dimension of great fun where much hoopla is found on television and in the press and radio. After the polls close on Election Day political party workers come to the "party." The "party" takes place whether the workers' candidate wins or loses.

For the winning candidate the voters are wise, attentive to issues, responsible, and selective. Losing candidates regard their supporters in that same way with an opposite view of the public who voted against them. The view that the public is not wise, selective, attentive, and responsible, finds support in the contradictory votes cast by any particular community for President, governor, senator, congressperson, and state and local offices. A community rarely picks candidates for each of the offices from the same political party or with the same liberal or conservative outlook. Usually the results show a mixture of winning parties, outlooks, and persuasions. There are few states in which all the congressional, senatorial, and gubernatorial office holders are from the same political party. The same inconsistency is true within the smaller jurisdictions of each of the states.

Election hoopla is found at political conventions noted by overflowing rhetoric and planned spontaneous demonstrations. In his nomination acceptance speech at the Democratic Convention in 1972 George McGovern quoted Woodrow Wilson saying, "Let me inside the government, and I will tell you what goes on there." In the atmosphere of distrust and suspicion during the Vietnam and Watergate times the promise of openness brought a thunderous response from the partisan crowd. The statement by McGovern and the response is a startling admission for candidate and audience. Ironically, the audience responded approvingly to the promise sixty years after Wilson had made the same promise.

Almost all candidates running for office claim that unlike the past they will let their constituents know what is going on. The candidate wants to establishe-subservience to popular control. The promise, however, confirms the basic point that the public lacks adequate information to assess responsibility and to understand the technical complexity of particular issues. Remoteness from all but the most immediate issues is found not only in the substantive policy areas but also in the voting process itself.

The pledge to inform the public is consonant with another phenomenon, that of candidates running against the office they seek. Candidates, even those who have been there for many years, present themselves as outsiders running against "Washington," that is, they run against the Washington mind set, or against the respective state capitals or state legislatures. The outsiders are saying that they will share with the public the information previously withheld and that they will do things in a new and different way for the benefit of the constituents. The consistent success of these campaigns validates the challenge to democracy on information grounds.

Broad based citizen's lobbies like Common Cause espouse popular control. They present themselves as seeking "government of the people" and opposing government by special interests. Built into their claim is the assumption that government is not currently "of the people" but is controlled "by special interests." The phenomenon of interest group activities involves a give-and-take process for reaching public policy decisions. Within this phenomenon there is a debate between "pluralists," who advocate the interest group competition process for making public policy decisions, and "anti-elitists," who distrust the interest groups. The anti-elitists view the interest groups as infringing on the primacy of popular control. In this debate both sides accept the same view of democracy. Both favor a decision-making process of public input and differ only on who is to be its preferred provider.

Pluralists prefer interest group rivalry as the major determinant of policy. They join the anti-elitists in opposing "authoritative" policy making by "government experts." On the other side, anti-elitists want popular determination of policy. The public interest groups and the regular interest groups urge their members to speak as "the public." Members are not directed to say, "As one of 250,000 national members of group X . . ." or "As one of 1.8 million members nationally of group Y. . . ." Each group member writes or speaks on behalf of the group and of the public even though constituting an extremely small percentage of either. Their claim to being heard is on the grounds that democracy is popular control and they are the public. Democracy's illusion or myth is manifest in these claims since the members have no more technical knowledge of a particular policy area than what is contained in an "action alert" from the group's officers or a monthly newsletter discussing current issues. For an individual to be one newsletter closer to an issue provides no depth of understanding.

French author Jacques Ellul in *The Political Illusion* observes that the people influence the course of political events but their influence is all for the worse since if the public is not aroused nothing can be done and, in his view, if it is aroused, moderate, equitable, and provident solutions are no longer possible. His comments, though cynical, question both public influence and political leadership. Leadership is ultimately to be found in neither the public or in elected officials. Ellul finds it in hidden elites of the bureaucracy, those who handle day-to-day responsibilities without fanfare or public awareness.

Since the public cannot control the specific policy decisions or the decision makers by electing them on any semblance of full knowledge, elite guidance is the only interpretation of democracy available. In democracy elites function by way of increasingly expensive elections instead of by way of private appointments in authoritarian systems or blood relationships in hereditary monarchies. The logical criticism of popular control claims that traditional democracy has its own elite, usually elite of wealth, even though it may be well hidden. Elite leaders need not know or acknowledge their elite character since the democratic myth is so ingrained. In Almond's words it is a "sustaining myth." Even when elite guidance comes disguised as virtual representation it still means that the public does not control. The verdict of the majority does not prevail.

The Third View: Popular Selection

If popular control is the essential and defining difference of democracy from other forms of government, then the lack of popular control relegates democracy into elite guidance. Elite guidance, whether by virtual representation, benign monarch or self-serving tyrant, is juxtaposed with popular control. The critics and proponents of democracy speak exactly in these terms. Popular control and participatory democracy's advocates see themselves at odds with power rooted in possession, privilege, or circumstance. Both defenders of democracy and its critics see democracy as the verdict of the majority, that is, of actual representation. That polarization must be resolved.

Central to the preceding discussion is its form as two equally unacceptable alternatives: "Yes or no, have you stopped breaking the law?" "Yes or no, have you stopped cheating on your taxes?" Given the choices there is no acceptable answer. It may be best to answer questions of that nature with a personally chosen alternative. Politicians accused of never answering direct questions, have developed the skill of regarding all questions as "Yes/No alternatives." For that reason they respond to questions by talking around the subject instead of jumping into the questioner's alternatives. Reporters, whose job it is to ask such questions, admire the politician's skill at avoidance of their traps.

Who said that democracy requires public control? The answer seems to be that the traditional view requires it and all the critics do the same. The focus is on control, the verdict of the majority, and public determination of policy. The focus is the problem.

Aristotle states a simpler view when he classifies democracy as "the good form of government by the many." Some writers look at Aristotle with historical interest only; some have formed a prejudice and give him even less attention. Nonetheless, if what is said is of value it should be considered no matter who said it and when it was said. The classification of democracy as good government by the many distinguishes it from other forms. No mention of control is made. This classification differentiates democracy from other good forms of government in terms of numbers, that is, the number of persons eligible to participate in the ruling process. Democracy is of the many. Monarchy and aristocracy are of one or few.

Another distinguishing quality in Aristotle's classification is with respect to the "good" as opposed to "bad." The bad forms are tyranny, oligarchy, and mob rule. The feature of bad versus good turns on whether the rule is for the sake of the good of the people or for the benefit of the ruling person or group. The monarch rules for the good of the people and the tyrant's rule is only self-serving. Aristocracy is for the common good and oligarchy for the benefit of the few. Democracy and mob rule are likewise opposed. A modern prejudice exists against anything that does not proclaim itself democratic, but that implies that anything before modern democratic times could not have been good. The "monarch" need not be a king or queen. It can be any one person who rules for the good of the community. During World War II Winston Churchill was in many respects a monarch, one man who ruled for the sake of the good of the people. England, the Crown, Europe, and most nations might not have been saved except for his single-handed efforts to gather many to the cause of defeating Hitler. Many historical governments could be looked at as serving the same beneficent role. Whether any contemporary regime might be looked at in this way will not be entertained here.

Monarchy and aristocracy are usually referred to as "elite" because of the limits to the number of persons eligible to seek office. If only the oldest male or female heir of the current ruler or if only those who have an exceptionally large amount of property are eligible for office, then the mass of citizens are excluded. In Aristotle's qualification criteria democracy is "non-elite." It is defined in terms of numbers of people eligible for office. On that initial criterion if the office holders are selected from the many and changed on a fixed schedule by rolling dice the democratic form would be distinguished from the other forms where fewer are eligible, fewer participate, and the turnover is infrequent. The essential character of democracy is in the selection criteria where the many are eligible to rule and in fact rule by reason of frequent turnover. It is precisely this democracy, people rule, as prescribed by the constitution of Athens that was so much discussed by Socrates, Plato, and Aristotle. In ancient times officeholders could be chosen by lot. Modern democracies prefer elections to the roll of dice.

The criteria of rotation and numbers give expression to democracy as the form where all are eligible to rule and all select the rulers. The term "all" actually means "the many" insofar as children and non-citizens, though part of all, are not in the group of those eligible or those selecting rulers. Earlier forms of democracy that excluded women from an active political role were nonetheless democratic in the sense that all of the adults thought at the time to be eligible were in the selection pool to rule and to select. In today's democracy women are included in the community of eligible participants but children and non-citizens are not. And so the basic distinction between the many and the whole community, the all, is retained. For this reason it was pointed out above in the context of town meeting democracy that they all were representative since even the popular assembly of all adult men and women would represent the other members of the community, children and invalids, for example, not present.

In a democracy the specifics of who can be included and to what extent they may participate can vary widely. The fullness of participation in Athens, Tokyo, Boston, or Harare (Zimbabwe) is affected by rules about the number of offices in the government, the length of the terms, whether successive terms are possible, qualifications for specific offices, the mode of elections, and the condition of the franchise. The original point of such provisions in any particular country is usually to ensure democratic rule, to see that all have their turn at office, and to insure that the process is orderly. Although not always with full awareness of the effect on the democratic character of the regime, modifications in the application of the rules occurred over time. Likewise, unchanged rules need periodic scrutiny to ensure that they remain true to their intent. Rules and procedures once in place do not automatically fulfill the original democratic intent without regular monitoring.

An example of the need to monitor rules in the fulfillment of the democratic intent can be seen in the modern financial reality for winning and holding office. Normally there are no property or wealth qualifications for office since that would render the supposed democracy an aristocracy. If, as seems increasingly the case, wealthy individuals have a disproportionate ability to mount a successful campaign and hold office then an aristocratic dimension is unwittingly injected into the democracy. Attention to this phenomenon is imperative for the democratic character to be maintained. However, vigilance alone does not guarantee success. Efforts to regulate campaign finance have occurred for decades so as to prevent wealthy individuals from having an undue influence and yet these efforts are challenged on grounds of undue interference in the freedom of individual expression. No formula to resolve this dilemma has been discovered.

Elite guidance excludes the public. Popular control limits efficiency and wise rule. In its formulation by Aristotle, democracy is about the people ruling in turn which means that no individual holds office for a prolonged period. Such a concise formulation presents a solution to the elite versus mass dichotomy encountered in the two previous perspectives. Embedded in the Aristotelian formulation is that the public does not so much control as it "selects." Democracy is not altered nor are the activities associated with it. "Selection" better explains the totality of democracy than does "control." The explanation does not change the reality. It only changes the description of it. What must be evaluated is whether the new description better fits the reality of democracy.

Control, as seen in section one and two, means that the verdict of the majority ought to prevail, that actual representation should be the practice, that immediate and direct impact by the public on policy should be realized, that if the public wants a war turned off it should be turned off, if they wanted taxes lowered they should be lowered. Because control is so unvarnished it is easy prey for its critics as seen in section two above.

Popular selection, on the other hand, says that the public only selects the rulers. Selection has an indirect and mediate impact on policy, not an immediate and direct one as inferred in popular control. In this depiction of the democratic election process officeholders are selected from the available candidates and they then determine policy. Any one officeholder is only one among an elaborate system of many officeholders. No democracy has but one officeholder elected by the people. The Assembly in ancient Athens co-existed with the Council, the Courts, and the Ten Generals. The Council was a rotating group of 50 members representing the 10 tribes of Athens picked by election and lot and serving for 1/10th of the year. Checks and balances existed between these institutions. This multiplicity of officials and institutions has always been the reality of democracy. It is so, and has always been so, in the United States and other "democratic" countries.

The reality of many officeholders in many institutions makes selection real. It makes control, in the sense of immediate and direct public determination of policy, a fantasy. In the election the candidate may claim that the public's fate resides in their making the correct choice. Reflection shows that each official is but one of many and one official alone does not decide policy.

Voters may know the position of the many candidates on some of the issues, but the public does not know the position of all the candidates for all of the offices on all the issues. In knowing candidates and issues the voters may have erroneous information, their votes may be contradictory on specific issues and particular candidates. The voters may be almost completely uninformed. Any two individuals may vote for a particular candidate for opposite reasons. The same two voters may be equally informed, or equally uninformed. In the best of cases the voter is only partially informed.

How the Public Selects

Only ten percent of the public are careful followers of the news. Yet being a regular follower of public affairs does not confer policy-making capability. Though being informed is important, what the voters do, and all that they need do, is select between candidates A and B. The concept of popular selection recognizes the limitations on information available to the public and on the public's ability to use it. It has the public select candidates on whatever basis they choose. Confidence, personal comfort, credibility, party affiliation, the influence of a family member or a neighbor, and accurate or faulty memory may all be factors in the selection.

The notion that selection is based on personal comfort and compatibility may shock. It is especially troubling to those operating from the traditional perspective of the "rational man-intelligent voter." This traditional perspective is part of the theme that the public controls policy and therefore the voting act must be intelligent and rational. This theme is prescriptive rather than descriptive. It assumes what it would like to see instead of describing what occurs. The perspective places an undue and dangerous burden on the citizen as voter. If citizens are told repeatedly what they are expected to know in order to vote wisely and they know that they cannot possibly measure up, that is an argument to not vote at all. The logic of popular control, the logic of insistence on the intelligent voter is that few should vote. What the voter actually does, however, makes sense and is more realistic.

Selection is decided on the basis of comfort, personality, and a myriad of other factors. Decision based on personality judgment is within the realm of individual experience. It is a familiar foundation for everyday action where individuals make frequent decisions about friends, associates, and casual contacts. Background characteristics, neighborhood, school, church, club, ethnic origin, family, sports activity, employment field, etc., are factors for initial attraction of individuals to one another. Acquaintance follows the initial contacts and builds on the background and interest. If compatibility is not found or reinforced, individuals drift apart or completely break off contact. Background characteristics serve as screens for judgments. Successive contacts are more refined screens by which more judgments are made.

Voters go through the same steps in judging candidates as individuals in assessing friends or associates. There is the first impression, followed by getting acquainted, and then there is a preliminary judgment as more information becomes available. Political parties, organizations, affiliations, and all the normal individual factors mentioned about serve as background characteristics for screening candidates and officeholders. The election campaign serves as the refining screen that reinforces or diverts first impressions. Party affiliation serves as the initial screen for meeting candidates. The screening process is not normally so rigid that other "outside" factors cannot in time supersede. Individuals do on occasion meet new friends "by accident," though personality judgments still prevail in the end. Voters on occasion make new political acquaintances by accident though they will eventually fit them into their political comfort level. A lifelong Republican may vote for a Democrat or a lifelong Democrat vote for a Republican but that voter will not deviate from a normal voting pattern for other offices in that election or in the next election. The normal pattern will prevail unless continuing factors reinforce or strengthen the deviating choice. Even when the first deviation is an indication of a change in general pattern, the voter is acting according to a personality judgment. Personal comfort directs the individual rather than the idealized and unrealistic rigidly rational and scientific choice of candidates and issues.

The voter's behavior is sound since elections do not so much decide policy as determine who shall decide policy. Elections cannot be the final poll on a campaign of issues since issues as articulated in a campaign lack precision and are mixed with all the personality factors of advertising hype. All that can be said of an election campaign is that when it is over there is a rough approximation of the public will. Despite its faults this mechanism of selected office holders in periodic elections is more reasonable than the pretense of voters by themselves determining policy. It certainly is more reasonable than the tyranny of no public input at all. Voters regularly acknowledge their limited awareness of candidates, political parties, and their programs.

Only one reasonable conclusion can be drawn. Either democracy is indeed a myth or the popular control definition of democracy is incorrect and popular selection is all that democracy intends. In the selection perspective though the candidate's personality is the focus of the voter it is the personality of the voter that is the locus of the judgment. The voter may, but need not always, begin with the candidate's personality. The starting point may instead be some particular issue, party, or friend's recommendation. Eventually a decision will be made to vote based on the voter's comfort, on the candidate's or the party's credibility, or on some other default mechanism. In this way the personality dimension is a starting point for many factors to follow. The voter's first competence is never set aside. The voter always casts a ballot with which he or she is comfortable. That assumption gives much more credit to democracy and the voter than does the hyper rationality of popular control.

Even the seemingly simpler choice in selecting between the two major parties is one on which very few can confidently qualify as intelligent. The Republican Party cannot once and for all be classified as conservative nor can the Democratic Party be classified as liberal. Each party has a mixture in different parts of the country of liberals, conservatives, and moderates. The public does not have available to it an easy and accurate categorization on which to judge parties and then candidates. In a decidedly one-party state or district that easy categorization may hold but even they change over time. Even the terms liberal and conservative cannot be readily defined and so the very beginning ingredient for sorting out candidates and parties is unavailable. Easy categories are for the convenience of the media in generating interest and, perhaps most importantly, entertainment value in their reports. With complex information about candidates and issues the media would lose a large part of their audience, which is small enough to begin with in this area of politics.

Subscribe to the New York Times?

Some years ago a former United States ambassador to Southeast Asia and later the ambassador to the United Nations commented that everything one needed to know to make a sound judgment about U.S. policy in Vietnam could be gained from a daily and careful reading of the *New York Times*. At a time of widespread public demonstrations it was consoling to know the source available to correct White House policy, "Subscribe to the New York Times." There are several things wrong with such a proposition. For one, the New York Times may or may not be the single best public information source but its readership is far from universal even in New York City. Further, although the ambassador's comment is traditional, it patronizes the public with something patently false. If it were true that all one needs to know can be found in a leading newspaper, the United States or any government could be well advised to scale down on special intelligence gathering and policy research activities and instead simply subscribe to the newspaper. Any reasonable person will acknowledge that the public has neither the latest information nor the immediate capacity to know what to do with such information if possessed. Jacques Ellul observed, "Undigested up-to-the-minute information is not enough. We have to know what to do with it and how to utilize it." The normal voter wants to make the decision that taxes should be lowered, that public services should be increased, and that the neighborhood elementary school should not be closed. All instances of such direct public decision making only serve to prove the occasional and temporary folly, to use Aristotle's word, into which democracies can get themselves. The public may have some of the facts, but it does not know what to do with them.

Public Intelligence

In some jurisdictions where it is possible to get tax cutting or tax-limiting referenda on the ballot folly becomes evident. The public approves such proposals as redounding to their benefit. They have no notion that the primary beneficiaries of property tax cuts are really large landlords with little or no corresponding benefit to renters. While the small property owner realizes some decrease or cap in property tax, the ultimate results are not entirely salutary with increases in weed-abatement and trash removal fees, and larger costs for other services. In school districts where the voters must approve tax increases the referenda frequently assume an emotional tone over the future of the marching band or interscholastic sports. In similar fashion when university students succeed in arguing against a tuition increase, non-tuition fees increase. The benefits of public referenda are more apparent than real. And, frequently they are devices used by politicians to shift the burden of hard decisions to the public. Instead of the triumph of popular democracy, referenda might well be looked at as symptomatic of its weaknesses and misuse.

In the period of a political campaign voters may be convinced of one candidate's superiority over another and later find out that they were mistaken. A "credibility gap" may emerge because of promises not filled or because of inconsistencies in positions over time. When a breakdown occurs between the initial expectation of the public and the perceived performance, the public may express and record its changed view at the next election. The public gets to take out its frustration on that candidate, if standing for reelection, or on that candidate's party, even if neither is truly responsible for the policy that incurs the public wrath. In the new election the public may make another "mistake" on the individual selected. The most critical aspect is that if the public makes "mistakes," the situation would be far worse if matters of policy, war, peace, the economy, racial justice, were being decided in such a manner. When the voters of California threw out Governor Gray Davis in the 2003 recall election they might just as easily have picked on the entire State Legislature except that the mechanism did not work that way. Whether they got the correct culprit and replacement is an open debate. In the meantime other issues and other emotions arise and the appropriate sorting out may never occur.

The central democratic thesis therefore becomes evident. Faith in the good sense of the average human comes about not in the assumption that the public is infallible in all of its choices of particular candidates. Faith in the average human choice is a result of the large number of well-chosen officials who are responsible for any one decision. This good-sense will prevail unless the collectivities of decision makers are wholly corrupt and the public is wholly corrupted in choosing them. In instances where particular officeholders lose public credibility the official either resigns, chooses not to seek reelection, is defeated, is opposed by an even worse opponent, or harm occurs. No system is without its potential for folly. The goal is to minimize it.

In democracy an otherwise fallible public does not become the profound arbiters of the public good. Democracy requires a process whereby the ordinary competences of members of the public are utilized to produce extraordinary results. Members of the public choose between candidates and parties that seek office. They also agree to stand by the results of the selection process until the next election. The public does not have extraordinary competence. The system of periodic selection has that competence. The system takes normal capacities and uses them to produce extraordinary results.

Retrospection And Perspective

Three views of democracy have been presented: (1) That it is popular control, (2) that popular control is a sustaining myth, and (3) that democracy is better understood as popular selection. The criticism of democracy as a myth is logically strong. The information requirements for real popular control of leaders and policy is lacking for the public. The solution often offered is for the public to be better educated, that more information be supplied to the public, and that more news programs be available. This solution will not work since the problem is essentially not a matter of the amount of information available.

The percentage of people in the United States with some college education has grown by greater than a factor of ten since 1940 when 7.5 million people had attended some years of college to 85 plus million now, but it does not make popular policy making more tenable. Popular control and its informational and educational implications give an excessively rational interpretation to democracy. Though such an interpretation is appealing it is misleading and dangerous because it gives encouragement to, if not gives way to, popular demagoguery.

Popular selection changes the perspective upon which democracy is conceptualized. It does not change democracy. It changes only the description of it. Popular selection gives greater credit to the system of selecting candidates than to the determination of policy issues by the public. This depiction does not revive elite guidance disguised as virtual representation. Popular selection insists that virtual representation is the logical and natural result of the reality of popular participation and selection. In that reality the essence of democracy is, in the classical phrase, "the public ruling in turns." Any manipulation of the selection process, by wealth or any form of corruption, is tyranny, not elite guidance.

Popular control itself manifests the character of tyranny by distorting and imposing an unrealistic interpretation on the selection process. Popular control expects the public to both select candidates and determine policy. For the public or anyone to determine that which they are incapable of is a tyranny. The popular selection view is a more modest one. It sees the process of selecting candidates as affecting the long-term character of the community. That is the democracy of which a republic can be proud.

The discussion has been predominantly from the American perspective. In unstable countries the pretense of popular control is particularly transparent except when it is offered as a revolutionary alternative to the living reality of elite dominance. In that setting to speak of popular selection would be more credible if given a chance. Unfortunately, moderation in rhetoric is not a quality found in turbulent circumstances. The ruling elites, even those who have come to office by use of the democratic process or who advocate eventual restoration of democracy, are blunt and apodictic about the capabilities of the masses. The entrenched elites disparage a conception of democracy entrusted to people who "do not know how to brush their teeth or bathe;" they hold fast that a country should not be looked at with American eyes when seventy-five percent of the people are illiterate. The disparagement of the public may be well taken except for the fact that the elites have ruled for a very long time for their own benefit and of little benefit to the many poor. This would be precisely Aristotle's definition of an oligarchy of the few who rule for their own good. Truly an aristocracy is possible where the few rule for the good of the public, but it must be asked how long the public must wait for its good to be realized. The mass public uprising to throw out the elite in favor of popular control is a product of that prolonged wait. It is difficult in those circumstances to urge patience and the wisdom of popular selection when the accretions of time have given no encouragement. This argues the heavy responsibility of incumbent leadership. It is only the beginning to be elected to office.

In the situation of developing nations there is a dilemma that popular control is unrealistic and yet without it there is no guarantee that the elite can be checked. Democracy has a powerful hold on the imagination insofar as it suggests a restraint on arbitrary power. So powerful is the appeal that revolutionaries use it to substitute the established elites with themselves. And the elites use it to maintain themselves in power. Continuing events in Latin America, Southeast Asia, and in Africa confirm these points. Developing countries are really the battleground of competing traditional elites amongst themselves and between them and revolutionary elites. In a pessimistic global perspective one could look at the whole world as offering the alternative between unrealistic popular control and inevitable elite guidance. Even American elections, where candidate images are manufactured and presented in the same way as clothing style or cell phone commercials, could fit into this pessimistic picture. Though the cleverness of the spin of campaign commercials may be admired as an art form, political purists despair for the corruption of sound decision making. The only saving alternative is for those who want to study and talk about democracy to view elections in the more modest perspective of popular selection. The saving insight from the selection perspective is that the public in their role as consumers have sorted through the embellishments and misleading statements of product sellers for a long time. A primary merit of an election in the popular selection view is the ability to freely reject unconvincing candidates. The process of turnover is what preserves democracy. The challenge of democracy is for those who are elected to do their jobs in such a way that they clearly help the public. This would obviate many criticisms.

Coming Next

The remaining sections of this book can be read completely independent of the discussion of democracy. Those sections, however, can also be found to provide material to support one or the other of the three interpretations just discussed. At times those connections will be brought out. At other times the reader can make the connections on their own. The point of this opening chapter has been more than just to discuss democracy. The point of the chapter has also been to plunge directly into a substantive question in the study of politics. At the outset it was pointed out that the proper relationship between individual and society, between the ruler and the ruled, is among the oldest problems in political discussion. The intention of this first chapter was to plunge in, to splash around, to be immersed in, and to almost drown in a real-life political question.

The water has not been especially deep. Metaphorically it has been in a lake, not an ocean, of the political world. Though deep enough to drown, the discussion has been limited to a consideration of the relationship of the public to leaders and policy. Not considered were other aspects to democracy: as a way of life, as an economic phenomenon, as a part of the legal process through a jury system. In ancient Athens the courts were the heart of the system more so than the popular assembly. It would be necessary to go into these other dimensions and to show their parallel to the alternative views of democracy to cover the topic thoroughly. Enough has been done, however, to establish the principles of democracy.

The next chapter will also use the plunge-in approach. There the subject is the political system. Unlike the current chapter the discussion is not of a real-life political question. It is instead about a real political science. In the end we will pull ourselves out, crawl to the side, dry off, and examine where we are. Examining where we are at will occur in the third chapter in which the discussion will be on what political scientists do and the different ways they go about it.

Chapter 2

The Political System

Most know "the state" as the basic political entity. State is used interchangeably with nation and country. Within the last fifty years many political scientists began referring to the basic political entity as the "political system" thinking it more universally applicable in fitting emerging political entities that lack the familiar ingredients of identifiable boundaries, kings or sovereigns, constitutions, written laws and all the trappings of legal systems. Political system was thought to be more scientific with differently defined components than those of the older reference to state. The newer frame of reference does not change reality, only the way reality is described. Knowledge of both state and political system is needed. This chapter deals with the political system. Later chapters will deal with the nature of the state and sovereignty.

Those political scientists who use political system do so as a way of presenting complex realities in an initially simplified manner. The political system is a model or a simple, organized portrayal of the things of the political world. Models are "good" or "bad" depending on their accuracy and their aid to understanding. Like maps they can help as well as confuse. Here system will be described first in its most elementary respects and then it will be adapted to the political world.

System Model

A "system" is an identifiable whole composed of identifiable and interrelated parts. There are initially three parts or functional operations within every system: input, core-conversion, and output. The parts are interrelated and together define the inner boundary of the system. An example might be a toothpick-making system where the input is pieces of wood, and a machine which splinters and smoothes the wood into fine, thin pieces is the core or conversion process of the system. The output is toothpicks. The toothpick process could be modified by enlarging the wood splinters slightly, adding some sulfur material to the input and finding some means of combining the sulfur compound and the splinters in the conversion process. The output would then be sulfur matches. More elaborate ingredients lead to more sophisticated output. A piece of fine furniture or a piano is the product of enormous numbers of input items and an elaborately designed conversion process.

The political system schema is an attempt to look at the political world in the fashion of the simple system. In a political system the inputs are public interests and demands. The core is the process of making decisions about the demands. The output is public policy. The boundary or size of the political system changes according to the amount of input, conversion, and output activity. The larger the domain of interests, demands, and public policy, the larger the system. The political system operates, as do all systems, within an environment of outside forces. The political system operates within the milieu of many other systems. The milieu includes the economy, the geographical setting, and the demographic factors of size, density, and distribution of the population.

Political Interests and Elections

The obvious input of the political system is the expression of political interest and elections. Substantive political inputs are demands, supports, and apathy. The two diagrams found in Appendix A (*Appendix A*) depict the various parts and activities of the political system. (These diagrams are adaptations of designs from the 1960s by political scientists Marian D. Irish, and James W. Prothro, *Politics of American Democracy.*) The simpler diagram shows input as public interest, core or decision process, and output as public policies. The second diagram shows more detail and depicts the flow of the system.

Interests and apathy appear to be opposite, and the latter appears to have no part in the system. Yet, it is an input even though it is usually assumed by definition to be of no consequence. A calculus of demands and support by themselves are expected to lead to a response. Still, apathy is a reality of politics and it requires decision makers to have a breadth of concern greater than that of immediate and identifiable demands. Apathy seems to reflect an attitude that either the status quo is satisfactory or that effort is useless. In reality, attention must be given to apathy because in many American elections it has a larger role than actual votes, since more potential voters do not vote than those who vote. Thus the non-vote is as much a determinant of results as the actual ballots cast. A curious anomaly in American politics is that winning modern presidential candidates have received less total votes than the number of eligible voters who fail to cast a ballot. "None of the above" would always have won if apathy had been tabulated in that way. The description of apathy is an acknowledgment of its place in the schema; it is not an endorsement of conduct to be emulated.

Functionally described, input constitutes the expression of various interests and the selection of leaders. Demands, supports, and apathy are substantive expressions of interests and choice of leaders. The functional input and the substantive input are carried on continuously by individuals, groups, political parties, or even by governmental units themselves. Correlatively, interests are advanced because of the leaders selected. The diagram suggests that the information processed by the system is one-directional but that is misleading since interests play back and forth between individuals, interest groups, political parties, elected officials, the bureaucracy, and many other community actors. To count and weigh the importance of each of these vehicles of input suggests to some a way to gauge and predict outcomes.

Authoritative Decision Making Agents

For the political system the core or conversion process consists of the decision-making agents or agencies that convert input into output. In the United States the core is congress, president, and courts. In England it is the parliament and the prime minister. A decision-making operation or core exists in every political system but the exact agency performing the function differs from system to system. In the former Soviet Union while the legally designated Supreme Soviet technically made decisions in reality those decisions were actually made by what was ostensibly an input mechanism, the Communist Party. It is important in any system to locate and designate the agency that actually performs the function instead of judging by the title of the agent. If the political party boss rather than the legal official makes the important decisions, that functional distinction must be recognized. Though sometimes the distinction may be politely overlooked, it is important to recognize the difference between what is polite and what is actual.

Public Policy

Public policy is the product or output of the decision-making process and it is understood to be laws that are made, enforced, or adjudicated. In the United States there is an inclination to link in a commensurate way substantive parts of the core of the system to the output in the manner, "Congress makes the law, the President enforces the law, and the courts judge the law." Similar correspondence of roles is assumed in parliamentary and other systems. For the present decision-making without attribution is sufficient.

Reaction to Policy

Output, whatever its form, will substantively constitute a reward or a deprivation to those affected by it. A new Medicare prescription drug law will reward those who receive increased benefits and, temporarily at least, be a deprivation for those (perhaps the same beneficiaries) who pay increased tax withholdings. A popular court ruling may appear to be beneficial to all lovers of justice but years later harmful consequences may become evident. In this way rewards and deprivations become "feedback." Feedback is a response, a reaction. It may be expressed in the form of new interests, more support, or less apathy. More benefits and less taxation may be demanded as one is respectively rewarded or deprived. A reexamination of the justice system may be insisted upon as the effects of earlier rulings become more evident.

The political system gives the appearance of an ongoing process of input, output, and reaction or feedback. An historical example of such a closed loop system would be the passage of the Eighteenth Amendment and its subsequent repeal by the Twenty-first Amendment. The Eighteenth Amendment came about as the result of the demands of a few, the support by some, and the apathy of many. Prohibition, the public policy result of the amendment, produced a reward for some and a sensed deprivation for a great many more. A secondary result was the creation of new demands, that is, feedback in the form of more insistent demands accompanied by more active support and much less apathy. A byproduct effect was black market production and distribution of alcohol and increased law breaking. Public dissatisfaction led to notable feedback and a speedy reversal in policy.

Milieu

Interaction of the basic operations of the system takes place within the milieu of other systems that affect the political system, such as the economic system, the system of basic ideas of the community (usually referred to as the "ideology"), the class system, the demographic or people dispersal system, the geography, and the culture in general and more specifically, the political culture. All these systems interact and influence one another and the political system. This interaction can be illustrated in the way just two of them, people and geography, affect the political system.

Think of Japan. (It's marvelous what the mind can do in response to one word, isn't it?) Japan has an area roughly equivalent to that of California, yet it has a population a little less than half that of the entire United States. Because of this combination of population and area, the political system in Japan would be different from the United States as a whole or, for that matter, the response mechanisms of California. California often shows concern over its large, from its perspective, population and makes efforts to curb it. California would be much more concerned about size if it had to contend with a population almost four times as large, which would make it comparable to Japan. A political demonstration of hundreds of thousands of participants would take months to organize for Washington, D.C., weeks for Sacramento, and twenty-four hours for Tokyo. Accordingly, the system (the response mechanisms, the traffic control arrangements, the public and portable comfort facilities, and the overall political system response) would be different in one place over the other. Extending the illustration, Canada has an area roughly equivalent to that of the United States and a population roughly equivalent to that of California. The two factors of people and geography alone would induce a different response mechanism in Canada than in California, the United States, or Japan.

As indicated previously there are many more than two factors needed for a complete analysis. People and geography were used merely to suggest the environment's affect on the system. To bring the point home about additional factors, family and residence may be substituted for people and geography in analyzing influences on the individual. In that case personal attitudes, educational background, and many other social factors must be reviewed to understand the many systems in the personal milieu.

In the political system other factors such as the economic system or the class system may be more important than people and geography. The economic setting is of enormous importance, yet no priority of systems within the milieu need be established. It is sufficient to acknowledge the impact as a whole. That acknowledgment implies only an influence and should not imply a determining effect on the behavior of the system. It speaks of the immense context of the integrated social and political universe that is the subject of political studies.

Assumptions of Application

The schema just described is a universally applicable framework found in any country and at any level of government. As the model is applied to successively lower levels of government within a particular country, the surrounding higher levels of government become part of that lower level's environment. The United States has the international arena as part of its environment, Tennessee has the United States as part environment, and Chattanooga has Tennessee as part of its environment, and so on. The system schema applies horizontally and vertically. The value of the schema is that it gives a framework by which the political world can be grasped in an orderly fashion.

A completely separate, but extremely important, question is whether the orderly framework of the schema is a deductive imposition deceptively suggesting an order not warranted by reality? At this juncture it is important to see the organizing utility of the framework and to use it without prejudice. The value assumption of the framework imposing an unwarranted order will be given more attention later in the discussion of methodologies. Many political scientists employ the political system model. Some use it rigidly while others merely employ it as an organizing framework making use of the language for the convenience of the terminology.

Political Culture and Socialization

The political system model can be extended to a consideration of the internal workings of the political culture and how it affects the system. Political culture is part of the environment and affects the operation of the entire system. An integral part of political culture is political socialization, which is the process whereby political attitudes are acquired. Culture can be understood as something given and socialization as something done. Culture is relatively fixed but it nonetheless has to be acquired by children and by individuals who change their physical residence or move to a new country. Culture is the way people go about doing things, their habits.

Socialization is the way habits are learned. Many political scientists pay a great deal of attention to political socialization. For some it is the principal way of studying the political world, that is, by describing the process whereby attitudes, orientations, and practices are acquired and transmitted. Political socialization will be discussed again in the chapter on constitutionalism and that on political change. Here listing some points in connection with political socialization will give an idea of the variety and breadth of the subject.

Political socialization is distinguished from nonpolitical socialization in order to differentiate between direct learning about politics and indirect learning. Formal political socialization is the deliberate effort to instruct in certain attitudes or values by parents, school, or society. Informal political socialization is incidental, coming about as the result of other events. There is also cognitive socialization, which is what hopefully takes place in government courses. Affective socialization, like affective learning, is the development of feelings about personal and group characteristics. In addition to these topics, specific attention can be given to the political socialization of children, political socialization of adults, and role socialization. The specific agents of socialization like the family, schools, peer groups, mass media, and traumatic events are important since all these agents shape attitudes and practices. One important realization is the non-uniformity of socialization, that the agents and events that influence attitudes and practices do not have identical effects on everyone.

At times the process of acquiring political attitudes and habits may seem very definite while at other times it is less clear. Inclinations to be Republican or Democrat, liberal or conservative, politically active or apathetic, are acquired in early years around the family dinner table. That grasp of how attitudes are acquired works well until thought is given to a sister or brother who is almost completely opposite in political orientation with no apparent difference in socialization. That reflection tells us something about the inexactness of knowing how socialization works.

System Model Applied To A School District

The political system model applies horizontally and vertically. The general adaptability can be seen in its application to the school district, the lowest or closest to the people level of government. The consideration of the school district also extends the earlier examination of democracy.

A convenient way to start is with the *core*, authoritative decision-making. In a school district either the board of school directors or the superintendent sets policy. Legally the responsibility is that of the elected officials! Practically, even though appearance supports the elected officials, the superintendent sets the policy by the options presented. The relationship between the board and the superintendent can be visualized in an old story about the relationship between a married couple, George and Martha. As the story goes, upon first being married the couple agreed that Martha would make all the little day-to-day decisions and that George would make all the big decisions. After many years of married bliss George found that there had been no big decisions. The elected board is George; the superintendent is Martha.

In the school system problems are analyzed, options are developed, and solutions are presented to the board by the superintendent. A series of little decisions or agenda alternatives are decided or scheduled by administrators. This does not say that school boards do nothing. They spend an almost inordinate amount of time on school matters. They have committee meetings to examine alternatives, they hold public hearings, and they examine budgets in great detail. In this connection there is an unfortunately common story about a school district in which candidates had to be recruited, even begged, to serve on the board. The recruit was told, "Look, it's only one evening a month!" Being convinced of the civic duty the individual gets on the board and finds the one evening a month is at home with the family.

The stories illustrate the problem of identifying functional roles. In the school situation, boards do not so much formulate policy as ratify it. The same principle applies at higher levels of government. It is bone of contention between the President and the Congress, particularly in the area of foreign policy. Who makes the big decisions and who manages the little day-to-day decisions is a constant contention between executives and legislative bodies at all levels of government. Maybe a political magnifying glass would aid in revealing who is responsible, maybe not. Nonetheless the system schema assists in asking questions about the core.

Specifying *input* aspects of the school district is likewise not a simple matter. Discovering the vehicles of interest articulation and leadership selection is more complex than generally assumed. Here the quest is for how demands, supports, and apathy are fed through the system to be brought to bear on the decision-making process. The agents of interest would be individuals or groups such as parents, teachers, unions or associations of teachers, local political parties, voters, taxpayers, and maybe even students. The relative value of input vehicles is hard to say. The extent and weight of each of the groups would have to be determined according to the peculiarities of the particular district before any accurate impression could be established. At one time one group may have more influence—parents who support the band program for example—only to be replaced later by a taxpayers group who could care less about a drum line or new uniforms. Thus input agents are no more static than any other part of the system.

Rather than as input students might more likely be found on the *output* side of the system. In that respect they are products that reflect the qualities of the system rather than simply the raw input processed by the core. The output of a school system is difficult to measure because the time for optimal measurement cannot be easily determined. It cannot be measured simply by the percentage that graduate from high school after a four-year enrollment or measured in terms of the average SAT scores or the number who go on to college and promising careers or the number who finish college or the number that learns "worthwhile" values or the number that lead a "good" life. While all these criteria are interesting, none are definitive and all have problematic or impossible time spans.

Even before the would-be measures of a school's output are contemplated it must be recognized that they address only a few of the functions of a school system. Although the educational function of learning certain courses and their content may still be thought of as primary, school systems today do many things other than simply instruct in reading, writing, and arithmetic. Schools have social, health, nutrition, welfare, and entertainment roles. They provide athletic training grounds, music, theatre and art programs, and general physical development. They teach job skills, combat drug abuse, provide sex education, inspire loyalty to the country, train good drivers, feed many of the poor with breakfast and hot lunches, run adult centers, and care for many children who otherwise would have little adult influence both during school hours and after. Many of these functions have been around for a long time even though it is only recently that they have been separately recognized in public discussion.

The job of the system model is the identification of roles, not prescribing them. The concern here is over the criteria used for measurement of success. This debate establishes a useful backdrop for reflection on the earlier democracy issue. The functions of the schools and the competing legitimate standards of success reveal the limitations of accurately grasping and subsequently judging the performance of even this familiar governmental activity.

The environment of a school system is no less multifaceted than the input, decision process, and output. In this instance the environment consists of all other systems. Even though education is generally nonpartisan, it is never completely independent of the political community. What is more, the local subculture, the local economic system, particularly the tax base, and the State Educational Code are all part of the larger environment of a school district. The State Code is surprisingly broad and detailed in what it requires of a local school system. It specifies the legal liabilities and responsibilities of each district, the minimum number of days the district is to operate each year, the certification requirements for teachers and administrators, building requirements for air circulation, whether corporeal punishment (spanking) is allowed and under what circumstances, the minimum content of the curriculum, minimum and maximum age of attendance, the size of athletic fields and classrooms, and much more.

Beyond the provisions of the Code, the tax base more than anything else determines the extent of the program of one particular district as opposed to another district. Affluent suburban school districts have a high tax base and a low tax rate while urban districts have just the opposite. The revenue from taxes makes it possible for one district to afford programs that another district cannot. Tax revenue means that the benefits to children are affected by a factor over which the school directors have little control. This factor is not likely to improve soon; instead it is likely to get worse because state-mandated tax systems rely primarily on local property tax revenues. Property tax systems encourage the movement of tax ratables from city to suburb as businesses and individuals seek more favorable tax opportunities. If a business now located in the city can move to the suburbs where the tax rate is lower the city loses and the suburb gains. The suburbs are not likely to discourage such a move.

Only the political environment of the state legislature or, at an extreme, the judicial environment of the state or the United States Supreme Court can bring about a change in the taxing system with its drastic affect on schools. Such a large environmental change might occur rarely although it is currently under discussion in California, Texas, Pennsylvania, and New Jersey to mention only a few. The local school district is clearly circumscribed in its ability for independent actions as it is affected by factors over which it has little or no control. Neither the central city nor suburban school boards in themselves can control the larger political question of the appropriate and fair tax system.

Relationship Of System Model To Democracy

The discussion of the local school district shows the general applicability of the system model. The basic framework readily applies to the school district; further examinations, however, show complexities that cloud the original picture. Elements become difficult to specify, such as who should decide on appropriate schoolbooks, the number and kind of required courses in the program, or the range of high school elective courses. Additionally, should parents or teachers or principals or school boards or the state legislature make the decisions? Should legislatures, local districts, professional experts, or the U. S. Department of Education decide on mandated testing programs? When is a district itself too small for viable programs and who decides to consolidate it with a neighboring district? That school districts can fail has become manifest in recent years as the schools in major cities as well as in small cities have been placed into receivership and have come under management by outside private companies. The failures of the particular school system occurred long before those recent drastic receivership measures were taken, but the basic questions remain: who knows, who decides, and when?

The above issues and questions are a challenge to democratic assumptions. And, there are more challenges. For example, the school district is the level of government with which citizens have the closest direct contact for the longest continual period of time but few citizens know the name and number of elected school officials, their term of office, the pay of the school board members (usually nothing), the names and numbers of administrators, or simple budget figures. A few actively involved parents at the time their children are in the schools know the names and number of board members but even these parents constitute a small percentage of total parents at any one time.

It is of more than trivial interest that the local school district spends more tax dollars, on an average in a ratio of two to one, than the local government which has responsibility for police, parks, trash, fire, traffic lights, stop signs, etc. In other words, in terms of total budget expenditures the local government is known better even though it does less. The local citizen may know the town mayor or manager yet is unaware of how the most important school district official, the superintendent, is selected and what he or she is paid (usually a great deal).

When democracy and the system schema are combined in application to the local school district the myth of popular control comes back with a vengeance. Indeed, it may be speculated that as the complexities of the local level are revealed the myth may be more appropriately applied there than at higher and more remote levels of government. It is a commonly held view that citizens know most about the level of government to which they are closest. That assumption is not contradicted here. What is challenged is the degree of citizen knowledge of and the corresponding degree of control. The degree of knowledge is sufficiently low at the local level to support the contention of elite guidance, whether in the person of superintendent or the self-perpetuating members of the school board. Periodically a school board election may involve an aroused citizenry of some issues of immediate concern. The appearance of popular control surfaces briefly only to be submerged in non-involvement for a succeeding prolonged period.

PERSPECTIVE

The principal reason that popular control is questioned on the local level as well as at other levels of government is that the complexity of government is beyond the grasp of the ordinary citizen. The political system model, instead of simplifying understanding, codifies the complexity of political life and the myth of popular control.

It is not new to say that government is complex. Edmund Burke wrote on that theme, "Why Government is Complex?" in his *Reflections on the Revolution in France.* Most other political writers reflect his views on complexity, although many do not have his courage to speak of it openly. Some want to argue that government can be grasped and controlled by ordinary citizens. They hold a basic simplicity of governmental issues. The discussion of the system model suggests complexity. It is not clear if the connection of democracy and complexity was the intention of the originators of the model. In any case, complexity is confirmed.

Albert Einstein, in explaining why his writings on politics were not as clear and easy to understand as his writings on physics and relativity, said, "Politics is infinitely more complex than physics." Einstein knew well the meaning of the word "infinitely." He must have understood what some political scientists and many advocates of popular control have not grasped: the problem of elite guidance versus popular control can only be resolved not by dissolving complexity but by recognizing it. This recognition is especially needed when the system model is combined with the democracy issue in the setting of lesser-developed countries. In that latter setting it first appears that the model is especially helpful in identifying performers of functions and roles. In the process of identifying the decision-making agents and the leadership selection process in various settings the subtleties of the process are discovered and the simplicity assumption evaporates.

As the scholars who study them dispute the nuances and intricacies of government of a particular country, the citizens of that country can hardly be expected to understand in these complicated scientific terms. It does not follow that elite guidance is the only alternative. The alternative of popular selection with regular rotation of officers is particularly applicable, analytically at least, in these situations. Popular selection has a handicap, however, in that moderate proposals lack appeal in the context of a developing country where strongly presented alternatives of popular control versus entrenched elite rule are more attention getting.

Surprisingly the limitation of alternatives in the developing context is the ultimate advantage of the popular selection view. Later discussion of the nature and end of the state will bring out sufficient dimensions of political life that a better grasp of the profound nature of understanding democracy can be gained. When alternatives are set forth in future chapters, especially when there are at least three, the richness of political reality and political discussion become evident. The discussions of democracy and of the political system give an introduction to that richness.

Where This Leads Us

Long ago Cicero spoke of the state as a *res populi*, a *res publica*, a thing of the people, a public affair. While that view did not necessarily imply democracy it did give a sense of the intimate relationship between the people and the state. That point is intuitively grasped. The eternal challenge to government and to political thinkers is to find a balance in that relationship. The relationship is no less puzzling under the terminology of the political system model. The model has an appearance of "a place for everything and everything in its place." Complexity comes about by way of a great increase in "things" and "places." Some imagine the systems model to be a means of bringing state and people into closer proximity by increasing awareness of the vast network of interrelated forces and interests. If that awareness is achieved it can only be to the point of realizing more fully the earlier words of Cicero.

Criticism And How Knowledge Is Used

In this discussion the political system diagram has been referred to as a schema, a framework, and a model. Though interchangeable the more common usage is model. Model suggests a formal and scientific character, which is why it is preferred. That appearance, however, may be misleading since it creates the impression of an order where order may not exist. It gives the impression of a causal relationship where there may be merely a co-existence or at best a correlation. Model suggests a significance which reality may not warrant. Consequently, although the model may accomplish the task of bringing an orderly description to the understanding of the political world, it by no means is the agreed upon, one and only, accurate and verified approach to the understanding of that world.

There are many competing models, of which the political system is one, on how best to describe the political world such as: the group model, the game model, the rational choice model, the power model, the psychological model, the communication model, the institutional model, and the legal model. Professional students of politics do not agree on which are acceptable. It is fascinating that the criteria for judging an acceptable or valid model are, with a few modifications, similar to the classical tests put forth for good literature. Those tests are that the work should be congruent with reality, that the work direct attention to important aspects of life, that it suggest insights, communicate its points well, and have a message of some worth. In literature, each author shapes the final product in his or her own perspective. With models there is the aura of scientific authority. It is this scientific authority and the precision implied which is the point of debate for political scientists.

As mentioned in the discussion of socialization the mechanism by which child socialization affects development of later orientations is not known. It is not known why a brother or sister even at high school age has completely different political orientation even though raised in an identical environment. Information about the percentage of inclinations in one direction or the other may establish probable predictions of behavior or attitudes but it does not establish certitude and it certainly does not help explain the family disagreements. Accordingly, while the information about socialization may be extremely fascinating and generally enlightening it is not particularly practical. Though additional knowledge is gained, it is not clear whether or how that knowledge is to be used. This is true of all knowledge whether it is called scientific or general.

The question of whether and how knowledge is to be used in particular situations is a moral consideration. It is a good point here to end the discussion of the political system because it is a reminder of one of the central concerns of politics and of disagreements among those who study it. The question of the use of knowledge brings to the surface an often-neglected dimension of political learning. Political scientists and others in the social sciences and the humanities widely agree that scientists whose studies make the building of bombs possible should be concerned with whether and how their scientific knowledge is put to effect. Though that conclusion about scientists may or may not be correct for the physical scientist, the point does seem to apply at least to the social scientists and others who make that case. It therefore seems appropriate to examine, as will be done in the next chapter, political science as a discipline and to see the procedures about study and their views about the use of the information they possess.

Chapter 3

Political Science: Scope And Methods

Discussion of the discipline of political science, its scope, and its methods appear to be more theory than real. That is true only to the extent that eyeglasses are less real than the world we see when using them. We have always heard that it is important to know whether a person is viewing the world through "rose colored eyeglasses." The information in this chapter is about the various lenses through which the political world is viewed. Thus something is learned about the real world in knowing the different ways it is studied.

What Is Political Science?

Political science is what political scientists do. Scope and methods in political science is a consideration of the range of their study and how they go about what they do. Some of what political scientists do has already been experienced in the chapter on democracy and the chapter on the political system. The scope is also seen in the approaches that will be examined and in the consideration of how the social sciences differ. This chapter will also describe the various methods used by political scientists to organize their descriptions of the political world. There is no unanimity on the lenses through which the political world is studied. A dominant method may exist today, but there have been a succession of dominant methods in the past. That succession in itself is instructive in understanding political scientists and the society they study.

Approaches

By "approach" is meant a broad way of looking at or investigating the political world. This can be understood by considering the political system diagram discussed in the previous chapter (and found in *Appendix A*) and asking: What does it portray? What goes on there? What permeates it? What does it tell us? What should be going on there? What is missing?

Policy Approach: From one perspective the political system is no more than the ongoing process described earlier. From this perspective the world it portrays is a closed loop system, an elaborate process that can be known in large relief or in minute detail. The object of political science then is to know and describe the observed process. The next step is to point out possible insights and is referred to as the "policy approach." In this approach political science is viewed principally as a "policy science" that looks at the refinement of the input, conversion, output, feedback process, and find where the output may be improved.

Political science would point out the important public problems, the important output or policy issues (e.g., crime, welfare, taxes, defense), show how other social sciences can be coordinated in bringing about solutions to these problems, and provide the principles and know-how for making decisions about these solutions. The focus in this approach is on the process, its continued functioning, and the avoidance of dysfunction. In some respect policy study is akin to management studies with their interest in improving the way a system runs. The approach has some traces of what used to be called public administration. The intention and perspective is broader than just administration, though it does look on the political world as a process that can be managed.

Power Approach: Another way of looking at the political world is to say that the system and the process are a façade for what is really the essence of politics, namely, power. This view holds that what dominates the political world is power and struggle. Peel back the veneer of the political system and the "real" politics will be revealed as a world of power brokers, bosses, power elite, Fortune 500, Forbes 400, the powerful few, and the powerful nations. Instead of seeing politics as an orderly process subject to systemic models it is a hidden world of arbitrary wills, capriciousness, competitive struggle, fiat, and actions that must be discerned below the surface or between the lines.

The power perspective suggests that some individual or group dominates in such a fashion that the operation of the system is explained more in terms of nonobservable activities than in terms of the surface processes. Simply put politics is a study of power, how it is acquired, used, and maintained. Hans Morgenthau, a distinguished political scientist, in *Politics Among Nations* wrote from this perspective. It is the dominant way of looking at politics even when it is presented in the language and form of policy or the methodologies of law, behaviors, or history.

Morgenthau's perspective was not new. A disputant in Plato's *Republic* argued that justice, or politics, is merely the interest or preference of the strongest element of the community. Machiavelli and Hobbes saw politics as primarily a matter of power possessed by the strongest and most skillful person. Marx saw power in an economic system determining all other behavior. Many modern political scientists, focusing on globalization or local politics, see conspiracies of social and economic elites maneuvering to maintain and increase their power. Some see revolutionaries as alternate elites in the power struggle.

The point of the power approach is that politics is not so much a function of reason as it is of will. Approaching politics from this perspective is proclaimed to be the most practical and realistic way to understand and explain winning and losing in the political world. Like the policy approach, the power approach both leads and follows reality, that is, both find support in reality and they in turn shape a view of reality. Power can be found in the real political world ("A" influences "B" to do 'C") and then that finding can be used to explain. In the policy terms "A" (input) influences "B" (conversion) to do "C" (output), which leads to a systemic explanation. It is left unexamined in both cases whether "C" as an impersonal goal has more of an influence on "B" than the person or impersonal "A". For both approaches the possible independent quality of "C" as a "goal" is unexamined. Both approaches are well established in political science and both have many adherents. Neither approach concedes much to the other or to the suggestion that both might be deficient.

(What should be made clear here is that the description is about broad approaches, starting perspectives, not methodology. Methodology, which will be described shortly, is the particular way one operates within an approach or perspective. Each of the methods described later can be used by any of the approaches.)

Moral or Goals Approach: The third broad approach is concerned with the direction and goals of politics. The purpose of power and the goal of the process is its focus. It is called the moral or goals approach. "Moral" is used in the sense that right or correct are appropriate considerations in the study of politics. These are qualities not discerned in "what most do," "what most favor," or "what the most powerful prefer," but in nature, character, and appropriateness. What is involved is concern for the range and limits of politics, for the purpose of politics, government, and the state.

A moral approach considers the facts, understands the process, and is aware of power and its use. It must also consider whether there are any external limits to the political domain and whether there are any internal objective factors that can affect its shape. Within the moral approach there are disagreements. Because of these disagreements many avoid it and concentrate on processes and power, which is thought to be easier. This tendency focuses on what is near perhaps at the expense of what is important.

Like the power and the policy approaches, the moral approach has classical elements in its efforts to comprehend the political world. Aristotle, and Plato before him, was principally concerned with the end of the state. Plato's concern was the good and just state, though he did tend toward overly rational process-like answers. Aristotle saw politics as the master science. He called it architectonic, though that does not mean a philosopher-king approach as in Plato. For Aristotle politics meant concern with the internal workings of the state as well as its purpose, its justification, its relationship to all other sciences and to the ends of life. Aristotle's wider concern does not necessarily make it better. His approach is teleological, which finds meaning in design or purpose. Over time the moral approach has made important contributions and so it must be included in the study of politics.

The discussions in later chapters will parallel these three approaches. No extended attempt to draw out the parallel will be made though their fascinating dimension will be ever present. What approach is best may be answered in terms of what is best for one's own particular purpose. Though it may be unsatisfactory to those who want ready-made answers, that response is not unprincipled. As the ensuing discussion unfolds, a fuller appreciation will be gained for the variety in political science as in political life. Making the undogmatic answer more acceptable and complete is grounded on the assumption that there may indeed be a one right answer to any question but its formulation is not agreed upon. An insistence on the truth as opposed to the relative contingent is important. There is room for much debate and dialogue, which is the heart of politics.

Political Science And The Other Social Sciences

It is useful to compare political science to other social sciences to understand its focus. The social sciences considered are sociology, psychology, economics, and history. Many other academic disciplines would contend for attention since there are divisions and combinations in each of those mentioned. Though a brief description will be given of each much more could be said and for that the reader is encouraged to go to appropriate sources like the International Encyclopedia of the Social Sciences or discipline specific source books.

Some may take initial offense at what is said about the other social sciences. Upon full consideration an understanding will be established and any offense will disappear while its subtle accuracy will be remembered.

Political science has an architectonic or master science relationship to the other fields. This relationship reflects both the nature of the discipline and the nature of politics itself. Politics is authoritative in that it is concerned with all aspects of life. It can command, for example, that actions be taken or even that courses be studied that affect life itself. Defense and military sciences are examples. The well-being of the community and the promotion of science are more general examples. Political science as a discipline is architectonic in its concern with the things of politics. The master science relationship applies to its concern with the extent to which the other sciences are helpful to politics. Political science is not authoritative. That is, it does not interfere in the other disciplines or tell them what their conclusions should be. It is authoritative only in pointing out the extent to which the others might be used. Political science or politics does not interfere in the "truths" of the other social sciences. If the other disciplines affect political decisions, political science wants to know that. Therefore to know the focus of the other social sciences is important.

Psychology

Psychology is interested in the general ways in which all human behavior is influenced. Political science has a much more specific concern than the general propositions of the psychologist. The psychologists may give the political scientist much useful information on how people acquire attitudes, what shapes opinions, what might influence actions, or how crowds may behave. The psychologist stops at the general information on human behavior while the political scientist takes the information and seeks its application to the political world.

Psychologists describe patterns of human behavior, authoritarian personalities, and obsessive-compulsive characteristics. It is for the political scientist to show whether and how this information is applicable to the specifics of the political world. Political science is cautious about pronouncements of psychologists because psychology itself, like political science itself and all the social sciences, is rife with internal competing approaches and methods. The solidly held views of one expert in psychology may be disputed by another expert. Psychology has its psychodynamic or Freudian approach, its behavioral or Skinnerian approach, and its humanistic-existential approach. Methodological rivalries abound.

Economics

There is a strange phenomenon about economics in that it is often ridiculed not just by its critics but also by its practitioners. Economics is frequently known as "the dismal science." Some maintain that economics does not exist, or that if it does exist it ought to be abolished. The "dismal science" title was attached to economics in the nineteenth century when the predictions on population and poverty by the English economist Thomas Malthus foretold a gloomy future. Whether the title is still deserved is for its friends and foes to debate. The confidence with which many proclaim the saving power of economics is sharply undercut by a quote by a former president of the American Economic Association, Kenneth Boulding, when he said "I have been gradually coming under the conviction, disturbing for a professional theorist, that there is no such thing as economics." Boulding's utterance is redoubled when Gunnar Myrdal, a Nobel Laureate in Economics, called for the abolition of the Nobel Prize in economics because it is a "soft" science. Soft is euphemistic for inexact as opposed to the "hard" of the physical sciences. Myrdal's proposal was occasioned by, but not aimed directly at, the awarding of the prize to Milton Friedman, who held widely divergent views from Myrdal. Others defend the retaining of the prize since peace, for which a significant Nobel Prize is also given, is likewise not a hard science.

The dispute shows some of the heat that can be generated over a normally civil matter. No one questions whether economics really exists. Boulding is not saying that the discipline in which he and others have spent a lifetime is all smoke and no fire. What he was doing is acknowledging that there is no one way to approach it. The general disagreements over the strategies of the Federal Reserve Board seem to confirm this view. The Board's activities are more genuinely economic than those of any other governmental agency. Fluctuations of the money supply, for example, occur because there is not a single agreed upon definition of the simple term "money." Though that disagreement is of a highly technical nature it does reflect the fundamentals that keep economics from being one unified discipline.

The disagreements within the approaches and methods are the product of many factors. The disagreements stand in contrast to the image of the hard sciences (physical, math, etc.) that are regarded as operating from a unified perspective. The contrast motivates some to seek greater unity in their respective disciplines or in the social sciences generally. Others view the diversity in the "softer" sciences as a strength manifesting the internal natural liberty of human endeavors. The challenge is not to homogenize but to accept and work with diversity to bring about either cooperative accomplishments or respected divergence. The imagined abasement of the soft/hard contrast evaporates in the good-humored observation that the hard sciences always have answers in the back of the textbook and use different colored chalk in the classroom to try to make their points clear whereas the soft sciences lack ready-made answers and use only white chalk. The comparison proves nothing, although it does raise questions concerning the assumptions about hard and soft approaches.

Some of the social sciences, particularly psychology and even more so economics, take on the appearance and character of the physical sciences with experimentation, formulas, equations, and statistical and mathematical analyses. Insistence on pure economic handling of societal problems is attractive until considering personal options like a new pair of shoes for one's self versus piano lessons for one's child. A pair of adult shoes can be the equivalent of ten piano lessons. Despite the reasonableness of the economist's imagined "economic man" making only optimal rational choice the explanation is still a generalization. The vision of making decisions purely on costs is contrasted with many piano lessons even when there is no expectation of an economic benefit. Choices are made on non-economic principles all the time. Even government makes many of them, as its support for the arts attest.

Because of the diversity of both economic and political views no government can operate on purely economic principles. In a democratic society at least no reasonable person or party is so certain that a particular plan will be successful that they will stake everything on a single approach. The effect of a single approach is so massive that society could not handle it. Governments and presidents often announce a single new economic plan. Proponents and opponents talk about the plan for years. Nonetheless the actual operation of successful governments and administrations always operate by mixed plans. Single plans are great in textbooks but are never perfect in practice.

Some, notably Marx, but he is not alone, have appeared to argue that politics and economics are identical. This is a theoretical as well as a practical proposition with problems in both spheres. Here that debate is not addressed and the academic discipline of economics is viewed solely in terms that it deals with among other things the production, distribution, and consumption of goods and services. Divisions among economists occur over the weight and value of all these factors. Still, the conclusions about them are of interest to politics and political scientists alike. It is imperative for anyone interested in political science to know economics. Economists stick to their charts and figures. Politicians, and consequently political scientists, must pay attention to those who press for action instead of analysis.

History

The focus of history is the *past*. Such an attribution may offend some who like to point to the contemporary importance of knowing history. Nonetheless the first effort of the historian is to accurately describe and portray past events. The tools and training of the historian are designed to make them skillful at accurately discerning the past. Whimsically it may be said that the historian is an antiquarian, a collector of a type of antique. The historian collects and authenticates antique events and puts them in a certain order on shelves or, in their instance, in books. This description of the historian's work is not meant to be invidious. Events and antiques need to be authenticated if they are to assume proper importance. From time to time they have to be rearranged and displayed differently to appreciate the material in a new or better light. Through rearrangements historical events stand out more clearly. In this way collectors and historians are similar. A thoughtful reader might respond that not much credit or significance is given to the historian's work in this description. That observation overlooks the value inherent in knowing the past and ironically imputes value only to external utility of that knowledge.

David Herbert Donald, a historian, got to the value of historical study in a little piece surprisingly entitled, "Our Irrelevant Past." Donald, a professor of American History at Harvard and the author of a Pulitzer Prize winning biography of the abolitionist Charles Sumner, wrote in the *New York Times* op-ed page (September 8, 1977) that since the past was an age of abundance and the present one of paucity, the lessons learned were "not merely irrelevant but dangerous." The role for a historian in our "new and unprecedented age" was to "disenthrall" undergraduates from the spell of history, "to help them see the irrelevance of the past, to assist them in understanding what Lincoln meant in saying, 'the dogmas of the quiet past are inadequate to the stormy present.'" An even more important role, he suggested, was "to make it easier for some to face a troubled future by reminding them to what a limited extent humans control their own destiny." Donald takes a profound lesson from history. His lesson is not deterministic, cynical, or presumptuous. Donald's lesson is the limited extent to which humans control events. He does not deny some control, but he does not exaggerate it either. He seems to be saying that a proper appreciation of the past should make us humble, but not fatalistic. In that balance there is extraordinary room for both courage and determination in our, or any, unprecedented age.

The role of the historian involves a proper appreciation of the past. Lessons can indeed be learned, although they are not to be exaggerated. The lessons can relate to current politics and correspondingly to political science. Still, the primary efforts of the political scientist and the historian remain different by reason of their particular focus.

Sociology

The focus of sociology is the *present*. In a respect sociology is the history of the present. Some may not like this depiction. As with history the purpose is not to caricature but to bring out a focus of the discipline. Sociology's forte is attempting to accurately describe the many different aspects and dimensions of society. To collect vast amounts of data, to find patterns in the data, and to describe in a meaningful way is a task of great challenge. With such information accurately gathered and presented society gets to know itself.

Just as it is false to claim that history leads to politics so it is false to claim that sociology leads to politics. The proposition that "history repeats itself," or that "those who are ignorant of the past are condemned to repeat it" cannot be proven scientifically or logically. Professor Donald made a reasonable claim for the modest practicality of history. Similarly, a claim that some particular future is contained in a sociologically demonstrated present is unjustified. Though the propositions about the past or the present may contain elements of truth in an abstract sense they cannot be tapped in any practical way.

Sociologically, like historically, determined outcomes are unverified and unverifiable. Claims about the meaning of past events or predictions about the future are romantic generalizations at best. Sociology attempts and succeeds in giving society a better knowledge of itself. Properly understood, it does not pretend to know all that must be known to verify any determinism. Political science makes use of sociological information, but is not led solely or exclusively by it. Political science has a focus different from sociology or history or the other social sciences.

Political Science

Political science's focus is the *future*! The earlier depiction relating history to the past and sociology to the present were accurate and not contrived even though they contribute to the unusual focus stated for political science. The focus of political science needs justification much more than do the other two disciplines.

This focus on the future is not to say that political scientists gaze into crystal balls or predict events by other methods. Political science is concerned with the same thing with which the political world is concerned, namely, in politics any action, any decision, any policy, can affect nothing except the future. The past or the present cannot be changed since they are already settled. This is a truism. It is a truism, however, which instead of being banal, clarifies.

All governmental acts, even the slightest local ordinance that alters the flow of traffic at an intersection, have only a future impact; no government, no matter how powerful, can change the traffic pattern that caused last week's collision. Acknowledging this simple truth is what gives pause to the policy maker or traffic coordinator and propels them to consider carefully the consequences of their actions. By insisting on attention to the future, decision makers are drawn away from dependence upon the historical record or contemporary demands alone. The actions of Congress, the President, a governor, a king, or a dictator are similar in their futurological implications.

The futurity of political actions is axiomatic. No political figure can ever change the past or the present. Someone, perhaps a person who is close to a President, may change eighteen minutes of a tape-recorded conversation needed in a legal proceeding. That erasure does not change the past. It changes only the record of the past. Such an erasure, however, drastically affected the future of a former President.

Definitions in political science today are usually in terms of government or power or in terms of derivations of "political" from the Greek word *polis*, meaning city-state, and the Latin word *scire*, to know. These definitions tell us little.

It is like being told that orchestras are about sound. "Future" adds something. Aristotle perceived this element in his *Ethics*, which is understood to be the first book of his Politics, where he observed that, "No one deliberates about the past but about what is future and capable of being otherwise." Dante observed many centuries later that legislative acts deal with "general issues of the future." Paul Samuelson, the Nobel laureate and economics textbook author, grasped this too when he observed, "economic activity is future-oriented." While he was talking about economics he was really speaking of the consequential character of its concern and hence of its political dimension.

Politics, and hence political science, is responsible, like it or not, for decisions that set the framework in which choices are made. Decisions about health or economic policy, social security, tax programs, defense strategies, or the local traffic light all have a delayed, general orienting effect. That is the essential nature of a political decision; it effects the community on a long-term basis.

That long-term effect makes politics different from all other activities. Political science, the academic discipline, follows politics in this way. Later it will be seen, in the discussion of the nature and purpose of the state, that this point about the character of politics is the subject of disagreements. One's view of political science is influenced by one's view of the political world and vice versa. There is an extraordinarily rich relatedness to the political world. What is being done in this book is sorting out some of the elements of politics and putting them back together gradually. The end product should be a clear awareness of that richness and variety of views.

METHODOLOGY

Methodology or method is the particular procedure or set of procedures of a discipline. No matter how one defines politics or its approach, some particular method is followed. The method may be random or it may be systematic, regular, and replicative. Several methods will be described below. Each has been used by the three broad approaches. Each has proponents and opponents and is ultimately tested by how accurately the political world is understood. Each is affected by the way one understands science, which, surprisingly, is not univocal (although we will attempt to treat it that way). Rivalry about approach and procedures is common to all social sciences and is likewise found in the physical sciences.

There is the inherent problem in applying the so-called scientific method, as modeled from the physical sciences, to the social world. No one pretends that the laboratory experimental studies of the physical sciences can be copied in political science or sociology or economics. Nevertheless the general procedures or outline of scientific method can be employed in the social sciences. That claim will be explained below.

Every effort at science involves *observations* and attempts to classify and analyze the observations, the formulation of empirical *concepts* that organize the observed phenomena, the discovery of laws or *generalizations* that state relationships between the concepts, the construction of theories that are collections of logically related generalizations, and, finally, *explanations* and *predictions* based upon the theories and generalizations. Political science makes some claim to working within this framework. The objective examination of the discipline, as was done by Alan Isaak in his *Scope and Methods in Political Science,* in terms of these criteria reveals serious shortcomings beginning with the very basic level of concepts. "Concepts" means that terms must be agreed to and "power," one of the most basic and most ubiquitous, is also the most problematic. In a step beyond concepts, political science can be empirical and scientific only in a very general way since it lacks universal generalizations needed to relate concepts. For this reason Isaak comments that political science is "relatively immature" as a science even after many decades of arduous strivings.

Many in the social sciences get carried into the specious logic, otherwise known as wishful thinking, that because objective science is important it is possible and must be pursued. This imperative quickly forgets the weakness in political science's use of concepts, generalization, and theories. If an intuitive grasp of power is all that can be effectively formulated then the scientific prospects of the study are circumscribed. Arnold Brecht in his *Political Theory: The Foundations of Twentieth-Century Political Thought* speaks of the importance of attaining "intersubjective transmissible knowledge." Put simply, that intriguing phrase means "an agreement on terms." It is desired because it does not exist. That admission speaks directly to the missing concept level building block.

Someone desirous of a scientific study of politics should not throw the book down at this point because the discussion is only beginning. The admission that rigid scientific study is not possible in political science is feared as likely to drive prospective students from the discipline. To the contrary, that political science is no more than it realistically can be ought to be an inducement. The statistical, mathematical, and other quantitative efforts in the areas of voting studies, decision making, coalition building, and the like, give the impression of a rapidly advancing scientific discipline. Much is accomplished in these areas, but reflection would mitigate a conclusion applying those successes to the entire discipline. Gabriel Almond, the past president of the American Political Science Association cited in the chapter on democracy, described the character of political science as being "more cloud-like than clock-like." That is, there is a precision and exactness to clocks and an inexactness and imprecision to clouds.

These views are not to advocate tearing down political science departments and replacing them with pool tables and a coffee lounge. As will be discussed later, systematic efforts in particular areas have been productive. Knowledge gained through all the different efforts in political science may not be perfect, but it is superior to random opinion, whim or caprice. The review, below, of the different methodologies will give a holistic positive perspective.

Psychologist B. F. Skinner is known for his lifelong insistence on subjecting all human behavior to scientific study. This study has come to be known as behavioralism Skinner sought "a technology of behavior," "a science of human behavior." In his novel, *Walden Two*, published in 1948, he has the principal character, who he acknowledges in a later edition speaks for him, proclaim euphorically the "fact" of "an effective science of behavior." Later in life Skinner acknowledged that behaviorism "is not the science of human behavior" but is "the philosophy of that science." There the commonly acclaimed father of the scientific study of human behavior admits that it is not a science but a philosophy, an approach. That acknowledgment enhances more than lessens the standing of the social sciences. Disagreements still will be present. The honest discussion of them, instead of one method claiming "scientific" preeminence, ultimately benefits all, especially the arch defenders of particular approaches.

Because of the variety of methodologies in political science it is important to describe each, to relate some of their history, and to attempt to show some order to them. Many different lists and possible categories are available. The particular methods presented here and the order of the presentation is used because of its historical-developmental and, what are thought to be, its logical character. Its validity, as in any proposal, is tested by the reality it accurately explains and by the insight it gives.

The list of methods to be described is: philosophical, historical, comparative, juridical, behavioral, and postbehavioral. The behavioral method is the most widely used within the discipline today. Some maintain that it is the only method worth much attention and that the others are only of historical interest. Appropriate credit will be given to the behavioral method. However, to fully appreciate it and the subsequent criticisms of it, a wider spectrum of methods must be reviewed. Furthermore, some of the other methods' usages have their own intrinsic merit and should not be neglected simply because of the number of practitioners.

Philosophical Method

In the philosophical method the investigator asks "why" questions: why the state exists, why some men rule over others, why we cannot get along without government, the "nature" of the state, the "purpose" of government, limits on rule, why states differ so much. The philosophical method is deductive, meaning that it proceeds from certain general propositions about man, for example, that he is a "social and political animal," and arrives at particular conclusions or applications. Plato in talking about the ideal republic used this method, as did Aristotle in his disagreement with Plato's design.

The "American fathers," Jefferson and Madison, proceeded in this manner. They started with "self-evident" truths, deductive propositions, and applied them to particular circumstances in the Constitution and governmental practices. Contrary to misleading impressions this approach is not a priori in the sense of operating without examination or analysis. It is not exclusively speculative since grounding in the empirical setting is a prerequisite to any attempt at political explanation. Aristotle's *Politics* may properly be regarded as a philosophical work but it is a mistake to forget the sound empirical base in his study of 158 Greek constitutions before his reflective efforts. Jefferson and Madison were men of experience as well as men of letters.

The philosophical "why" was not completed in ancient writings or in nineteenth-century revisions. Contemporary political scientists, even those of a decidedly empirical orientation, are known for their philosophical generalizations. Skinner, as mentioned above, saw the philosophical dimension of his work. The philosophical method today has an important, although historically smaller, place in political inquiry.

Historical Method

The historical method inquires into the conditions that gave rise to the particular institutions and practices about which the philosophical method speculates. The historical method is distinct from history as a discipline. Historians accurately portray the past. Some may attempt through extrapolation or through ideological predisposition to apply the past to the present or to the future. However, the historian's primary duty is in keeping us honest about the past, a valuable service that protects from charlatans who use the past to mislead.

While political scientists use the historical method by borrowing some of the historian's tools, they do not adopt the historian's primary focus. Political science, for example, may inquire into the origin of American political parties or the origin of the Electoral College. The inquiry is interested not so much in the details of the historical period as in the structuring principles that were present and may still be present or which have changed over time. In other words, the political scientist is interested in the implications of structuring principles and their continued relevance to changed circumstances.

The political scientist may show that the Electoral College's indirect system of selecting the President continues to apply, not because of an unyielding past but because the electoral principles remain constant even when the conditions that gave rise to that particular device no longer obtain. In the past most political scientists used the historical method. Some still do. It is as legitimate a method, as history is a discipline.

Comparative Method

The comparative method is in many ways a continuation of the historical method. As the latter inquires into the conditions that gave rise to the particular state or governmental practice, the comparative method inquires about whether others had similar experiences. No culture is totally the product of one historical condition and so the comparative method examines other conditions that influence particular or divergent outcomes. The comparative method expands the area of investigation. "Comparative Governments" courses in nearly every political science curriculum reflect this approach.

Each of the methods discussed can be used in a comparative way. There could be a comparative philosophical investigation, a comparative juridical investigation, etc. The comparative method is singled out for description at this point in the list because of its logical and chronological closeness to the historical method.

The comparative approach at times assumes a very large role within political science. At one time almost all political scientists engaged in comparative analyses. The particular techniques are derived from the parent method (philosophical, historical, juridical, etc.) and from the ordinary rules of fairness and scientific exactness. Comparative voting studies, for example, would take studies of American voting behavior and compare it to French voting behavior with due care about isomorphic settings and similar statistical procedures. A comparative study of institutions starts from legal structures or historical settings.

Juridical Method

The juridical method emphasizes laws, institutions, structures, and roles founded upon law. In this method, probably the one in use in most reader's first contact with the study of government, the Constitution, Congress, President, and courts were described, often in that order, with a few preliminaries about voting, elections, and political parties. Such a procedure is juridical.

The emphasis on law, institutions, and the Constitution and the progression of topics usually follows the outline of the Constitution. Much detail can be developed in using this method. The jurisdiction of the courts, qualifications for voting, the committee system in Congress, civil rights, court decisions, and how a bill becomes a law are all expressions of a juridical approach. In these studies the legal definitions are controlling. This emphasis is justified because law plays such a large role in society. Regarding the extent of that role later chapters will discuss rights, constitutions, and forms of government. The method is a model for many political scientists. In employing the judicial method they assume some of the aspects of a lawyer. It is the juridical orientations in political science that attracts many students to the discipline and to later entry into the study of law.

Behavioral Method

The behavioral method is interested in the actual behavior of political actors whether those actors are individuals, institutions, or groups. Rather than studying theories about the state's existence, historical conditions, or legal expectations it is interested in what actually happens. For example, the law may say that all citizens are eligible to vote but many do not. The Constitution may say that "Congress shall declare war" but the President may be the principal initiator of war in ninety-five out of one hundred historical cases. The courts may rule in favor of constitutionally guaranteed equal protection of the laws but actual behavior may deny it to many minorities.

The behavioral method maintains that it makes its inquiries without juridical or other presuppositions. It seeks only to know what happens as opposed to what is supposed to happen or what has happened previously. In this way the behavioral method presents itself as objective, empirical, scientific, and value-free. Statistical, mathematical, and other quantitative analyses of vast amounts of data are part of the behavioral approach. These tools work to guarantee scientific objectivity. Value judgments are eschewed, while data collection and analysis are prized. A look at most quarterly issues of the *American Political Science Review*, the premier journal of the premier political science association, bears out this point.

A chasm is set up between the behavioral method and all previous methods on the grounds that the behavioral is "scientific" and all the others are "normative." The philosophical, historical, and juridical methods are said to be normative in the sense that they reflect some norm, some predisposition or starting point, some "value." They are said to assume some preexisting values in the settings, conditions, theories, or institution from which they begin. Assumptions about the conduct of war from the Constitution or assumptions about voting from the eligibility rules are examples. The behavioral method claims freedom from presuppositions by reason of its scientific procedures. This claim will be examined further in the remainder of the chapter.

THE LOGIC OF THE METHODS

The five foregoing methods are listed in the order of their chronological development within the discipline as dominant methodologies. The chronological development applies in a very broad way from the beginnings with Plato and Aristotle and it works through the present time. The chronology also applies to the narrower development of political science specifically within the United States. The interested reader who seeks to pursue the detailed chronology of the discipline can look for that in one of many other fine texts about the discipline such as, *The Development of American Political Science* by Somit and Tanenhaus.

Logical Development

A curious aspect about the broad chronology is that the list of methodologies moves from the most deductive to the most inductive. The philosophical method is deductive in the sense of arriving at conclusions about particulars by inference following necessarily from general or universal premises. The historical method is more inductive than the philosophical but less so than the comparative, and so on. This ordering is used in an ordinal and not an interval sense. No suggestion is made that there are increments of deduction or induction from the philosophical to the behavioral method.

The proponents of the behavioral method in describing its emergence in the period after World War II spoke of the previous approach and methods as being too limited in scope and of their desire for a new, more comprehensive approach. That comment can be made about each new methodological development. The historical method could claim that it was more comprehensive than philosophical speculation. The same comment could be made by the comparative approach and in turn by the juridical approach. Juridical comprehensiveness comes in the fact that historical and other background information is culminated in the basic law or constitution of a country. By concentrating on the constitution the usually belabored historical and comparative studies could be circumvented. Work, from their perspective, could begin on "true," juridical, political matters without the necessity of plowing through historical material.

The behavioral method claimed the previous approaches concentrated on what was familiar, illuminated peculiar characteristics of systems, and tended to focus on institutions, legal norms, rules, and regulations. Desired was an approach that was broader, focusing on performance, interaction, and behavior. Along these lines new effort and experimentation in the post-World War II period sought a more comprehensive scope, greater precision, greater realism, and a new, more comprehensive theory. The political system model, described in the second chapter and in *Appendix A*, is an outgrowth of behavioralism. Its comprehensiveness is seen in the inclusion of "everything" in its range of investigation. The core authoritative decision-making agencies are included as well as political parties, elections, interest groups, policy output, feedback, communications, political culture, the economic environment, socialization, and all their linkages.

With a play on an old television crime program the behavioral approach might be called the "Dragnet school of political science." Sergeant Friday, the lead detective in this early police show, questioned all the witnesses by asking for "just the facts." So the behavioral method wants just the facts, but the facts it wants are all the facts. No presuppositions are made about voting, war powers, judges, or constitutions. No values are to intervene. Objective, empirical, scientific, and value-free investigations are made into the moving forces behind political events through careful observation and analysis. No philosophical, historical, juridical, or moral preconceptions get in the way of the scientific study of the facts. This is the behavioral credo.

POSTBEHAVIORALISM: A NEW METHOD?

In the words of a song from the musical *Oklahoma*, with the behavioral method political scientists appear to have "gone about as far as they can go." If the philosophical approach is on the deductive end of the scale, the behavioral is at the opposite end. One cannot be more inductive than gathering all the facts. Surprisingly another new method, "postbehavioarlism," came upon the scene. Its legitimacy is denied or at least disputed by many behavioralists. Similar contentions about succeeding methods occurred all along the chain of development. The test, however, of a new approach is what it accomplishes.

It is intriguing to see again the pattern of claiming that the previous approach was too limited in scope and that more comprehensiveness is called for. It may be difficult to imagine how behavioralism, which includes "everything" in its domain, can be too limited. How can a new method be more comprehensive when the previous method includes all the facts? The answer relates to what by definition behavioralism leaves out. Proudly and determinedly it leaves out "values."

Values PostBehavioralism

The behavioral method declares itself "value-free." Postbehavioralists would include values. Taking values into consideration as an object of study is not the point since behavioralists do that. According to the postbehavioralists the point is "having" values. Postbehavioralists want to proclaim their value preferences. They want to make value judgments about the politics they study.

In their effort to be objective and to leave out all presuppositions, the behavioralists study only the facts. Postbehavioralists criticize this as conservative, antidemocratic, and antipolitical. That is their way of saying that the behavioralists are too limited and that the discipline must be more comprehensive. According to Charles A McCoy in the introduction to his *Apolitical Politics* the behavioralists are conservative, anti-democratic, and anti-political. Apparently the postbehavioralists would prefer that political science be instead liberal, democratic, and political. Behavioralists are conservative in two ways: First, that an empirical science is inherently conservative since it only studies what is and not what will be or ought to be. Secondly, there are inherent values of equilibrium, stability, balance, and internal self-direction in the system that is their base. Thus "functional" and "dysfunctional" denominators of activities within the political system are hidden status quo norms that work against entertaining the possibilities of dramatic change. The conservative characteristics do not show up in the private life of behavioralists as some proclaim themselves to be political liberals, yet they talk about wearing two or more hats, suggesting there is a separation between their private conduct and their professional conduct. The critics are saying that the two-hat argument is specious.

The antidemocratic charge refers to reports and studies on the low level of democratic participation in voting and in other areas of citizenry involvement. The professional response of the behavioralists is that their responsibility is to explain the phenomenon, not to change it. Low levels of citizenry involvement contribute stability to the system by providing a cushion of those undisturbed by passing events. Postbehavioralists see such an evaluation as antidemocratic in that it fails to promote democratic values and they criticize this assigned functional evaluation of apathy. It is on similar grounds of scientific neutrality that many behavioral social scientists refuse to take sides on many social issues exposed by their research.

Behavioralists justify detachment as scientific and professional requirements. Laboratory professionalism does not allow influence by particular sets of values. Because of this detachment they are said to be antipolitical and that their imputed objectivity, value-freeness, and scientific pretension predetermine and limit the content of political studies and leave out the very political dimension of the world. Topics are selected not by any criteria of political significance but rather by the methodology, that is, whether it is subject to empirical verification. The postbehavioralists called their predecessors "pseudo-scientists."

Postbehavioralists want both professional and private engagement with the issues of the day. They want value-oriented interest to lead studies on social issues, war and peace issues, health and welfare concerns, poverty issues abroad as well as at home, and myriad of other issues that rarely fit into the scientific parameters of the behavioralists. The postbehavioralists felt that to merely continue to study the functioning system was to endorse it. For them a true sense of values, a true politics, demands change and the profession must be directed to bringing that about.

The value preferences of the first postbehavioralists were not hidden. They had clearly expressed attitudes toward American foreign policy, civil rights, domestic political orientations, and toward the behavioralists. A subtle point now arises. The behavioralists are not being charged with not having values, although according to their credo that would be an acceptable charge. They are being charged with having unacknowledged norms or values. They are not so much value-free as value blind or dishonest. The place of values in political science from the postbehavioral point of view is clear and definite. That is their postbehavioral characteristic. This normative quality is explicit with the postbehavioralists and implicit, though unwittingly, with the behavioralists.

Other Forms of Postbehavioralism

Postbehavioralism comes in other forms. Some researchers with more formal mathematical orientation want to go beyond the statistics used by behavioralism. They would use *mathematical models* for "a calculus of voting," "game theory," and "decision-making analysis." Approaching the world of events from a statistical perspective gives a set of answers dictated by that method and its implicit values. Mathematical analysis is open to a wider range of options. Formal modeling becomes a tool for insights that otherwise cannot be explored. Some of that work is done in the study of voting patterns, decision-making, comparative regimes, and other large or detailed conceptual schemes.

Other postbehavioralists are concerned with *biopolitics* on the claim that the social sciences attempt to build a superstructure based on merely the past two or three thousand years. Society could better be comprehended by understanding it in the context of biological origins of a million years. Inquires into the extent to which crowding, birth ordering, body rhythm, nutrition levels, and biological instincts influence behavior would be more profitable. Crowding, for example, produces biochemical changes and stress in animals and it may do the same on humans. The way medication for physical ailments affect behavior can be explored more effectively through biology than through sociological techniques of behavioralists. Like other forms of postbehavioarlism they propose doing more, being less limited in scope.

Evaluation of Postbehavioralism

While the postbehavioralists have pertinent criticism of behavioralism they are precisely *post* behavioralists and not *anti* behavioralists. They come after and would go beyond the contributions of the behavioralists. Each of the postbehavioral groups would add a dimension to political studies such as values, formal mathematics, or a biological base. The value group does not seek to reopen a discussion of values such as characterizes classical political theory; their values and insights are presented as unquestioned values and insights. A particular war is to be condemned, forms of pollution should be controlled, and globalization must be rejected. From their perspective implementation must begin! Mathematical formalists would add a dimension that, from all appearances, is arrived at deductively. Why one model is preferred over other possibilities is a deductive choice of the investigator. Likewise the biopolitical approach arbitrarily adds a new dimension to the spectrum of methodology that needs its own justification.

Why the particular values, why the particular mathematical models, why the biological base rather than an astrological base? These "why" questions return to the beginning philosophical method. The linear progression of methodologies is now curvilinear. A corner has been turned; the methods of political science can be seen as a whole instead of a rigid progression from the marginally useful to the scientific. Each methodology looks at the same political world but each sees it differently. It is as if each methodology is a listener occupying different sections of an orchestra hall. Some occupy more seats than others, some are in the balcony, some claim the conductor's perspective, some the composer's understanding. Each in fact enjoys the same event but from a different perspective.

Equanimity on methodology has always been possible. Critics of behavioralism prior to the postbehavioralists were not necessarily antibehavioral but they were often looked at as such. A singular contribution for the postbehavioral development is that all participant methodologies can view the whole in larger perspective. The method is "best" which is most appropriate to a particular task. No one method alone is definitively best. Each has something to offer and each is limited in certain respects, as the other methods point out.

Conclusion And Perspective

Near the end of the nineteenth century, in a general infatuation with the accomplishments of science, Seurat and some other neoimpressionist painters proposed techniques for making painting an exact science. They proposed that lines, color, proportion, space, etc., could be subjected to mathematical analysis and formulation. Their immediate technique is known as pointillism, a process whereby the picture on the canvass was constructed out of dots of color. Many of their paintings are very beautiful and most fascinating. They created a brief stir in the art world and have long since given way to the ongoing creative efforts of other artists.

Some people in the world of music and other performing arts attempt to adapt their artistic field and science. Such endeavors are not without justification. Music has an exact mathematical basis. Still, scientific formulation can never capture the creative, emotional dimension of art. Shakespeare, Beethoven, or Monet cannot be expressed in a mathematical formula. Some of their work may be better appreciated with the insights contributed by scientific studies, but their creative spirit cannot be captured except through the imagination. Even the effort to scientifically create the acoustically perfect orchestral hall has defied success. The architecture of such construction is as much an art as the works on display within them.

The shades of interpretation and appreciation of a work of art are as varied as its audience. The political world has also had a fascination with scientific analysis. Much of the political world can be captured to a greater degree by science than the world of art, but only to a degree. The part captured by science may be, as the postbehavioralists suggest, the least interesting and the least important. The contributions of such endeavors have to be proven by results and not be assumed from a methodological beginning point.

It would be unusual to expect that political science has arrived at a definitive way of understanding the political world. If a "correct" approach had been found the path to the door of the discipline would be trod with individuals and leaders seeking solutions to the every sort of problem. From time to time some scholar is thought to have uncovered a remarkable new way to understand and bring order to political reality. In any lifetime such new discoveries will come and go and the world will remain pretty much the same. The world is not obstinate. Discoveries are just not as useful as they first appear.

More than twenty-four hundred years ago Plato proposed an ideal republic with an elaborate educational system that would remedy the defects of the political world. Aristotle (*Politics,* II,1264a) also saw the defects of the political world yet he opposed Plato's solutions because they "disregard the experience of ages," that "in the multitude of years these things, if they were good, would certainly not have been unknown." It is not that the world perversely avoids things that will work. Rather, Aristotle's comments are in agreement with those of Einstein about the greater complexity of the political world and the difficulty of understanding it through purely rational constructs. Rational efforts are not to be disregarded. They should, however, be in accord with the experience of the ages. The same is true of the methodologies of political science.

Chapter 4

The Nature Of The State

The nature of the state constitutes the base from which democracy forms. It is the classical alternative to the political system discussed earlier in Chapter 2. Though at times neglected, the state is still viable focal point of political science. While it is known and experienced by everyone, the state is also unknown. It has components or attributes that must be explained in order to begin an understanding. The "poetry" of "state" must show its "scientific" parts.

Some political scientists, notably some behavioralists, disown the concept of the state, regarding it as an inappropriate orienting idea in analysis and research. For them the concept of the state is badly culture-bound and the origins of the state and related concepts are viewed as intimately tied up with the rise of a centralized monarchy and a territorial national state in the West. These critics object to the theoretical or ideological disputes evoked over the state in earlier political literature and are reluctant to return to that framework, in light for them, of the assumed successes of the newer methodology.

The clarity and measurability of the assumed scientific language of the political system is set off against the ambiguity and divisiveness of the traditional language about the state. While there is richness to the political system approach, as explained earlier, it also had its problems. There are valid concerns about its direction, origin, purpose, and justification. Though the political system was consciously designed to avoid such concerns it is those very concerns that must be addressed if the system is to attend to the reality beyond its world of ideas. These are value questions that cannot be avoided on limited methodological grounds without circumscribing the comprehensiveness of the study.

To be sure there is inexactness to the term "state" and there are profound disagreements about its meaning and application. Nevertheless, as the previous discussion about behavioralism and postbehavioralism revealed, to simply substitute the term "political system" for the term "state" does not magically purify political science. It only replaces one set of assumptions with another. As discussed earlier the new set often has hidden implications that only later become evident.

A consideration of the various theories of the state will not harm the political system model if the theories and the system are presented fairly and objectively. Seen as alternative points of view based in reality, the theories of the state will constitute a backdrop against which the system model can be viewed, proving its resourcefulness and perhaps revealing limitations. The chapter on methodology concluded that the best method is the one most appropriate to a particular task and that each method made a contribution. From this perspective, examination of the state has a contribution to make even to the political system approach.

Another criticism of the term "state" maintains that recent discoveries of the non-Western world uncovered societies without sovereigns in the Western sense. Accordingly, the conclusion is drawn that either such societies had no politics or the definition of politics embodied in the concept of state was inadequate and that therefore the study of the state must be abandoned. The conclusion is quite overblown. Seventeenth century Englishmen made the same discovery when they met native Americans and responded in confusion. Still, they had to deal with some formed entity, some authority's presence, whether in stealing land or fighting wars. It is the nature and origin of the particular society, no matter the ambiguous authority structure, that those who deal with the nature of the state or sovereignty concern themselves.

Further, proponents of the power approach view the political system assumptions in the same manner as the system proponents view the state and sovereignty. Each views the others as starting from undemonstrated assumptions. The perspectives reflected in the three broad approaches to the political world are repeated in a surprisingly parallel fashion in the traditional debates about the nature and purpose of the state. Formulating new language to avoid old problems may save initial time, but the reemergence of the methodological debates plus the debate about such fundamental terms as democracy show that the problems of authority, power, and theory remain despite the wishes of those who would prefer them to go away.

It might be easier if all students of politics and all political scientists used the same terms in exactly the same way. Arnold Brecht, mentioned earlier, with his notion of intersubjective transmissible language, sees uniformity as the goal of the humanities in general and the major contribution of political science as a "science." Such uniformity may be debated as a goal. It obviously does not exist at the present. Whether the uniformity should exist is a point that requires an understanding of the alternatives and cannot be foisted without disservice. Therefore the nature of the state itself as well as its historical and comparative worth, its origin, it purpose, and sovereignty follow.

ELEMENTS OF THE STATE

The foregoing comments assume the reader's familiarity with the concept of the state. To become familiar with the concept of the state what needs to be done is to extract identifiable elements that all "states" have. These elements are people, territory, government, and some unifying principle tying the first three elements together.

The "unifying element" comes in three forms: organismic, mechanistic, and a third that requires discussion even to give it some name. Each unifying element claims exclusivity as the correct binding force, or glue, of a political community. The very terms may be unfamiliar, which stands in contrast to the seeming clarity of the basic elements. People, territory, and government are material, tangible, familiar, easy to recognize, and, at least the first two if not the third, are measurable. People can be numbered. Territory can be calibrated. Government has nominal status and it has degrees of effectiveness, or at least it can be measured in the sense of either the state has it or it does not.

A caveat on measurement can be instructive with respect to the degree the (imagined) familiar state is known. Most readers, when asked to list the top ten nations in the world according to population, will include Japan, Germany, England, and France along with China, India, Russia, and the United States. Italy is usually included at some point and the tenth country mentioned is often Israel, Spain, Argentina, Canada, Brazil, or some other country in recent headlines. That Germany, Italy, England, Spain, and France are not among the top ten is never considered. In fact only Germany and France (by current count) are among the top twenty. England (properly the United Kingdom), Italy, and Spain are in the twenties, and Canada in the thirties in a ordering of countries by population. A current almanac is helpful in constructing a list of the top fifty or sixty countries in the world by population. In so doing countries and their size are discovered beyond what is expected. The list changes almost on a yearly basis because census data becomes available at different times from various parts of the world. Some states are growing rapidly and a look at birth rate minus death rate tells even more. Many states in the top ten and certainly many in the top twenty would astonish most readers. Indonesia, Bangladesh, and Nigeria are in the first group of ten and Vietnam, Ethiopia, the Philippines, Turkey, Iran, and Thailand are in the second group.

The assumed knowledge of the familiar concept of state is challenged by the suggested exercise in population ranking. Reflecting on the list gives pause as to what is familiar and what may not be. An additional exercise is to rank order the states based on land area. This would be a more permanent list since area never changes (except through conquest or destruction). Once again the list would be instructive with countries like Kazakhstan and Algeria, little known to most people, ranking ninth and tenth. A mental correlation of preconceptions and actual size rank surprise most of us. An additional category, which might be reflected upon in terms of areas of political tension and tranquility, might be density (size combined with population).

MiniStates

Size and comparative size information raises issues about votes in the United Nations, the determination of political importance, and the very recognition of the basic term "state." Americans think it unfair that countries much smaller than states in the United States have votes in the United Nations. At least 130 countries have populations less than that of the Los Angeles Metropolitan Statistical Areas, MSA. The New York MSA, Tokyo, Mexico City, and Sao Paulo are even larger than Los Angles and according to population projections by 2015 Dhaka, Bangladesh will be the second largest metropolitan area in the world. These large cities as well as large countries such as China and India in comparison to small states have understandable complaints about their single vote in the General Assembly of the United Nations.

The opposite of the large countries are those that are exceedingly small, some in population, some in area, and many in both. Still, they are all members of the United Nations. Seychelles has a population of 80,000; Sao Tome & Principe a population of 110,000; Grenada, 89,000; St Lucia, 161,000; Maldives, 318,000. By contrast the four hundred and thirty-five congressional districts in the United States are based on an average population of 650,000. (In seven states with the lowest population there is one congressional district no matter what the size. Montana has the smallest population of 494,000.) There are one hundred cities in the United States with a population greater than 194,000.

Some years ago the United Nations attempted to address the problem of size, not with the size of existing members but of potential members. According to its charter the United Nations is open to all "peace-loving states," that is, any entity claiming statehood and being peace loving is eligible for membership. The Secretary General at the time described potential members as "entities which are exceptionally small in area, population and human and economic resources, and which are now emerging as independent states." That they were described in the definition as "states" gave the problem away since there is no one that is not "peace loving." Back then the conservative Wall Street Journal proposed an arbitrary quantitative means test of "a population of at least 10,000; a territory of at least 360 square miles; a budget of at least $15 million a year; and a foreign trade worth at least $15 million a year." By these criteria most universities and small towns within the United States might consider seceding in order to petition the United Nations for membership and then applying for United States foreign aid.

The size issue at the United Nations was not playful speculation. Nauru, a small South Pacific island, cited as an example of potential United Nations membership, was reported one year to be 3000 and the next year it was reported at 4914. The increase would seem to confirm their peace-loving status. Nauru became a United Nations member and its population is currently around 13,000, clearly having passed the Wall Street Journal test. This interest in Nauru was not an idle exercise in Charter requirements and United Nations membership. Nauru at the time controlled 98 percent of the world supply of phosphate giving the state a strategic importance as well as exceedingly high per capita revenues. Since then the phosphate reserves have been nearly depleted with environmental damage from strip-mining so severe that Nauru has become a problem of an altogether different sort for the United Nations.

A further eye opener is that Nauru is only the second smallest current United Nations member. Tuvalu, a nine island chain in the southwest Pacific and composed of coral reefs, is a member with its population of a little over 11,000.

To complete this story, there are other small members of the United Nations, among them, in ascending order, Palau, San Marino, Monaco, Liechtenstein, Saint Kitts and Nevis, Antigua and Barbuda, Andorra, Dominica, Marshall Islands, Seychelles, and Granada. All have a population of less than 100,000. Vatican City, which certainly qualifies as peace loving, with a population of about 800 is not a United Nations member.

The issue of size and United Nations membership is not the main concern here. The chief issue is what makes an entity a state. What makes Tuvalu a state and not Maine or Pensacola? In a momentary return to the issue of political science terminology, whether Tuvalu is called a state or a political system would change nothing. In neither case are there any minimum specifications for population, area, etc., since Tuvalu possesses the criteria whether these are people, territory, government, and a unifying principle or input, output, feedback, and authoritative decision-making agents. Maine and Pensacola are not states according to standard understandings. While other states will be added to the United Nations in the future, possibly even Pitcairn Island with an area of 1.75 square miles and a population 54, Maine and Pensacola will not.

Imaginations can get carried away in thinking about population and area and the specifications for statehood. As there are no minimum specifications for the size of the "measurable" population and territory elements of the state, so also there are no maximum specifications either. China is accepted as a state because it has "always" been called a state, as has India. China and India as well as many other countries could break into many parts, making for a great proliferation of United Nation's members. Given an agreement on essential elements it is easy to conjure a world state consisting of the human race as the people, spaceship earth as the territory, and the United Nations as the government.

Since there are no self-evident minimum or maximum specifications to ordain or preclude mini- or maxi- states the answer to the challenge of statehood must be found elsewhere. In the world of fashion it may be asked, when is a miniskirt no longer a miniskirt or a necktie no longer a tie, in either direction? Answers for skirts, ties, or states are arbitrary. The answers are not necessarily right but they set the current parameters. The point has been that the assumed familiar and measurable aspects of the state become less familiar and more immeasurable after a brief examination. The topics of a world state and disintegration of large states will be dealt with in later chapters. Especially pertinent will be the discussion of federalism where Maine and Iowa are not states while, of course, the United States is. Whether the United Nations might fit is also of great interest.

THE UNIFYING ELEMENT

The size issue shows that the unifying element of the state is not alone in being unfamiliar. The unifying element will not unravel the mysteries of the minimum or maximum sizes. Answers to those questions will continue to be arbitrary and political, as occurs at the United Nations and in the relation between states. The examination of the unifying principle looks into what it is that holds a state, any state, together. It can be understood as the "glue" that holds a certain people in a certain territory under a certain government. Sociologically or behaviorally the adhesive holding a people together is referred to as "patterns of allegiance." No matter what it is called it is a mystery challenging us to go beyond the measurable and approach the classical issues of political thinking.

Political theory traditionally speaks of three alternate theories of the unifying principle of the state. It should be understood that the theories discussed here and in the following chapters are exclusive, meaning that each theory presents itself as the only correct view of the nature or unifying element of the state. No theory can be dismissed out of hand. Each has the premises with deep logical and historical roots.

The topic of the unifying element of the state may appear unimportant to the practically oriented. The practical reader may view "the Palestinian state" as a real political problem in need of solution, so also the decades old conflict in Northern Ireland or the lingering problem of two Chinas, although diplomatic niceties have finessed the latter until most recently. With the Palestinian state there is a serious question for some about whether it is or should be a state. If it is a state there is the further question of what holds or can hold it together, what is its exact territory, and who determines the acceptable parameters? Interestingly it is a question not unlike that raised by some at the time of the creation of the modern state of Israel following World War II. Proponents of the Israeli state would be aghast at such a thought because of its decades, if not centuries, of waiting. For its proponents the same thought process applies to the contemporary issue of the Palestinian state. In Northern Ireland, like in the Middle East, there is not only domestic turmoil; there is also the long standing historical question of rightful jurisdiction, arbitrary force, and popular will. The same questions still linger about the China of Taiwan and the China of the mainland. These are but three contemporary political question areas relating to state identity to which the practical mind wants to turn.

There are, however, similar problems or potential problems in almost every state in the world. In India, for example, there are twenty-four or more languages spoken by one million or more people, which is a possible unity problem. Potentially explosive problems remain in Afghanistan and Iraq. If someone were to stir up the Kurds in Iraq or other factions in either country to seek their own "national unity and statehood" the repercussions could be earth shattering. Similar problems exist within Spain, France, and in a great part of central Africa. For many years the problem seemed to be the same with the French in Canada and with Puerto Rico within the United States. In the latter cases the situation has eased, but for how long is always uncertain. The communities along the Mexico-United States border and the Canada-United States border are often reported to have much more in common with themselves than with their respective political centers. While the identity of these border situations have never reached any level of active interest, why they do not is as much a curiosity as why they do in other localities.

What makes each and every claimant to separate identity truly a state or not may in the practical setting be settled arbitrarily, as with the question of size. Individuals, groups, and other states throughout the world do not accept the claimed statehood of many prominent states today. The problems of globalization, colonialism, imperialism, and nationalism are all expressions of or reactions against, or at least can be expressed in terms of, the unifying bond of the state.

The discussion of the unifying principle of the state will lead to an appreciation of the depth of the issues involved and the intensity with which the contending parties hold the positions. If it is necessary to be practical, a reasonable perspective in any political consideration, about this appreciation, there is a humanizing and potential problem solving utility to understanding fully the position of opposing parties in any dispute.

Organismic Theory

The organismic theory maintains that the state is an organism where the parts are intimately tied to the whole. No part acts except as the whole acts. The parts may not be consciously aware of their role as functioning on behalf of the whole, but it is the obligation of the theory to explain how that is the case. There are two viable variations on the organismic theme. One speaks of a spiritual force, the other of a biological force. The force controls human actions in organizing, moving, and directing the state. In either form the overall action is not subject to human control even though the actors may think of themselves as controlling. In either form the organismic theory may appear preposterous. Reflection shows that not to be the case.

The early nineteenth century philosopher Hegel provided an intellectual setting for more recent and familiar renditions of the theory of organismic unity. Hegel's theory is an historical rendering of the state subject to a spiritual force. He views the state as the embodiment of the "Divine Idea as it exists on Earth." The individual's worth derives only through the state and the state receives its worth only by the Divine Idea which controls it. All parts are uniquely fitted into the controlling whole. He views the state as the march of God in the world and only through it is freedom realized. For Hegel, neither man nor the state itself controls the dynamic by which the state comes about. The dynamic is all a product of the larger unfolding process. It is this force, this power over which men have no control, that holds the state together, not men's separate wills.

Hegel's "divine" can be viewed without theological or religious meaning. It can be understood as simply a force over which humans have no control. That is the way it is viewed in modern expressions. The biological version of the organismic theory, for example, does not grant a spiritual dimension to the state. Nonetheless the factor of control is the same. The biological form regards the state like any other organism where the part cannot act separately from the whole. As the hand cannot live separately from the body so the state and the individual are seen as having the same dependent relationship. Some versions of this theory ascribe birth, maturation, reproduction, and death to the state. A state is seen as initially founded, grows in strength, becoming imperial, having colonies, withering under the stress of time, and eventually dying from internal or external causes. While this sounds as no more than analogy, more is intended.

Popularized versions in the form of biopolitics or sociobiology maintain that human behavior can best be explained in the general terms of animal behavior. Expressions of this view are found in the writings of Robert Ardrey: *The Social Contract*, *Territorial Imperative*, *African Genesis*; and Desmond Morris: *The Naked Ape*, and *The Human Zoo*. These writings contain fascinating accounts about human and animal behavior. They contain interesting stories with an underlying theoretical position.

B. F. Skinner, the behavioral psychologist, presents the same theory, namely, that a force over which they have no control directs humans. With Skinner it is much more evident that his is a definite theoretical position despite his every intriguing stories and arguments. According to Skinner human behavior is conditioned and reinforced by all the factors of the environment. While there is uniqueness to the individual for Skinner, there is for him no individual control or free will. Humankind can only design ("respond" is the more accurate technical term, as Skinner suggests in his *Walden II*) more or less efficient ways to operate within the environment. Human social response is no different than biological evolution. For Skinner, as for Hegel, people are controlled by some external power.

The organismic theory is not flattering since human beings like to think of themselves as in control. The theory's affront to human pride, however, is not reason in itself for dismissing it. The conclusions of Hegel, Skinner, and others are based on observed facts. Put simply, the organismic position might be expressed in this way: (1) men exist and so does the state, (2) men's existence is ephemeral compared to the state, therefore, (3) the state (or the environment in Skinner's words) is of paramount importance and men ought to be seen as serving it.

There is cogency to this argument. Thinking just in terms of personal existence, it can be acknowledged that the state existed before the individual and will in all probability exist long after. In that respect the individual is ephemeral; the state lasts for centuries. Like the animal herd, humans live in the political community not by individual choice but by reason of some force over which they have no control. Particular examples of apparent independent action do not refute the theory because the examples are small relative to total numbers. Independent acts can be dismissed as mere aberrations. The organismic theory has to be faced in its own terms. The total picture has to be grasped and it has to be dealt with in terms of the weight and merit of the premises and conclusion. Though independent actions can give pause for not accepting the theory outright, it has to be evaluated in comparison with alternative views.

The organismic theory says that manifestations of the underlying unity are seen in common language, culture, beliefs, ethnic qualities, and habits. One state is distinct from another. Political arrangements, like boundaries and autonomy, are but reflections of the more basic unity. Events that appear to contradict this unity, as in the federation of disparate groups or the fission of an established state, are explained as manifestations of a yet unrecognized greater unity or as isolated deviations. The underlying unity explains the individual's place within the state. The roots of nationalism are found in this unity. So also can be seen in skeletal form the theory of socialization, which says that one is conditioned and reinforced to certain relatively constant behavior. In whatever version, the organismic theory says that individuals act primarily as parts of a whole and the whole controls.

An interesting but clearly unintended expression of the organismic view is reflected in an observation by Robert Strauss, a respected former government official and chairman of the Democratic Party, when he said something to the effect that: "Everybody in government is like a bunch of ants on a log floating down a river. Each one thinks he is guiding the log, but it is really just going with the flow." Strauss was making a rhetorical political remark, not a philosophical one. Taken philosophically, the remark can be viewed as consistent with the organismic theory. The theory holds that the human role is merely to know and describe the state and its parts, not to change it.

Mechanistic Theory

In the mechanistic theory the state is viewed as completely subject to human control, human beings control the unity of the state. A machine, a watch, and an automobile have mechanistic unity. The parts are put together at the direction of the person who designed the machine. It is the way of modern science. The mechanistic theory is at a minimum flattering.

The mechanistic view argues that: (1) as long as states have existed they have been directed in some fashion by people, whether one person, a few, or many; (2) perennial complaints about the direction the state is going implies that it could be "directed" better; (3) therefore, human control is the constant in political life. As with the organismic theory there is cogency to the mechanistic argument. The organismic theory regards the supposed "direction" of the state as no different from the behavior of the "alpha" or lead animal in a herd. The lead animal does not control its actions any more than the other members of the herd. Hegel saw the same relationship between Caesar or Napoleon or any leader and their respective armies or empires. While the mechanistic theory concludes that there is human control, the organismic concludes the opposite.

The mechanistic understanding of the state is that it is artificial in its origin and mechanical in its nature, that it is a function of human design. The state may not be subject to the design of the individual who at the moment is in disagreement with the government and its policies. Thus, to that individual the state assumes an organismic character. That individual is assuaged by the promise, however, that with a gain in support for his or her position the direction of the government may change. This possibility of changing the government on the basis of popular appeal argues human control and shows traces of traditional democracy discussed in Chapter 1.

Practical examples of the mechanistic view, signs of human control, are found in the fixing of territorial boundaries by treaties, the establishment of states by compacts agreed to by previously feuding factions, and the specification of the role of the government by contracts or constitutions. All such arrangements are humanly determined; they are arbitrary and artificial. There may be "natural" borders along cultural, language, or traditional lines, but they may not be respected. Where the boundary is located is ultimately determined by human agreement. Occasionally an individual may not be happy in a particular location and will move. Or, a person may attempt to get the boundaries redefined or the constitution amended. All this manifests human control.

The organismic theory maintains that the mechanistic can only point to the "appearance" of control. The respective theories make sense from their given premises. Since theories affect conduct the mechanistic theory dictates the type or at least the range of solutions that can be considered. To maintain that the state is completely subject to human control argues the ability to impose in some way a temporal human will on all. Whether it can be done or not, the prospect raises concern. It is one thing for the mechanistic inclination to disagree with the organismic position and the lack of human control. It is quite different to accept complete human control as the only alternative.

Lack of human control promotes the desirability of human control while, on the other hand, the prospect of complete human control does not automatically create an escape. Both the organismic and the mechanistic theories have strong arguments in their favor and both are subject to lingering doubts. One scares and the other seems contrary to normal experience. With problematic alternatives, compromise that combines elements of both seems appropriate. The combination must, however, reflect reality and not just words.

Synergistic Theory

In the past the third unifying principle of the state was termed "organic." One problem with the term was its confusion with the first view, "organismic." Another problem is that the term organic has far too many different usages in the history of political thought. Aristotle's theory of the state is said to be organic; so are the theories of Hobbes, Rousseau, Burke, and others. Since each of these thinkers present full stories about the state that are greatly different from one another, to use the term organic invites ambiguity where clarification is sought.

The title "synergistic theory" is offered here because synergy means combined action. It refers to the behavior of a whole which behavior is unexplained by the behavior of the parts or any subassembly of the parts. At first glance synergy may imply compromise, but strictly understood, compromise is not involved. An example of synergy is the tensile strength of alloy steel. The alloy is greater in strength than the separate strength or the conjoined strength of its components. Buckminster Fuller, who cites the alloy example of synergy, also gives the strange formula that one plus two equals four whereby taking three equi-edged triangles, stacking them together edge to edge as a three-sided tent inadvertently produces a fourth equi-edged triangle at their base. Out of the three triangles a tetrahedron is formed synergistically.

The synergistic theory holds that events are subject to human control but they are also to some extent uncontrollable. The components are combined but the exact results are unexpected. The term synergy makes it possible to explain an ancient concept of the state in a new and more effective way. It is opposed to the organismic lack of human control and the mechanistic view of complete human control. Many years ago the Sperry Rand Corporation, in an interesting series of ads, claimed itself to be "synergistic." It had several corporate divisions producing quite unrelated items or at least to the unsynergistic minded the different corporate divisions would appear unrelated. One division made hay balers; another made typewriters; others made electronic amplifiers, computers, and electrostatic copiers. The ads claimed, "We do a lot of things at Sperry Rand. And we do each one better because we do all the rest." They add, "We're synergistic!" They said they made a better hay baler because they make electronic amplifiers no larger than a pinhead even though these two divisions and their products had not visible connection. All divisions and products came from different facilities in different parts of the country. The divisions and products were unrelated in an ordinary, mechanistic or organismic, sense. They were related synergistically.

Synergistic unity, Sperry Rand claimed, made them a success. That synergy was lacking, it was implied, in the mechanistically organized competition. The truth of Sperry Rand's claim will not be examined. Synergy versus mechanistic versus organismic unity, however, is crucial. Synergy implies that what holds a social entity together and what makes it work is a force subject to human control and lacking human control. The other two theories speak of either complete human control or no human control. The compromise implied in the concept of synergistic unity may be outwardly appealing but it may be totally artificial and must be investigated for logical and practical substance.

Synergy says that individual human efforts contribute to the existence of the state similar to combining divisions in a corporation or stacking triangles into a tent to form a tetrahedron. As in the nonpolitical examples, individual efforts could break up the corporation or pull away one triangle and cause the tetrahedron tent to collapse, so individual efforts can destroy the state. A partially hypothetical concrete example of political building and destroying is Lebanon, which was built using some natural foundations in the 1920s and destroyed in the 1970s and 1980s. It would be best if this destruction did not take place, especially because of the many innocent victims of such a tragedy. The problem may be that there was no real, synergistic unity in the beginning. The building of a corporation and the stacking of three triangles are human efforts. The results are unexpected. The state is the product of human efforts and it can be destroyed by human effort even though the exact steps in each effort may not be fully understood. In other words, the state cannot be completely controlled, even synergistically. It will not completely collapse like the tent or the corporation. It is reconstituted in some new form, either broken into many new states or dominated by some external power. It may be that Lebanon was put back together, but it may be artificial and not real.

The continued existence of the state can be explained in terms of these three theories. Each explains the unifying principle, the internal adhesive, differently. How the state exactly comes into existence is a separate topic examined later. The focus in this chapter is on the nature of the unifying glue and whether it is without human control, completely subject to human control, or a combination of these two. As in the first two theories, there is cogency to the synergistic view and there is a realistic base: (1) individuals do act independently, (2) there are things about the state which individuals do not control, and (3) most human endeavors, including the state, are conducted in similar fashion.

CONCLUSION AND PERSPECTIVE

At this juncture the inclination is to favor the third theory of synergy since it combines reasonable elements of control and the lack of control. The discussion appears convincing and compromise is persuasive, but a conclusion is premature. What has been accomplished is the juxtaposition of three different views of unity in the state.

Until the other characteristics of the state have been considered, judgment about a preference should be suspended. In the remaining topics, sovereignty, origin, and purpose, three views will be presented which parallel the three just considered. Although the topics will not be systematically woven together, three distinct and coherent views of the state will emerge. At that point a conclusion may be in order. Still, even then it may be better to avoid a decision altogether. To have knowledge of the three views and the principles involved, to have recognition of the distinctness of the theories with no judgment between them may be too academic, but it is consistent with the synergistic position about hesitation in leaping at expectations that all necessary knowledge has been accumulated. An appreciation of and a respect for profound differences may lead to understanding more than conclusions do. When dealing with principles of politics, as is being done, understanding is a virtue.

If a preference for the third theory is suspected at times, that inclination will be balanced when upon examining the purpose of the state its full dimensions become evident. Then the theories will stand in full balance as three equal alternatives whose distinctness is based on their fundamental assumptions. At that point with the alternative views of the nature of the state appreciated the reader may comfortably choose between them or choose not to choose.

A word should be added about immediate practical applications of this topic. In developing countries there is an especially evident struggle with problems of identity and allegiance. Most emerging nations, although claiming historical roots frustrated by colonial domination, are themselves the amalgam of diverse groups welded or bandaged together by the will of a dominant or temporarily dominant force. An examination of these countries in the light of the three theories, although never considered in this way by those involved, reveals the character of the contending forces within such nations. Some groups or individuals, in an organismic way, seek to dominate by right and will. These forces are oblivious to any separate point of view. Others, in a mechanistic form, contend that they act for the majority. It is a separate and usually unexamined question how the majority is discovered. Some synergistically act on behalf of the community good, with no indication how that good is determined. Warring factions with these different points of view is the common tribulation of developing nations.

Once in exploring the question of unity and identity in a large and diverse country it was asked, "Is India a Nation?" The same concern can be raised about China and many other countries. Pakistan, Lebanon, Ethiopia, Congo, and many other African countries, the Middle East in general, Northern Ireland, Bosnia, and many others are beset with problems of internal composition and national unity. Our practical, engineering, sense wants to step beyond the theoretical, to go to what will make things work. A resolution to the problems of particular countries will not come about from solving the question of the correct theoretical unifying principle. A consideration of the theoretical unifying principle can give insight into the depth of the conflict and making clear the patience needed to avoid exacerbating existing divisions. Theoretical knowledge will compliment the historical, economic, cultural, and sociological aspects of any such situation. All factors must be known and utilized in any attempt at improvement.

Human beings meet in many different ways and levels. In any meeting there is the contact of behavior, opinion, attitudes, beliefs, values, and theory. It is easiest to meet and interact with the person, but what is that person? Sometimes we meet the person from their theory dimension, sometimes their opinions, attitudes, and beliefs, and sometimes purely from their behavior. Each step further into the person is complex. Theory attempts to describe and understand. Though difficult it should not be avoided. If the state is to be explained by starting from behavior, there is the risk (as was discussed in the chapter on methodology) of never reaching beyond the level of statistical generalizations and partially sufficient conditions. Theory goes further.

Chapter 5

Political Authority/Sovereignty

It will disappoint to learn that the previous discussion has not been necessarily about the state. The discussion could easily have been about corporations. Political sounding terms such as state, government, citizens, and territory have been used. Nonpolitical terms could just as easily have been used; corporation, management, personnel, consumers, and property fit nicely. The theories of the unifying element can then be applied to corporations. Sperry Rand (mentioned above) claimed to be synergistic in its corporate makeup. Another's unity could be mechanistic. In the mechanistic case the corporate whole is merely the sum of its component divisions. DaimlerChrysler might fit the mechanistic category. A third corporation could be organismic where a spiritual force inspires and guides their existence. Claimants to this structure are rare in American experience, with the possible exception of the original Amana. The claim is not as rare in non-Western settings.

What Makes the State Different?

The use of political or nonpolitical terms does not determine the character of an entity. Some unique quality that explains why one defers to the other, that is, why normally corporations defer to the state, determines what is political. The unique feature of the state is said to be "political authority" or "sovereignty." Some political scientists say the term sovereignty is badly culture-bound and should not be used. It needs to be explained.

Origin of the Term "Sovereignty"

The origin of the term sovereignty is tied to the rise of the centralized monarchy and a territorial national state in Western Europe. Jean Bodin, a French theorist, coined the term in the late sixteenth century under circumstances of great religious feuding that threatened the breakdown of the state. Bodin felt that the disagreements about the responsible implementation of authority could be avoided by recognizing the king's "supreme power over citizen and subjects." This supreme power he called sovereignty. Bodin's notion of sovereignty can only be understood in terms of his purpose which was to focus attention on the king and the state in order to get away from scandalous religious disputes that he found destroying France.

The focus of political discussion did change, France survived, and the term sovereignty became widely used. The concept or reality that the term represented, however, was not new with Bodin. Supreme power over citizen and subject is not fundamentally different from the "supreme authority" to which Cicero had referred seventeen centuries earlier, nor is it different from the "supreme power" of the state referred to even earlier by Aristotle and other classical authors. However culture-bound the term, the concept is ancient. It continues today to accommodate the diversity of Greece, Rome, and Europe, as well as America, Africa, and Asia.

Three Views Of Sovereignty

There is an important debate about the meaning of the concept whatever the history of the term. To avoid the debate on the meaning of sovereignty, one of the structuring principles of politics, a basic element in understanding the range and limit of political decisions is overlooked. Three views of the nature of sovereignty must be described.

Absolute Authority

On the one side (the terms sovereignty and authority are used here interchangeably) it is maintained that authority means the absolute, complete, and unlimited power of the state over the life, rights, and duties of every one of its members. In a word this position views the state as "absolute." The government is obeyed because that's just the way it is. Deviations may occur but order should be restored and the law enforced when there is a departure from absolute rule.

Relative Authority

The relativist position is opposed to the absolutist view. The relativist view holds that the state is on the same level as other institutions; it denies that the authority of the state is essentially different from that of corporate associations. Authority is viewed as "relative" to time and place. From this perspective prior to the sixteenth century the state was not absolute, but during modern times the state may have become absolute. For a variety of reasons, according to this position, the situation has changed and the absolute state is in the process of being replaced by other social arrangements.

John Kenneth Galbraith, a widely read economist and public figure of the mid-twentieth century, talked about the emergence of the "corporate state" (*The New Industrial State*) and Charles E. Lindblom (*Politics and Markets*), a Yale professor of economics and political science, spoke of public policy made by corporations. Such views are within the relativistic perspective on the nature of authority. Those two authors do not address the theoretical topic formally, nor do they advocate a relativist view as such. They simply describe what they observe in the behavior of corporations and governments. The corporation may become or may already be dominant as witnessed in the United States in the way corporate decisions affect local communities' tax base and witnessed nationally in job outsourcing in many fields of employment. Decision makers in corporations are neither elected nor answerable to the affected community. The inability of the government in developing countries to change public policy because of the ingrained power of corporations further supports this claim of the relative nature of sovereignty. Also giving credence to the claim is the influence that pharmaceutical companies and health insurance companies have on attempts to change health and prescription drug policies. Though these may not be Galbraith's or Lindblom's versions of the new industrial state, they give some perspective on relative sovereignty.

Responsible or Proper Authority

Opposed to both the absolute and relative view is one called "responsible" or "proper" sovereignty. This third view strikes the logical (or verbal?) alternative to the other two. It holds that the state's authority is or should be neither absolute nor relative but instead there is or should be a certain "proper" activity for government and all units in society. In this perspective the authority of the state is neither too great nor too little; government will not interfere unduly with corporations nor shrink from intervening where appropriate. This third view strikes a nice rhetorical balance, but it does not immediately specify what is proper, where the line of responsibility can be drawn, and what is appropriate. Unspecified content makes this third position appear weak. To specify the content of responsible authority requires inquiry into more concrete experience of authority before the theoretical positions can be debated.

Popular Sovereignty and Legal Sovereignty

Sovereignty occurs in political literature previously in two ways, as popular sovereignty or as legal sovereignty. Popular sovereignty, sometimes called *political sovereignty*, is associated in American and English tradition with authority coming from the people. It is a notion that the authority of the state resides in and flows from the people. In exactly what manner it resides in or exactly how it flows from the people is usually unspecified. Government deriving its "just power from the consent of the governed," as stated in the Declaration of Independence, is an expression of popular sovereignty. History texts and introductory American government texts frequently explain sovereignty only in this way. Sometimes popular sovereignty is associated with direct democracy, suggesting that since the people possess authority they can rule themselves directly without any specific ruling personnel. The chapter on democracy explained the theoretical and practical arguments about the assumptions of direct democracy. That caveat, however, need not weaken the character of popular sovereignty. It is perfectly possible for the authority to come "from" the people, as Cicero's *res populi* and the Declaration of Independence suggest, without it being exercised by them directly. This will be discussed more specifically later in inquiring into the historical and logical origin of the state.

The context from which the term sovereignty may be known is that of legal sovereignty even though few may remember direct contact with it, often thought of in the sense of never having a monarch. Nonetheless, it is experienced in courts and other legal bodies that make binding decisions. Whether a simple traffic ticket, a zoning law, or a major constitutional issue some final rule-making authority is accepted. That decision or the framework within which it is made is the *legal sovereign*. It is definite and specific in comparison to popular sovereignty. It is found in some agency or person. A claimant knows that there is a final disposition to a case and knows who decides the case. All states have some identifiable final authority, a legal sovereign.

In matters of legal sovereignty there is no vague reference to a decision by the people. Occasionally there may be an allusion to a constitutional amendment or a decision by the ballot box in controversies. For the most part such allusions are more rhetoric than substance. The rhetoric occupies the attention of many people. Appeal beyond the legal authorities, despite the rhetoric, does not change the legal decision. Proof of this can be found in the lack of popular referendum amendments to the United States Constitution. The only amendments that might have been brought about by popular acclaim are those on women's suffrage and prohibition, and each has its own separate problematic that undermines the popular aspect. The other amendments are extensions of the legal environment instead of the other way around.

Attributes of Legal Sovereignty

The specific or inherent characteristics of an item are its attributes. By knowing the attributes of legal sovereignty it will be possible to appreciate better the claimed unique authority of the state. And, understanding the ascribed attributes makes it possible to finally decide between the absolute, relative, and so-called proper views of political authority. The plan is to describe how authority behaves and how it is regarded in order to determine whether it is absolute, relative, or proper. This will make it possible to decide whether sovereignty is indeed unique or merely an historical convention. Here the attributes ascribed will be reviewed in order to understand their implications. This information will bring about a fuller appreciation of the state. Once the state is better known more general questions of the range and limit of its authority can be entertained.

Determinate

The attributes of legal sovereignty are determinate, indivisible, and omnicompetent. Determinate means that legal authority is found in some definite agency, person, or other specified entity. In England it is located in Parliament. In an absolute monarchy it is located in the one predominant ruler. In the United States it is located in the national government. Some would prefer to say that in the United States legal sovereignty is located in the Constitution or in the ratification and amending process. Saying that legal authority in the United States is found in the national government temporarily avoids difficulties associated with American federalism (considered momentarily, and then separately in a later chapter), with the American separation of powers doctrine (likewise considered below, and in a later chapter), and avoids the lack of concreteness in ascribing it to the Constitution or the amending process. In this ascription there is the vagueness and diffusiveness of popular sovereignty.

In every state, in every political system, some specific rule-making, decision-making, or policy-making person or entity can be found. There is no question that "authoritative decision making" is central to the political system whatever the process of input, environment, or feedback. Wherever decision-making authority is found there is the determinate legal sovereign. Such a role does not disappear when the name changes from state to political system. The functional role of some person or body making decisions is the determinant authority.

Indivisible

Legal sovereignty is also indivisible. If it takes both houses of a legislative body to pass a law then the combination of houses is the determinate legal authority. If it takes the agreement of the legislative and executive branches and the acquiescence of the judicial branch to make law then legal sovereignty is located there. In most countries other than the United States there is no question about the legal authority being indivisible. Most countries are like England in governmental form where there is one universally recognized authority; previously it was the king while now it is parliament. Non-democratic countries are merely following the earlier part of the English example.

In the United States it sometimes takes all three branches for something to be legal. At other times one or two branches is adequate for a binding legal decision. The point on the indivisibility is that no two decision makers are equal such that they both can make binding but opposite decisions. At times it may appear that legal authority is divided in the United States. Periodically the media speak of lively debates about which branch of government is legally superior and different answers come according to particular historical settings. Despite the excitement the branches of the government do not represent warring factions. If they did the result would soon be a divided country. Rivalry between the branches is overstated, as is that between the political parties. This is developed in Chapter Fourteen.

The idea of federalism is a graver challenge within the United States, or any similar designed system, to the notion of indivisible authority. Federalism means to many that authority is divided between the national government and the states. For the present, and to the point of indivisibility, it should be noted that the issue was argued at length in the early years of the nation. Most especially sovereignty was argued in the famous Webster-Calhoun debates of the late 1820s and early 1830s. Daniel Webster, supposedly arguing the position of the North and in defense of the nation, presented the so-called federal notion. He argued that "sovereignty is divided between the states and the national government but the nation is one." John C. Calhoun, spokesman of the South, argued in more eloquent rhetoric and in more consistent logic, as Professor Harry Jaffa (*Equality and Liberty,* 131) points out, that sovereignty was "like chastity; it cannot be surrendered in part."

Calhoun was as sound in his theory as he was vivid in his imagery. He was also wrong. Specifically, he was incorrect in the application of his theory. The states did not have sovereignty, as Calhoun would have liked. The national government had it. Some readers of historical inclination may want to dispute the locus of sovereignty. To blunt that quarrel until it is addressed in a late chapter, it must be acknowledged that for Calhoun, Webster, or anyone else in any specific situation some one final decision-making authority settles disputes, which is the point of sovereignty being indivisible. The national government and the states cannot make equal but opposed decisions. If a decision must be rendered some<u>one</u> must make it. The rhetoric of federalism, of divided jurisdictions, hides from this reality of nationhood.

The reason some comments about the locus of sovereignty in the United States are in broad constitutional terms is to avoid the federalism debate. It was not avoided here, nor was it settled. The complexity of government to be appreciated must be acknowledged and then held in abeyance while additional information is gathered. The attribute that sovereignty is indivisible can be appreciated in its theoretical form even though its exact practical specificity must wait. Federal systems in the United States and elsewhere have a creative ambiguity in order to avoid debilitating disputes. Nonetheless, undisputed decisions must be made if the regimes are to succeed.

From the perspective of the United States there is no difficulty in locating the undivided sovereign in other countries. Whether observing federal systems or unitary states abroad, the regimes are perceived as undivided. Disagreements occur from time to time over "who" possesses and exercises authority in observed regimes, but the disagreement does not center on equal division of authority. Occasionally in the rare, though real, case of secession ambiguity may arise about the locus of legal authority. Conflicts usually are worked out without great drama. The European Union, which has been in the throes of coming into being, is attempting to anticipate some of these issues before the Union reaches full development. The extent of its success will not be clear for many decades and will not be determined just when the final constitutional agreement is reached.

Omnicompetent

Omnicompetence, the third attribute, means finality or completeness. It means there is no restriction on legal sovereignty; whoever is the determinate and indivisible authority has full power. The legal sovereign could declare murder legal, it could abolish private property, or it could abrogate freedom of speech or religious worship. If some higher legal body could annul the earlier decisions, that later body is the legal sovereign.

The Parliament in England has omnicompetent sovereignty and could do all those things. There is no higher legal body in England to overrule Parliament. The same omnicompetence is true in all countries once the legal authority is located. In the United States the Supreme Court is frequently cast in the role of the body that makes unpleasant binding and final decisions. That viewpoint about the Court is not exactly accurate since Congress or the President can or could have a role in such matters. To avoid disagreement about the omnicompetent authority within the United States by offering the constitutional amending process as an alternative does not change that quality because then the amending process is affirmed as being precisely omnicompetent. In other words, refuge in the popular sovereignty does not disguise this attribute of legal authority as final and complete. (The relation of the branches of government will be dealt with in a later chapter.)

LIMITATIONS ON LEGAL SOVEREIGNTY

Having said that authority is omnicompetent, there is some need to consider if limitations exist. This further consideration is an extension of the examination of the attributes for the purpose of understanding the ascribed character of legal authority. That understanding is preparation for evaluating the purpose of the state, the nature and end of political authority.

Limitations on sovereignty are thought to be natural or moral law, human behavior and popular will, and the facts of international life. These three limits are called "natural" which suggests that the limits arise in some automatic manner to avoid the advance of despotism. They are assumed to be natural barriers to authority becoming all-powerful, absolute, and unlimited.

Moral Law as a Limit

The natural moral law limitation assumes that ethical and moral standards limit the state's jurisdiction and authority. It assumes that when the full character of an oppressive regime is understood the weight of moral suasion will turn against the perpetrators and the ruling structure will collapse. Those acts of the state that are contrary to morality, which abuse the dignity of human beings, are thought to lack legitimacy and are not binding on the individual citizen who can and will turn against the regime. Moral outrage sounds great. However, it has had no affect on the dictators of history, Hitler or Saddam Hussein for example. This alleged moral limitation was of no help to the Jews in Nazi Germany who were sent to ovens as victims of an immoral doctrine. (Imagine someone standing just outside the door of those crematoriums whispering in the ear of those who passed, "Psst, you don't have to go in there because it's against the natural moral law." It is not hard to picture who would be shoved in first.) The mass graves of Shiite Muslims uncovered in Iraq likewise show there was no escape until "the facts of international life," to be considered in itself in a moment, came to the rescue.

There is no guarantee that the moral law, be it "natural" or whatever, will prevent immoral practices. A careful student of natural moral law would recognize that its effect can be destroyed. Aristotle, though he argued in defense of natural moral law, acknowledged in the *Ethics* (VIII, 1151a, 15) that "virtue and vice respectively preserve and destroy first principles." He was saying that the first principles of moral law ought to be preserved but they can be destroyed. If first principles are destroyed by repeated acts that ignore them, then Hitler or other monsters are possible. That there are many moral citizens under such a tyrant guarantees no recourse. If the tyrant possesses sufficient power, the tyrant can prevail. This is not to say that morality will always be ignored. It is just to recognize that morality has been and can be ignored.

Human Behavior and Popular Will as a Limit

The same general observations made about moral limits are true with respect to the alleged limit on legal authority labeled "human behavior and popular will." This second limit contends that no matter how despotic a government becomes it can never totally ignore the customs, beliefs, and practices of a people. Thus it is maintained that the legally omnicompetent British Parliament would no more dare to enact a law abolishing freedom of speech or popular elections than Mussolini would have attempted to legally abolish the practice of Catholicism in Italy.

The contention is that even a tyrant is limited by the psychology of human behavior. In a practical sense, however, in the political world a dictator can effectively manipulate the psychology of human behavior. The skillful tyrant would see that it is not necessary to abolish Catholicism in Italy or freedom of speech or popular elections in England. At least the would-be tyrant would not do these things first. These items can be abolished later if it is still important to abolish them. In the meantime the tyrant's will is imposed. If the tyrant's will prevails in all things important to ruling then it is unnecessary to abolish the practice of a religion, freedom of speech, popular elections, or whatever. The tyrant will be happy to let the public have its "toys," so to speak. Hitler was popularly elected and popularly supported until the people could do nothing to control him. The skillful control of the flow of information was key to his establishing absolute rule.

Thus, contrary to the assumption of a natural limit, human behavior and popular will can be undermined. Mass brainwashing is possible. The people followed Hitler because they were led to think that what he allowed them to hear was true. Today it is known that they were misled. Back then the people's ability to challenge the regime was limited institutionally and circumscribed by governmental control of the media. Even the German Catholic bishops who have been criticized for not challenging Hitler discovered the limits of their ability to act. Guenther Levy in *The Catholic Church and Nazi Germany* pointed out that when bishops attempted to challenge practices of the regime, they found curates arrested and executed on fraudulently concocted charges. Their diocesan publications became the last free press when restrictions gave way to outright ban. Courageous criticism was replaced by forced silence.

What is known today is that Hitler was evil and "should" have been stopped. "Should" is based on the assumption that at any given time tyranny can be restrained by the popular conscience mobilized as a result of information available in a free media. It is assumed that by activating some mechanism present in a free society the oppression will end. Such an assumption overlooks the particular circumstances of the regime in question. A new experience is the popularized tyranny of recent decades where the only ones oppressed are those who claim the freedoms of normally constituted Western society. The assumption that a response can throw out the well-organized tyrant overlooks the opposition's fractionalized and necessarily part-time character. Watchdog international human rights groups emerge in an effort to have permanent organizations to warn about abuses, but experience show that though they do good, much evil occurs while practices are covered up. It is false to believe that by knowing the dangers from the past a futuristic *1984* and Brave New World can be avoided. Complacency in that belief of natural restraint makes the undesirable that much more possible. The word "eternal" in the watchword, "Eternal vigilance is the price of liberty," may just be too late.

The belief in popular will limiting tyrannical government is supported by cases where popular reaction has, indeed, overturned unpopular regimes and legislation. "People Power" in the Philippines and repeal of the Eighteenth (Prohibition) Amendment in the United States serves as examples. Next time, however, the tyrant may learn from predecessors' mistakes or sweeping policy objective as in prohibition may be accomplished by less direct means. In the latter case an "educational" campaign may be launched extending from nursery school through elementary grades and beyond, advertising of the item in question may be banned, and "opposed" commercials may be government sponsored. With such preliminaries there will be no need for a constitutional amendment. A glance at the statistics on the declining per capita use of tobacco by Americans confirms the ability of government to achieve an objective in a piecemeal fashion more effectively than with an outright ban. Winston Smith was allowed his "Victory Gin" in *1984*. Today he could not have a cigarette.

Facts of International Politics as a Limit

Hitler and Saddam Hussein, more recently, were eventually overthrown by "the facts of international life." Unfortunately the justification at the time action was launched against Hitler and Hussein was not because of what they were doing internally (that justification only came later) but because of some threat at the moment to the larger world community. What is intended by this third limit is that the mere existence of other states limits or eventually comes to limit the power of a government within its own boundaries. The effectiveness of this alleged limit might be questioned by atrocities discovered after the regimes demise as witnessed in many former tyrannies and most recently in Iraq. Usually an "international" incident must occur as an excuse before a sanction can be carried out by external states. Hitler's direct aggression against a neighboring state was what brought about his downfall. Rumors of internal atrocities evoked only disparate verbal reactions that were not sufficient to bring action. Likewise in the case of Hussein it was the case made against "weapons of mass destruction" rather than the reality of internal atrocities that was offered as justification for bringing down his regime. The skillful tyrant can learn from such cases so that the factors that provoke intervention can be reduced or eliminated in the future.

Today there is much appropriate concern about the abuse of human rights. Amnesty International is a voluntary group of international citizens that looks into alleged human rights violations in countries throughout the world. Abuses are found especially in, but not limited to, developing countries. Frequently the only recourse against such abuses is unfavorable publicity. However, publicity does not have a great effect in many countries, particularly those that control their media. Some countries become immune from sanctions and scrutiny, or so it seems since the problems seems to go on endlessly. Sometime the offending country is the ward of a larger state and inaction is the result of competing international interests. Sanctions against a "protected" country could result in conflict with the protector. Such are the intricacies and encumbrances on international sanctions for the abuse of internal authority. Again, the alleged natural limit does not necessarily limit.

Conclusion And Perspective

Natural internal barriers to the omnicompetent legal authority do not exist. A skillful would-be tyrant can overcome the alleged limits of moral law, human behavior, and the facts of international life. In final analysis omnicompetence means just that, omnicompetence. The government, any government, could become all-powerful, absolute, and unlimited. Technology makes this even more possible today. Even the United States government in its need to develop a capacity to know what potential enemies are doing has perfected a technological capability that enables it to monitor messages in ways never before possible. The interception of messages is not limited to military units but to all walks of life. Legislation creating the Office of Homeland Security (OHS) following the 9/11 attack was debated precisely on this point. The Office was established, but the arguments over potential threats to traditional liberties have not been entirely resolved. The need to curtail terrorists is very real; imaginative new ways to ferret out the threat are needed. As the war on terrorism continues the debate of government efforts and the means employed will likewise continue.

Technology used to combat tyranny can also make tyranny possible. A political response to that possibility might be that vigilance is necessary. Jefferson and many others called for eternal vigilance, which is continually reflected in administrative decisions, the courts, and in congressional hearings. Vigilance may take the form of curbing the activities of the OHS, the CIA, the FBI, and the government in general, although there is also a sentiment for empowering them rather than restricting them. Vigilance is useful but it may be misguided since it can lead to vigilantism, an equal form of tyranny. If tyranny is to be avoided, a more formidable check might be in knowing more about control of the state, the subject of the next chapter.

Three questions have been left unsettled: (1) whether sovereignty in broad perspective is really absolute, relative, or proper, (2) the content of "proper sovereignty," and (3) the relationship between popular sovereignty and legal sovereignty, that is, how the one "flows into" the other. The first question was not settled in the discussion about the attributes of legal sovereignty or in the examination of the alleged limits on authority. The attributes and lack of limits only point to the possibility of absoluteness, not that it will necessarily come about. Thus the overall character of sovereignty is still open as is the content of so-called proper sovereignty. Answers to these questions will become available with an understanding of the origin of the state. The different views of the origin of the state reveal more fully its character and the basis to control it.

Chapter 6

The Origin/Control Of The State

Why do we have the state? The answer is simple: to avoid anarchy and disorder. There are those who hold that human beings can function, and would be better off, without the organized state. That challenge to the state existence, supposedly so obvious, provides an opportunity to review its justification. Justification contains the basis for control.

The existence of the state seems historically universal and an explanation of its existence need require only a brief reminder of particular origins. Given the history little more appears necessary. That is incorrect. There is an historical dimension to the origin of the state, which preoccupies many and is thought to satisfy required justification for its existence. Yet, it is critical to explain why any individual is obliged to the rules established by others. Historical information is not the answer. Why any individual should be obliged to follow what was done in the past needs a deeper explanation.

There is a double sense of the origin of the state. There is an historical origin. There is also a philosophical origin, or a "logical" origin. The logical origin is much more critical, even though the historical is what is constantly drilled from the earliest school days. The logical origin spells the basis for control of the state. It will be described at length after a brief look at historical origin.

Historical Origins

An unusual aspect of the historical origin of the state is that although it comes in three varieties (force, kinship, and social contract) all three can be true. In the unifying element of the state and in sovereignty, three theories confronted each other and only one could be correct. The same exclusiveness obtains for the logical origin of the state and later for the purpose of the state. For historical origin, that exclusiveness does not obtain because the three historical versions amount to only broad summary categories of what has occurred.

Force as an historical origin maintains that the state, a particular state, originated in the efforts of one great man or group who organized a diverse community into one nation. Charlemagne served this role in France. Simon Bolivar did so in a number of Latin American states. ***Kinship***, on the other hand, holds that the state is the product of an evolution from the family and a community of blood relationship. Many nations can claim this evolutionary origin. Examples are the biblical and current state of Israel, as well as many African, Asian, and nations of Eastern Europe. Secessionist movements within many other countries lay claim to kinship roots. The S***ocial Contract***, most prominently exemplified in the United States, maintains that the state is the result of community representatives coming together and agreeing to form a larger unit.

Those who study a particular country may dispute which theory of historical origin applies. Some may claim social contract origin for Israel by pointing to earlier agreements that brought about its independent status in May 1948. Some maintain that Israel both biblically and historically is a product of force. Looking to George Washington as an early Simon Bolivar, it could be held that despite the appearance of social contract, the United States is really an example of force origin. In many respects some economic interpretations of the origins of the United States wittingly or unwittingly fit into the force mold. France might be viewed as an example of kinship origin instead of force. The mixed picture of historical origin is possible in many countries with the depiction dependent on the presentation of the historian.

Summary views about the historical origin of states give information of value to those who have a historical predilection. The exact origin of any particular state and a generalization about all states can vary according to perspective. What is important, however, is that knowledge of historical origin does not have immediate practical value. As explained earlier in discussion of history as a discipline, the immediate practical consequences of knowledge about historical events are remote at best, although one would be foolish, indeed, to completely turn aside from it. Yet, no matter what the historical origin of a particular state no information is provided or justifiably implied in that origin that would bind an individual today to those earlier events.

A citizen in any state may be told that the "founding fathers" desired the acceptance of the rules and practices of the successive governments. The founders may, indeed, have desired this compliance, but there is no binding quality to that desire. Historical justifications in themselves always are arbitrary and artificial. They are subject to the convenience of the immediate interpreter, the convenience of the current holders of the keys of the state, their defenders or their opponents. Any skillful formulator who uses historical evidence can tie a story of origin to support their cause. Historical justifications are not acceptable even if, which is impossible, conditions have not changed since the beginning. To bind the individual today, to justify the individual's acceptance of today's rules of this particular government under this particular constitution in this particular state, some explanation must be given that transcends historical lines.

To oblige the individual, a justification must be given that goes beyond historical circumstances. The individual today in Poland or Brazil or the United States or any country must be tied in a nonarbitrary way to the state. Without personal ties, compliance and allegiance are nothing more than arbitrary. The philosophical theories of the origin provide explanations of personal involvement. Historical origins are shortcuts; they are poetical (as mentioned in the Introduction) and lack logical completeness. Historical explanations may persuade and emotionally bind. They cannot logically bind except insofar as each individual chooses to accept without question, which is a reason without depth.

PHILOSOPHICAL-LOGICAL-LEGAL ORIGIN

The "philosophical" origin is best renamed the "philosophical-logical-legal" origin of the state. The latter choice better conveys the concept it represents than does the shorter one-word name, "philosophical." (For convenience sake the shorter name will be used most often.) Philosophical origin as opposed to historical origin, like any philosophical examination of a topic, attempts to get an X-ray of the entity instead of an external description. A philosophical explanation looks inside rather than only from the outside. To know why an individual is bound to a state today as yesterday or a century ago is different from knowing what the forefathers did in that same period.

Philosophical origin comes in three versions and each maintains that it alone is the correct justification for tying individuals to the authority of the state. Each is applicable to any of the historical forms. Traditionally, the three logical origin theories are called divine, social contract, and natural. The theories answer the question of why the individual living now should accept the action of the founders or ancestors, who did not know today's circumstances. A visit to the beautifully preserved and restored Independence Hall and Park area in Philadelphia and the skyscrapers surrounding the low-profile original buildings provides visible evidence that the founding fathers were of a different age.

The divine, social contract, and natural theories respectively, answer the question of why one is bound to the state in the following manner, "God wills it," "the majority wills it," "your better self wills it." To these declarations it might be replied, respectively again, "Ergo I am not free," "I am oppressed," "I will it." The third response seems favored, but that impression will be offset in the elaboration on each theory that follows and in the next chapter. The short preview answers show that the philosophical approach is different in kind from the historical ones. Each links the individual to the state in a personal way.

DIVINE (OR DETERMINATIVE) ORIGIN

"Divine" or "determinative" origin, which need not be taken in any religious sense, means that some force over which the individual has no control brings about the existence and continuation of the state. This force can be God, Hegel's *geist*, a biological force, Skinner's environment, or the deterministic developmental stages of the Swiss theorist Piaget. Serious as well as popularized expressions of this divine origin theory exist. James I of England or Louis XV of France claimed that God ordained them to be king. The building of Israel or

Islamic states is explained as flowing from God's directive. Other expressions of "divine" intervention in affairs of the state are witnessed in President McKinley's claim that God inspired him to retain the Philippines after the Spanish-American War and when supporters of Ronald Reagan claim that he was spared from an assassin's bullet "by the hand of God . . . for a purpose." All these claims can be seen as real or rhetorical. As rhetoric they form a cover for raw power, imperial fact, or a hidden biological pecking order. They may be an elitist self-justification given in language to pacify the ignorant.

Hegel saw the state as "the march of God in the world." Many today see their brand of liberation or their version of national self-expression as God's intent. The origin of the state and succession within it are viewed in this philosophical theory as a product of spiritual, biological, or environmental forces. In biological terms the state's origin is found in a gregarious instinct as in the herding or flocking of animals. Various embellishments of this theory are found in recent writings on biopolitics and sociobiology. The popularized writings of Desmond Morris and Robert Ardrey give fascinating stories of parallels between animal life and human life. Embedded in those stories is the notion that the organization of human society is little different from that of other life forms.

The critical point of this divine or determinative theory is that human beings do not control the state anymore than an animal the herd. The origin of the state, and as a consequence its control, is in some force over which individuals have no control. Charlemagne, the founding fathers, the original clan, the historical majority, are products of the uncontrolled force, whether it be identified as the environment, culture, God, or instinct. Awareness of this uncontrollable force brings about for human beings a heightened appreciation of the human condition, of "man's fate" as Andre Malraux referred to it. For practical purposes no change can be effected by what is known. It is similar to the enjoyment of a familiar movie, opera, or play even though the outcome is known.

Hegel saw his theorizing as "painting gray on gray;" peoples' destinies are set and reflection on it is the only option. Political events are studied just as the daily astrology reports or the biorhythm charts are read and nothing changes. It may be consoling to know what is inevitable. From this perspective political science can move beyond false theories of freedom and dignity, to use B. F. Skinner's phrase, by seeing that behavior is patterned and predictable. By measuring men's movements sufficiently behavior is as predictable as molecules in a gas.

From "economic man" to econometrics, from "Freudian slips" to biological determinism, from "history repeating itself" to developmental stages, from "fate" to "futuristics," various forms of determinism find favor in scholarly and ordinary discourse. These disguised versions of determinism reveal its continued presence. Though the President may not be regarded as the father of the nation-family as the Japanese regard the Emperor or as Sadat claimed in Egypt, nonetheless, we may all be, in the words of Robert Strauss, like ants on a log floating down the river, each thinking we control its direction.

Like the organismic theory of the unifying element of the state the divine theory is not flattering. It also is not to be dismissed in a casual manner. Many popular contemporary philosophies, like those of Camus and Heidegger, although not admitting to nineteenth-century determinism, have humans as victims of a "human condition" symbolized in the myth of Sisyphus. Humanity is seen as being thrown in the absurdity of existence contemplating the nudity of the world. Such philosophies and attitudes toward the ruled and the ruler express the essential element of the divine theory of state origin that it is not subject to human control.

Social Contract Origin

The philosophical social contract theory holds that the origin of the state is found in some form of voluntary agreement and is the opposite of the determinative theory. It maintains that in some way, which need not be explicit or overt, humans agree to the existence of the political community. This agreement constitutes a "rational or legal legitimacy," in the words of the German sociologist Max Weber (just as determinative origin is a combination of Weber's traditional and charismatic basis of authority). The point of the social contract theory is that human beings by their choices control the existence and the direction of the state. It certainly is more flattering than the determinative origin.

There are three different versions of the social contract theory. What the three different versions show is that the general theory can fit, as the determinative theory can, the full range of historical situations. This flexibility must be elaborated on because there is an inclination to associate the philosophical social contract with the historical social contract.

The philosophical and the historical social contract are different. The historical refers to a particular state with supporting historical conditions. The United States and the activities of the Second Continental Congress are prime examples of an acceptable historical social contract origin. The philosophical social contract theory, on the other hand, explains all states, whether the historical conditions seem to support it or not. In other words, the philosophical social contract explains historical events like those of the United States and those of a Charlemagne in France or of states that have evolved from kinship origins. That the origin of the United States has all the characteristics of a social contract does not by that historical form commit it to the philosophical/logical social contract.

The philosophical social contract can be described (See *Appendix B*) as a sequence of events consisting of (a) a state of nature, (b) a contract which is a function of some human control, and (c) the state or the situation which exists following the contract. Described in this way the theory suggests a story line where (a) men originally live in a "state of nature" or some original, natural prepolitical condition, that (b) for some particular reason they enter a contract or agreement, and (c) they thereby bring about the existence of the state or whatever it is that the political community or the condition following is called.

Despite its historical appearance (A to B to C), the philosophical social contract is not intended to be historical. Unfortunately even established scholars frequently mistake it to be historical. The philosophical social contract intends just the opposite sequence from the historical sequence. It intends the sequence to go from "C to B to A." That is, the existence of the state or the existing condition is explained by way of a contract or agreement in order to avoid what is unacceptable, in order to avoid a state of nature. The leading theorists of the philosophical social contract (Hobbes, Locke, and Rousseau) are described below in order to document its adaptability to all historical situations.

Thomas Hobbes

Thomas Hobbes, in his *Leviathan*, (1651) argued that people originally lived in a warlike "state of nature" where life was solitary, poor, nasty, brutish, and short. In this state of nature the law of the jungle prevailed, meaning that each person had to fend only for him or herself. As the story goes, desiring to overcome this original condition, individuals entered into a contract that establishes the "Leviathan," they produced the absolute state. Hobbes's Leviathan can in many respects be visualized as a Frankenstein monster; it is made from the parts of many persons. In creating the state men, for Hobbes, in common agreement confer all their power on one person and reduce their will to his will.

Hobbes calls this product of common agreement a "Commonwealth" or, in other words, the great "Leviathan", or "mortal god." The term "leviathan" derives from the Hebrew term for a sea monster symbolizing evil, which is ultimately to be defeated by the good. Although Hobbes speaks of our debt to this mortal god, "under the immortal God," he twists the original scriptural use of the reference from a monster kept in check by God for man's sake to a monster that dominates men under God. This dominance of men by the monster is reflected in a curious drawing on the title page of the original edition of the Leviathan in which a crowned giant, whose body is composed of tiny figures of human beings, overlooks a town. Over the giant is a passage from Job 41:24 saying, "Upon all the earth there is none like him."

Hobbes's meaning is clear; there is a "real unity" in the ruler dominating all under the approval of the heavens. Hobbes does not mean to say that the state must possess and exercise all power all the time. The state must possess full power so that it can exercise whatever power is necessary to avoid disorder. The people desire or will the state in order to avoid anarchy and disorder. In 1651 the state would not need as much exercise of power as it might in the twenty-first century. In either case what is needed is enough power to overcome, that is, to avoid, the state of nature. The evils of the wars of individuals, of each against each, are such that absolute power is preferable. The ruler who does not possess that power should be replaced by one who does. Without enough power the community is in danger of falling into the state of nature.

Power is absolute even though Hobbes appears to say that there is liberty for the subjects as when he says that the individual may refuse an order to kill himself, though justly condemned. Yet, for Hobbes, such liberties are matters "praetermitted" by the sovereign, meaning that those matters left outside the law can later become part of the law. Even the liberty to disobey the command to kill himself can be abrogated when the refusal to obey frustrates the end for which the sovereign was created.

Hobbes's theme can be observed today in the rationale of martial law regimes and in the rhetoric of "law-and-order" candidates for elective office. The claim is that authoritarian rule is needed to overcome and to avoid general disorder and lawlessness. Easy criticism is thrown at these modern leviathans. Still, many prefer the authoritarian regimes to the disorders where there is no freedom to walk the street in safety or to tend one's shop or garden in peace. Some in Iraq after the overthrow of Saddam Hussein desired his return to overcome the lawlessness that followed the war. A fundamental preference for safety and order, in the seventeenth century or the twenty-first, constitutes the consent, the agreement, the contract of which the social contract theory speaks. The desire for peace, security, and safety that the regime satisfies is justification for its rules and its power. If the situation of lawlessness and disorder is grave enough then absolute exercise of power is justified.

This version of the social contract can be seen to strike a responsive contemporary chord where disorder ensues. It intends to apply to all states whether disorder is evident on the surface or hidden below. Hobbes argues that even in a tranquil setting the windows are locked and the doors bolted because a tendency toward the jungle lurks below civility's surface. It takes only slight experience with urban turmoil for a "tough on crime" candidate to successfully mount a campaign for public office. Incumbent officeholders are loath to be portrayed as weak whether the issues are crime, the economy, or responding to terrorism. Hobbes's social contract represents the public's desire for well-being and a low degree of tolerance for placing it in jeopardy.

John Locke

The most widely accepted of the social contract theories is that of John Locke. In his *Two Treatises of Government*, dated 1690, Locke's primary concern is with "limited government." Locke is usually perceived to view the state of nature differently from Hobbes. For Locke the state of nature ("a" in the sequence) is said to be peaceful, the contract (step "b") is said to be a function of reason, and the state ("c") is expressed as "limited government." Puzzlement about this version of the philosophical intention should occur. The story does not work. It is not immediately apparent why people would leave a peaceful state of nature to enter a contract and form a government, even a limited one. It is true that Locke insists, against Hobbes, that the state of nature is peaceful. He contrasts the state of nature with the state of war as a contrast between peace, goodwill, and mutual assistance with enmity, violence, and mutual destruction.

Yet, that commonly cited contrast by Locke must be put into the context of his earlier observation (*Second Treatise on Government,* paragraph 1) that men are originally in a state of perfect freedom to do as they think fit. Men may act in this perfect freedom without asking any other man for approval. He maintains that this is not a condition of license since a "law of nature" governs. The problem is that if the original condition is indeed peaceful there is no apparent reason to leave it. Locke recognized this peculiarity since he later goes on to describe the "inconveniences" in the state of nature even with its law of nature. The inconveniences arise from a consideration of determining the specifications of the law of nature. Who will judge the law, who will enforce it? To these questions Locke answers that enforcement is in every man's hands.

Assuredly it is an inconvenience when each individual must decide what the law is, when violations occur, and how to enforce it. In other words each individual is legislator, executive, and judge. And to these individual powers the words from Locke's opening passage would apply, that is, men acting "as they think fit." Contrary to the reading that sees Locke's version of the state of nature as peaceful, his portrayal camouflages the reality below the surface, the war of each against each. If everyone does "as he thinks fit," Locke's state of nature is not noticeably different from that described by Hobbes. This changed reading improves the understanding of Locke's theory. If the state of nature is warlike, inconvenient to use Locke's euphemism, then in the story line there is reason to abandon that condition. In the philosophical formulation there is reason to avoid the state of nature. Reasonable people agree to set up limited government to avoid the inconveniences of the state of nature. As it turns out then the major contrast of Locke with Hobbes is not in the condition of the fictional state of nature. The contrast is in the contract itself and the nature of the state that the contract supports.

The contract is a function of will or desire for Hobbes since human beings desire for themselves the good they see in others. For Locke the contract is an expression of man's reason, of his awareness that the state of nature is inconvenient. Government for Hobbes is or can be absolute. For Locke it is always to be "limited." The nature of Locke's "limited government" is of critical importance. It is both the individualism and the notion of limited government found in his argument that attracts many to Locke.

What Locke intends is that government be precisely limited from doing anything other than overcoming the inconveniences of the state of nature. He holds that every individual should be able to do "as he thinks fit," but the inconveniences interfere with this ability. Government limited to a minimal role makes it more possible for the individual to acquire wealth or do many other things of one's own choosing. Men subject themselves to rule for "the great and chief end" of the preservation of their property. Overcoming the inconveniences of the state of nature makes it possible for men to go about the business of accumulating wealth of plums, nuts, or more durable gold. His social contract easily accommodates laissez faire individualistic views of the state. Even his often acclaimed right to rebel must be understood as itself limited from "reverting" power to the individual to reestablish the inconveniences previously overcome.

Lockean theory and individualism can be recognized in contemporary political rhetoric, economic theories, and daily conversations. Locke's social contract theory says that the role of government derives from the common agreement that individuals do not want the inconveniences of enforcing the law themselves. They do not want absolute government; they only want to do as they think fit without uncertainty, insecurity, and harm. They do not want to be interfered with as they go about acquiring wealth. These qualities strike a very responsive chord. Even the poor are often persuaded that by limiting the purview of government their interests are served.

Jean Jacques Rousseau

Rousseau's theory differs from both Hobbes and Locke. Although he dislikes government, Rousseau sees a larger role for government even as he condemns its "chains." Rousseau, the most colorful writer of the three theorists, dislikes the state and prefers the state of nature which he describes as truly peaceful but unattainable. What is more, there is greater historical realism to his social contract story version. The historical quality should not make any final difference in the acceptance of the theory, but it is also striking that his story coincides with biblical depictions of a tranquil Eden.

The opening phrase of Rousseau's *The Social Contract* (1762) reads, "Man is born free; and everywhere he is in chains." By this he conveys his appreciation of the state of nature as free and peaceful; the state is enslavement. The condition of enslavement Rousseau made clear in an earlier writing, *Discourse on the Origin of Inequality*, when he related: that degraded man accepted the origin of society and law, which bound new fetters on the poor, and gave new powers to the rich; which irretrievably destroyed natural liberty, eternally fixed the law of property and inequality, converted clever usurpation into unalterable rights and, for the advantage of a few ambitious individuals subjected all mankind to perpetual labor, slavery, and wretchedness. The warlike condition described by Hobbes as part of the state of nature (the original natural condition) is instead for Rousseau a product of leaving the state of nature. Wretchedness came with the development of private property. Rousseau is critical of both Hobbes's absolute government and Locke's limited government since it protects private property.

Initially Rousseau's view that the state of nature is truly peaceful and that all forms of society is a form of bondage presents a double problem for the social contract theory. The first problem is that the story does not appear to work. If the state of nature is truly peaceful then there is no justification either in reason or will to abandon it. The second problem is that the general pattern of philosophical intention does not appear to work either. What exists ("c"), the chains, is undesirable and what is desirable for Rousseau, the peaceful state of nature, ("a") is unattainable. Both problems are resolved by Rousseau's transition step ("b"). By a combination of fate and consensus agreement to fate Rousseau fashions an intermediate step that makes his theory and his story cogent.

In the story for Rousseau, man leaves the state of nature because of a series of natural accidents. This expulsion compelled man to invent increasingly elaborate means of survival. What he has in mind is that by being set off from his original condition, man had to invent new devices to aid survival. He invented thinking, then property, and eventually government to protect both the barbarous and the weak. In this connection Rousseau (in his *On the Origin and Foundation of the Inequality of Mankind* as well as in his *Social Contract*) *is* particularly effective in describing the origin of private property. He credits the first person, having set off a plot of land and finding others simple enough to believe him, as the founder of civil society. With no one challenging the first claim humankind became subject to crime, war, murder, and the evils of civil society.

The accidents Rousseau has in mind at the origin of civil society are volcanoes causing the fusion of metals and the creation of implements, which led to agricultural tools and weapons. Other physical disruptions gave way to similar developments. Man learned to adapt. In the process mankind became enslaved to what was new. In other words, humans left the state of nature because they had no choice, nature forced it upon them. Here the story line and the philosophical intention conjoin. The "simple feeling of existence" that obtained in the state of nature, and which is the philosophical goal, is desirable. Unfortunately it is unattainable since it is not possible to undo nature. Humans must be resigned to their fateful chains.

Although human beings desire the tranquility of the state of nature it cannot be achieved since nature cannot be reconstructed. The human condition is the product of varying adjustments to the diverse circumstances produced by nature. All that can be done is to make the best of the bad situation. This is the role of the general will or consensus for Rousseau. The general will is an attempt to acknowledge human fate and to approximate the state of nature by being resigned to fate. Rousseau's writing is a combination of hope and despair, a resignation to chains and a rejection of them. His philosophical position amounts to an environmental determinism and an existential individualism. He would seem at home in twentieth century dour philosophy and literature.

Political fatalism and consensus are expressed when Rousseau describes the social contract and its accompanying general will. In his view each gives himself to all and in so doing gives himself to nobody in particular. Since each individual acquires the same rights he gains an equivalent for everything he loses. This is the strangeness of his "general will" whereby in uniting himself with all he obeys himself alone and remains free. A little later Rousseau acknowledges the need for a "legislator," in effect a dictator, who will instruct the general will. Here Rousseau's despair is clear, for he admits that to succeed such a legislator should feel himself capable of changing human nature. Unfortunately, from Rousseau's perspective, this change cannot be brought about because nature cannot be changed, the accidental disruptions at the origin of society cannot be undone. Rousseau uniquely and strangely combines appealing criticisms and irreconcilable solutions.

This combination makes Rousseau's fundamental theme appealing to the advocates of democratic popular control discussed in Chapter One. Criticism of elitism combined with unattainable idealism characterizes that version of traditional democracy. The Port Huron Statement's participatory concepts and hidden centrism are vintage Rousseau.

The three versions of the social contract theory are similar in that they impute agreement by the members to the existence of the state. The agreement need not be overt. It need not come about by way of a public referendum. It can be and normally is tacit. Passive consent, resignation, and implied consensus are its trademarks. The "voluntary contractual submission" of the social contract is not written. It can assume written form in some historical expressions, as in the United States (keeping in mind that the United States need not be an expression of the philosophical social contract). In the law-and-order monarchy or dictatorship, in the consensus "popular democracy," and even in the constitutional republic there is according to the social contract theory an agreement that comes before the regime. That agreement is the fundamental commitment to law and order or to limited government or to the general will.

The theories of the social contract purport that all mankind desires, finds reasonable, or is personally resigned to the basic circumstance of the state. The theories are not to be faulted because there is no historical or anthropological evidence that such agreements ever occurred. The theories speak of a philosophical or logical or legal origin of the state, not an historical origin. The explanation is "logical," not "chronological." Logical origin in a contract is about human control. If there is not enough law and order human control can change it, if the "limited government" needs more limiting it can be curbed, if the general will is unhappy it can be freshened.

The element of control or agreement stands in contrast to the lack of control in the divine or determinative theory. Each of the theories of the origin of the state carries over into respective theories of the purpose of the state. The linkage of origin and purpose will become evident in their general pattern. An appreciation of the continuity of nature, authority, origin, and purpose in three different ways will also become evident. This continuity shows that an understanding of the range and limit of government involves many things. Before the purpose of the state can be considered, the final theory of the origin of the state must be explained.

(Natural) Or Socio-Logical Origin

The third distinct theory of the origin of the state maintains that the management of the state is neither completely subject to human control nor completely beyond human influence. Frequently this theory is named "natural" on its claim that the state exists by way of human nature and is not an artificial construct. The name "natural" is not being used here since the other two theories also claim that they are natural. The determinative theory and the social contract theories read human nature differently; they nonetheless understand themselves as expressing a naturalness of origin. Fairness in the treatment of the theories requires a name that does not attempt to accomplish by preemption what it must demonstrate.

The term "socio-logical" is used here for the third theory. What is intended by the term socio-logical is that the logic of man's nature as a social and political animal explains the existence of the state. The theory is Aristotelian and holds that, "Man is by nature a social and political animal." From this view the state is not purely a product of human control nor is it purely a product of uncontrollable forces. To be naturally social and political means that "always or for the most part" man would live in society.

There can be exceptions to the rule that man is naturally social and political, but they are indeed exceptions. Aristotle expressed this by observing (*Politics*, I, 1253a, 27) that anyone unable to live in society, or who has no need because he is sufficient for himself, must be either a beast or a god. Aristotle did not spend time describing the beast and gods because they were so rare, they were self-identifying, and they were not in the realm of the political. An example that might be offered is the hermit with <u>no</u> societal contact. Pseudo-nonpolitical pretenders live, either figuratively or literally, on the fringe of society in a parasitical dependence on the established order. Nonpolitical pretense frequently purports godliness while bordering on beastliness. The so-called Reverend Jim Jones and his unfortunate People's Temple cult that entered a mass suicide of more than nine hundred members in 1978 in Jonestown, Guyana, is a gruesome modern day example. Most who claim that they are nonpolitical are a far cry from such bizarre events. They are also a far cry from being truly nonpolitical, since they live within and depend upon the existing order. Even those who desire to change the existing order to one of greater imagined autonomy for the individual are by definition political since they desire some order.

According to the socio-logical view, human beings live in society for two reasons, because of the necessities of life and because of fundamental human capabilities. In this view the state comes into existence originating in the bare needs of life, and continues in existence for the sake of a good life. The same two reasons apply when it comes to explaining the existence of the family. The bare necessities of life are provided in the family and in it is accomplished the ability to share and communicate in an intimate fullness. In the family the individual exercises capabilities that are not utilized either in private or in the larger political community. Intimacy of relationship is not present in more fleeting and larger social relations. A division of labor in the family provides for the daily material needs. There, one person is often the principal provider, another the principal processor, others are helpers. This division of labor is an economic dimension that, though important, is not the most important ingredient.

The economic dimension of the family is not its primary ingredient because the family remains a great good even when the individual no longer depends on it for the necessities of life. Independent young adults and college age individuals can appreciate this observation since, while frequently being self-supporting, they nonetheless love to go home for a holiday or to receive a letter or phone call or money from a member of their family. The visits, letters, or other contacts are part of living well. These contacts are non-economic even though a meal or a gift might have been included. The human community satisfies not only economic need but also social need and basic ability. Men, even when they do not require one another's help, desire to live together. Men cling to life even at the cost of enduring great misfortune, seeming to find in life a natural sweetness and happiness.

Every activity, like piano playing or social living, has its routine performance and its well performance, its performance at a level of quality. Human beings seek a type of "well" performance in community. That is, although men and women can live without the community, they can be beastly; they cannot in that manner live well. Aristotle observed (*Politics*, I, 1253a, 30-35) that "man, when perfected, is the best of animals, but when separated from law and justice, he is the worst of all." The family is an exercise in living well through an intimate sharing with another human being. Individuals leave their family of origin and begin to form a new family to fulfill a sharing in intimacy, for purposes that are not just material, economic and sexual. Individuals, usually young but also old, pair off in quiet strolls, dine in twosomes, and seek privacy in crowds. All life, its beauty, and its potential are the domain of these two "lovers" of sweetness and happiness.

The same two dimensions, economic and social, explain the political community or state. The state comes into existence for the bare needs of life and continues in existence for the sake of a good life. Economic sufficiency is a prerequisite of any state. Some states fail in the economic dimension, placing their political existence in jeopardy. This is especially troubling in the context of international economic globalization and threatened insolvency of smaller nations.

From the perspective of socio-logical origin, even if the economic needs of the community were somehow provided automatically forever in the future, the state would continue to exist to fulfill its social dimension. This continued existence idea is in contrast to contract theories as they imply that the state could go away if the ends of order or wealth are met. For Locke if the "inconveniences" were provided automatically government could be "limited" to the point where, as with the later theorist Karl Marx, it would wither away. From this perspective if the state merely provides a traffic cop function and that function is satisfied with electronic traffic signals, then the personnel-operated state can be set aside. In contrast, from the perspective of socio-logical origin the state comes into existence to facilitate the production, distribution, and consumption of material goods while *it continues in existence for the sake of the good life*. This better of social existence parallels the nonmaterial dimension of sharing and communicating of the family. It is real but nontangible. In the state it is a function of or an expression of the ability of the individual to extend to the universal community of humankind. The social ability of sharing and communicating expresses itself in art, education, religious ceremony, athletics, libraries, concerts, clubs, social service, and a host of other activities.

In the civil/political community sharing and communicating is less intimate and of a different character than that between two or a few individuals in the family. Though not intimate, the sharing and communicating are no less real or significant. If a person has the ability to communicate to many in a musical concert or in a demonstration of athletic prowess, that concert cannot be performed or the contest played in a chaotic war torn setting. Symphony orchestra concerts and international athletic competitions are not scheduled where turmoil prevails. Since a universal need and ability exists to communicate through art, through literature, religious meetings, athletic competition, and a myriad of other ways, the state's existence expresses and fulfills that capacity.

By presuming the existence of the individual, the family, and the state, socio-logical origin reflects an understanding of man as "multidimensional." Assumed are a private dimension, a limited but intimate social dimension, and an extended social dimension whereby communication is universal. The last dimension requires an orderly community for complete fulfillment of all capacities.

When the respective answers were offered to the question of why the state should be accepted, the socio-logical response was, "My better self wills it!" Now that "better self" has been introduced. It is the self who naturally lives in the orderly domestic and civil community. It is the self who is able to share and communicate in the family and with all humankind even if the sharing is no more than picnics and good music.

The socio-logical origin does not deny that one can choose not to live in the state. One can choose to destroy the state just as it is possible to disrupt the harmony of communities. It is better not to exercise this liberty of contrariety, to rebel against the givenness of things. To reject organized society is either beastly or godly. Control within the state amounts to paying attention to doing what is "right," "proper," "responsible," "correct." These control qualities are consonant with human nature. Their implementation is important though not automatic. Since disagreement exists about the content of human nature, no set behavior is automatic. Nonetheless to abandon an effort because it is not automatic or is difficult is merely to surrender to another theory by default.

Conclusion And Perspective

When asked at the beginning of this chapter why one should accept the particular laws of a particular government under a particular constitution in a particular state, three different answers were given. The three answers reflect three different possibilities of control of the state: God (a determinative force) wills it therefore I am not free; the majority (who specify the contract) will it therefore I am oppressed; my better (socio-logical) self wills it therefore I will it. (The oppression of the social contract theories is a function of the individual vis-à-vis the whole and hence potentially at any time in the minority. Rousseau, though he argued the general will's resignation to the state, precisely saw it as an oppression of chains.) This string of alternative answers appears to favor, in language if not in argument, the third theory. There is, however, in the third theory a hidden assumption about reality and the nature of human beings that has not yet been fully revealed. In the next chapter on the purpose of the state each of the theories will be examined for their full implications. In that final look the three different theories about the origin or control of the state, the three theories about authority, and the three theories about the nature of the state will be evident as three integrated systems. Though one theory may appear preferred, it comes with sufficient caveats to be not utterly convincing both to its adherents and to its critics. If it were so convincing no problem of divergent political views would exist. But there are many divergent views.

People take contrary positions because they view political principles, the fundamentals of politics, differently. It is an awareness of these deeply felt and well-founded principles that are at the heart of the discourse on the state in this book. The balance that can be gained from political principles is not just a balance on the scales of logic or worth. It is a balance of reality where all these theories are contending forces in the daily battles and conflicts of political life. To recognize that others have deeply felt, self-convincingly well-reasoned justifications is a basis for respect and a foundation for the ever-desirable harmony in the community.

Chapter 7

The Purpose Of The State

Collectivism, individualism, and the common good are the primary topics of this chapter. First, brief attention will be given to anarchism, which also purports to be a purpose of the state.

Anarchism

The word "purports" in the previous statement is not an objective introduction. The wording is deliberate for several reasons. Anarchism holds that the state should not exist and it regards the state as evil per se. In the anarchist's view the state should be eliminated since there is no justification for one person ruling over another. This view makes it illogical and semantically incorrect to include anarchism as a purpose of the state.

Anarchism comes in two varieties, evolutionary and revolutionary. Evolutionary anarchism awaits the state's eventual decay and collapse as a non-cooperation doctrine spreads from individual to individual. Revolutionary anarchists on the other hand cannot tolerate any delay in eliminating the evil. For them the evolutionary plan is too slow, perhaps even insincere. More direct and violent efforts to destroy the state are required. From such revolutionary attitudes and their occasional implementation all anarchists receive the reputation of bomb throwers.

There are nonviolent and quite peaceful anarchists who nonetheless should be recognized as anarchists. Thoreau is one, as are Kropotkin and Buckminster Fuller. Kropotkin in his *Conquest of Bread* (1913) and Fuller in his *Operating Manual for Spaceship Earth* (1969) and other writings would replace government and politicians with engineers and technocrats "who would make things run." It is as if engineering titles would preclude the technocrats from becoming politicians and taking the reins of government. It is imagined that society needs only bureaucrats putting things in motion and keeping them that way, that choices reflecting values can be eliminated. The view is simplistic. One can honestly wonder whether even the proponents believe what they say.

Henry David Thoreau, the American poet and individualist, was more generally critical of government than technically critical of it. He sought to live on the fringe of society, withdrawing to a cabin on Walden Pond to be free of the world. Many revere his poetry and his Walden retreat has been preserved as a National Historic Landmark. An ironic commentary, however, is that it took governmental action to preserve the Pond. It has parking fees for cars, and swimmers and sunbathers litter the beach. Crowds are such that no one can be "alone" there. *Sic transit gloria mundi.*

Anarchism receives an unsympathetic presentation. Realistically, what sympathy could be expected in a consideration of the purpose of the state that is practical? Some of the extreme versions of individualism will show a theoretical foundation for variations on the anarchism theme.

COLLECTIVISM

Collectivism regards the state as an "absolute good." As such it is the opposite of anarchism since it believes that all worth for the individual is found in and through the state. Hegel's organismic view clearly has this exaggerated role for the state. The whole, which is the state, is greater than the sum of its parts and the parts, the individuals, are intended to serve the whole. Alfredo Rocco, the philosophical apologist for fascism, maintained that society has purposes greater than the individuals who compose it at a particular moment such that the society and the individual may be in opposition. Rocco's conclusion is that such conflict is to be resolved by sacrifice, even up to total immolation, of the individual on behalf of society. For him society is the end and the individual is the means.

There are many different expressions of the collectivist view besides that of fascism. Communism is an obvious example. Collectivism is found, however, in other surprising locations as well. In a revealing reaction to criticisms of his book *Beyond Freedom and Dignity*, B. F. Skinner commented that rather than doing away with freedom and dignity he wanted to go beyond it in a quite progressive way. He maintained that for the continuation of our culture we must induce people to control population growth, environmental pollution, and other harmful developments. He saw his advocacy not so much as imposing restriction as inducing the present culture to take into account things that go beyond immediate personal satisfactions as Rome did to become great, as the Church did, as some contemporary economic systems do to further their survival. For Skinner, imitating this sacrifice is the only way for the survival of our culture.

Skinner, without knowing it, is pointing to the collectivist role of the state, and, in his view, the church and communism. He seeks "inducements" which allow for the perpetuation of the culture of today. He emphasizes the culture at the expense of the concepts of freedom and dignity of autonomous individuals because otherwise, in his view, some other culture will make a greater contribution to the future. Thus, culture becomes in Skinner's usage and intention as collectivist as earlier versions of the state or communism or fascism or the church. In each case the individual's role is to serve the whole, the thing external to the self in which the self finds meaning. The whole, the state, which has permanence greater than the ephemeral existence of the individual, is paramount. It is needed for the individual's survival in the same way that in the animal kingdom the herd or flock serves the members and the survival of the species.

Other contemporary versions of collectivism exist. Though Skinner, Hegel, and others appear abstract, their simple expression of serving something outside of the self actually gets to the heart of much contemporary thought. Those dedicated to the environment, to the fullest enjoyment of education or travel, to the undiminished growth of wealth and who acknowledge that there is nothing beyond them share a collectivist outlook. The more familiar form of collectivism is a statist one in which authoritarian decisions are imposed on the members of the community. What is at root in collectivism is the notion that there is nothing beyond the collective from which the individual benefits. Singular dedications to the environment, education, travel, wealth, or any economic system share that characteristic in so far as the thing external to the individual benefits while the individual passes away.

INDIVIDUALISM

As collectivism overemphasizes the role of the state, individualism underemphasizes it. Individualism sees the role of the state as minimal and as directed to the enhancement of the individual's private capacity. Government is a "necessary evil." Accordingly, "the government which governs least governs best." Those were views from Thomas Paine's pamphlet "Common Sense," published at the opening of America's conflict with England in 1776. Mistakenly, his views have developed an American identity. They are instead the views of Paine (pun intended) and individualism. They are not necessarily or correlatively American. Paine's words are colorful and have been adopted by many where he says that even at its best government is a "necessary evil." At its worst it is an intolerable evil. In, perhaps his second most colorful observation, he claims that government, like dress, is the badge of our lost innocence.

In Paine's view and in that of those who share it the individual is to be accorded the widest scope of freedom consistent with the freedom and safety of others. Government in the individualist's perspective is to be "limited" to maintaining order, protecting individual freedom and enforcing contracts. These tasks are precisely the inconveniences performed by government in the individual's behalf in the theory of John Locke. Other than this limited role, government is to "keep its hands off," laissez faire, the affairs of individuals and groups. It is best to allow individual competition and natural abilities to control the affairs of mankind.

Laissez faire found severe expression in the writings of the nineteenth century author, Herbert Spencer. Spencer argued against public assistance or what is called today welfare and social security. His attitude is labeled "social Darwinism" because of its elements of natural selection and survival of the fittest. (A curious thing is that Spencer spoke of these elements before Darwin dealt with them in his *Origin of Species*.) The viewpoint of Spencerian individualism is that to interfere with the natural laws of society or the physical world will do much harm and little good. Natural selection improves the species. Interference or the constraints of law destroy initiative and stifle incentive. The best policy, according to this view, is that every person be free to pursue individual interests to the highest possible degree. Spencer, in his *Social Statics*, lamented the sickly worker who cannot compete, the widow and orphan who must struggle for life or death, but when viewed not separately but in the interest of overall humanity these sufferings are full of the "highest beneficence." Spencer's view has been characterized as one of "'everyone for himself,' said the elephant dancing among the chickens."

Most individualism does not come in Spencer's form. The usual argument for individualism is attractively put in terms of individual ability, private initiative, doing one's own thing, the individual knows best, and rejecting government's intrusion. Elements of individualism can be found in contemporary conservative and liberal political rhetoric. Rhetoric is seasonal with political opportunity. (It is fair game to pick on government and to criticize its activities as much as at times it is common to constantly propose new programs for expansion of governmental activity. Such rhetorical appeals reflect in only a loose way a theoretical attitude toward the state and change as quickly as the personal attractiveness of candidates change. Necessary for the serious student of politics, young or old, are well-founded principles that stand as measure of the passing appeals.)

Large theoretical issues of politics may never be finally settled for many. The principles that stand firm give orientation to little decisions on budgets, policies, and conflicts. Theoretical principles also give meaning to individuals who seek to know their place and purpose in the vast political universe that affects them daily. Despite the legitimate confusion about the distinctness of the theoretical principles, they remain separate. Individualism has a trace of anarchism if the evils of the state were to be stressed instead of the necessity of the evil. Stressing the necessity of the state shows a trace of collectivism. The theories touch and blend. They are distinct in their emphasis: one on the individual, the other on the whole. The third theory of the purpose of the state, in a special way, emphasizes both.

THE COMMON GOOD

The third theory is "the common good." Unlike the other two it is not readily identifiable in the conversations of everyday life. It is initially misunderstood as a form of collectivism. When it is explained to be "the good of the individual as a member of the state" it is then mistaken for individualism. It is neither collectivism nor individualism. It is a separate and distinct position whose distinguishing features are important for practical politics.

What distinguishes the common good from collectivism is its respect for the integrity of the individual. What distinguishes it from individualism is its recognition of the individual as social by nature and the state as a natural instead of an artificial construct. The common good is the good of the individual as a member of the community, the good that the individual realizes from sharing and communicating. It is a good which is indeed one's own but of which the private benefit is not the absolute measure. For example, the good of the family is one's own good but it accrues to the individual by reason of family membership. The common good of the family is not the father's good, plus the mother's good, plus each child's good. It is not the sum of the good of the parts. The good of the family is each and every individual's good but it is a good which each shares by reason of the membership.

The Common Good, which is the state, is the good of the individual, even while it is the good of each and every individual in the community. That does not mean that the goods of each and every individual are identical. Each good is distinct from but not separate from the good of every member of the state. The good comes by way of the community, by way of its sharing and communicating. In one instance it may be the listening to beautiful music and in another it may be performance of the music. In one it may be living a tranquil life without paying attention to politics (even though being involved is a good thing) and in another the lifelong involvement in or study of politics. For one individual the common good may be in military service and for another it may be collecting antiques or painting homes.

The common good is that fulfillment of the extended social dimension of the individual under the socio-logical origin of the state. The "multidimensional" individual has a private dimension whereby things are uniquely and incommunicably one's own, a limited but intimate and in-depth social dimension, and, an extended social dimension whereby one communicates with universal humanity. The individual has goods that accrue by reason of each of these dimensions, private goods, the common good of the family, and the common good of the state. Private goods, those that are uniquely and incommunicably one's own, are limited to things such as the food that nourishes, the clothes that warm, and the virtues that perfect one as a private individual. Clothes may have a secondary social effect of appearing attractive but the secondary effect is incidental to the functional warmth and protection. The primary private virtue is temperance, whose incommunicableness and uniqueness is principally demonstrated when it has been lacking (as portrayed in cartoons when one complains of a certain type of headache saying, "You don't know the pain I'm suffering!"). Other than these few items there are not many exclusively private goods. Almost everything is the result of communicating and sharing. Education, books, patience, museums, jazz concerts, transportation, athletics, national parks, and most things are social goods.

The common good holds that the state provides an environment, material, social, and intellectual, which is most conducive to free, human living. That environment is consonant with human nature. It lets the ability of individuals thrive in fulfilling their capability. It presumes the individual and the various abilities of different individuals; it presumes the development of private, social, and universal dimensions. As in the family it is not the sum of the singular good of its members. It is the good of the individual and greater than the sum of singular goods.

Individualism views the state as the sum of singular private goods. Collectivism views the state as greater than the sum of the parts and something to which the parts must be subservient. The common good is greater than the sum of private goods but it does not subordinate the individual. An attempt to express these relationships in symbolic language is presented in *Appendix C*. All the relationships are fairly easy to appreciate. They all follow from the verbal descriptions already given. The common good, despite the distinctions that have been made and the descriptions that have been repeated, remains not entirely clear. As with many other things differences can be seen more clearly when examples are given.

EXAMPLES OF THE THREE THEORIES

It is difficult to give unambiguous examples. An exercise of eminent domain against ancestral property for public use is only mildly interesting because the differences blur. Collectivism would rejoice at the contributions that can be made to the state, individualism would moan at forced sacrifice by unwilling individuals, the common good would piously support doing what is right. The end result of all three is not noticeably different since the property would be taken, some payment would be made, and even the collectivists' approval would not prevent them from accepting the money.

Death in the Line of Duty

Other examples are similarly anticlimactic. All are unsatisfactory except one that is more ultimate. When the state asks the individual to act so that his or her life may be sacrificed in the line of duty the relationship between individual and the state is severely tested. Going to battle to defend one's country in time of war is such an act. There are similar sacrifices. Police work and firefighting are not as dramatic as wartime events but death in such circumstances is just as final. Other occupations exist where individual life is put in jeopardy for the sake of others. The purpose of the state is tested in terms of what the individual gains from the sacrifice.

The anarchist would respond that death in the line of duty is absurd. For the anarchist the state or government should not exist and therefore a request for sacrifice is out of reason. Individuals might make a personal choice of sacrifice but some outsider or intermediary does not direct the decision. Anarchism ignores reality and because of this consistently negative view of the state and of political reality as evil little serious attention is given to it. The absurdity of war can arouse understandable sympathy for the rejection of individual sacrifice. Yet, despite that absurdity, the unfortunate reality of war cannot be ignored. If sympathetic feelings formed the standard of the acceptable then application to police, the firefighter, and the emergency medical team would unravel society where individual sacrifice is no more or less meaningful. Certainly those personal sacrifices are not absurd.

For collectivism, death in the line of duty is unfortunate for the individual but meaningful within the whole where worth is determined. In collectivism the individual is the means and the state is the end. Mussolini depicted it well: "Fascism conceives of the State as an absolute, in comparison with which all individuals or groups are relative, only to be conceived of in their relation to the State." Individual service and sacrifice, he said, have worth from the contribution made to the state, "The fascist conception of the State is all-embracing; outside of it no human or spiritual values can exist, much less have value." Fascism's words are graphic, yet every form of collectivism is the same in seeing nothing beyond itself for the individual.

There is no question that for collectivism the individual can be called upon to sacrifice, even up to total immolation in the view of Alfredo Rocco, on behalf of the state. From sacrifice value is found since worth does not exist beyond the state. A distinction has to be made with respect to patriotism. The sacrifice of a Nathan Hale or the service asked for by President Kennedy differs from slavish subservience to a "totalitarian" state about which Mussolini bragged and which Lenin and Stalin employed. Unlike Hale or Kennedy, the collectivist totality takes into account nothing else that measures the goodness of the service provided. Hence the cultural value of Skinner or scientism or wealth gathering or environmentalism fits the category of collectivism for there is nothing beyond their principal value. The contribution and role of the individual remain in the same fatal relationship even if wars or sacrifice are not involved.

Individualism reacts to sacrifice of the individual on behalf of the community with skepticism or with the extreme of revulsion. Its most visible response is the one witnessed during the Vietnam era in the United States, where crowds of youth chanted, "Hell no, we won't go!" Unwittingly, the chant had a tinge of collectivism. The chanters meant that they as a group, or possibly as individuals, and not the government should decide what an acceptable call to duty was. If a majority of "I's" feels that a war should not be held or that an individual should not be called to duty, then the war should be called off. If individuals felt that they did not want to go to war, then they should not be drafted or sent. Within the same perspective, some of mercenary mind could take their chances and make up the fighting force. It is all a matter of personal choice. Individualism's closeness to anarchism is revealed.

According to individualism serving something beyond the individual is dangerously collectivist and to be avoided at all costs. A dilemma arises for the cost of service may be the survival of the liberal political community that makes freedom for the individual possible. The logic of the situation is either to ignore the danger at peril or deny it with bravado. "Peril or…bravado" is not an evaluation. The choice constitutes "an act of faith in the abiding good sense of the average human" and a confidence that in the long run the values of individual worth will triumph over the forces that threaten them. Until the triumph occurs extant individuals are sacrificed.

The common good's position appears contradictory: death in the line of duty is the good of the individual as well as the good of community. The good of the community is fairly evident, assuming the community survives. Benefit accruing chiefly to the community seems collectivist. But, to be collectivist there would have to be nothing for the individual beyond the service. The common good insists that there is benefit for the individual.

Death in the line of duty is an exceptionally individual act. The idea of individual benefit challenges credulity. The traditional justifications and ancient values such as the preservation of the community, of saving one's family, and maintaining order and the rule of law are not insignificant, yet there is nothing immediately apparent that accrues to the dead hero. No matter what the conditioning prior to service, no person rejoices at death as "feeling great." Though the individual may have been drafted into service out of poverty and extreme personal deprivation no apparent personal benefit accrues except the service rendered to the community. For the individual who dies there is no apparent good in this life.

The phrase "in this life" is new. Up to now no attention has been given to some dimension beyond this life. Considering a heaven in which individuals are rewarded according to the quality of their life or the quality of their death conveniently settles many issues. If it exists then everything follows in symmetrical fashion: as one lives a good or a bad life one will receive proportionate reward in the afterlife, and if one dies courageously one may make up for earlier deficiencies. This is the heaven/hell phenomenon of religious belief, of traditional thought, and of folklore. How it fits in a reasoned argument must be explained.

Pericles and Lincoln

From the time of Pericles, the Athenian general during the Peloponnesian War, to the time of Lincoln and beyond, war dead have been honored. Pericles in his funeral oration praised the ones who had died, saying that they sustained their own good while sustaining the good of Athens. The same principle applies to any who die in the line of duty. It is a belief that service merits a special reward and the afterlife is the all-satisfying locale. A "belief," however, does not prove personal immortality or an afterlife. Religions believe in those things, in heaven, hell, personal rewards, and punishments. Aristotle, that ancient pre-Christian philosopher, did not preclude the possibility of an afterlife and he spoke of the soul as separable from the body. These religious beliefs and philosophical treatments do not prove by proclamation. Though they fit into the discussion of the common good, though they complete the notion of the individual's personal benefit from heroic service, they do not prove the existence of an afterlife, of heaven, hell, and all the rest.

Afterlife is not the only way in which the individual could benefit from death in the line of duty. If instead of personal reward what is involved is less personal but equally universal *and real*, individual benefit can still be realized. If it is maintained that to be "courageous" or "good" or "just" is unqualifiedly better than to be "rash" or "cowardly" or "bad" or "unjust," then one's death in the line of duty is consistent with that better course of action. Similar to religious belief, the individual is not serving some state determined good or some privately determined good but serves an objective and real good. It is better for the individual to die courageously than to live cowardly, to die justly than to live unjustly. The individual shares in a true good that is objectively, not subjectively, determined. How it is made manifest is as mysterious as the afterlife itself or religious belief.

According to the common good the individual lives and dies in accord with real universal norms sustained by truth. The individual does not follow private or state determined goals. It is good that the community be afforded fire protection, police protection, and military defense. If the individual dies in service to these community goods, then the individual has done what is right even if the particular situations requiring protection or defense are questioned or are mistaken. The individual's benefit is not adversely affected by the misadventure of political leaders or even, in the case of war, by defeat.

Lincoln honored the men who died at Gettysburg. The men of Athens procured the common good, according to Pericles, even though it was later understood that their side lost the war. Although there is a real good for the individual in sacrificing for the community, life is not at the complete disposal of the community or the leader. The limit on leader and community is the difference between the common good and collectivism. The individual is not at the disposal of the community such that service is expected and is said to be of merit where service, not truth, is the only test of worth. The common good, as opposed to collectivism, presupposes and preserves the integrity of the individual. The difference between the common good and individualism, on the other hand, is that the service and the benefit are not determined solely by personal choice.

Collectivism and individualism, measured only in human terms, preclude the consideration of an afterlife or other factors beyond the whole or the individual. The common good's consideration of something beyond this life does not prove the existence of what they claim. The argument merely completes the common good system. For the common good it is something beyond the present life which gives integrity and independence. The individual has a higher purpose to serve, a purpose not contrary to the state but quite beyond it. Without this external something being real and true human beings make themselves or their creations the thing to be served. Aristotle commented, "Politics would be the highest science if man were the best thing in the universe, but man is not the best thing in the universe." It is the existence of something better than man in the universe that for the common good preserves and guarantees the freedom and integrity of the state as well as the individuals within it.

The common good makes human beings neither masters nor slaves. It is a good which is indeed one's own, but the private benefit is not the absolute measure of this good. The state is not the absolute measure of this good either.

Conclusion And Perspective

This chapter attempted to balance the three theories of the state and eliminate any advantage that the third system (synergistic unity, responsible authority, socio-logical origin, and common good purpose) might have enjoyed. It might appear that a balance has not been established; that instead the imbalance has been augmented or exacerbated.

The third system, the common good, includes more in its universe of discourse than do individualism or collectivism. What the common good wants to include, its extra dimension, is perhaps subject to more criticism and doubt today than at any time in human history. Contemporary philosophy has little to do with transcendent things outside of subjective artificial constructs. If the afterlife does not exist, if objective "truth" or "goodness" or "justice" do not exist, then all that remains in sorting out the purpose of the state are the human alternatives, namely, individualism or collectivism.

Whether politics should take as its fundamental point the part (the individual) or the whole (the state, culture, economic system, etc.) or "something better than man in the universe" is the distinguishing factor of the different theories of the state. The choices between these alternatives influence how individuals evaluate events and direct their actions. In their premises and the relentlessness of disciples the three systems are in existential balance.

The last four chapters have laid out alternative points to show the respective positions of the different approaches to the state. Since the "correct," once and for all, universally acclaimed, approach has not been determined or proven, all that is available are options. Personal preferences are made in the light of background, reason, religion, emotion, and comfort. The information needs to be considered in the light of conditioned preferences and anticipated consequences as well as logical reasoning. Unconscious and conscious factors of choice cannot be suppressed easily. To proceed as if only one view will prevail is both mistaken and impractical.

Despite a preference for one or the other approach it is to be recognized that other individuals cannot accept that choice. There are large numbers of individuals who share the preferences of each of the three basic approaches. Those alternatives have existed from the beginning of Western, if not human, thought. It is the start of political wisdom to know and to understand the differences. Only with that wisdom can human beings accept the diversity of those with whom they cannot agree. Only then can the practical business of the political world be approached realistically.

The different approaches are so diametrically opposed that violent conflict often occurs. Authoritarianism, Marxism, capitalism, laissez faire individualism, fascism, socialism, democracy, and anarchism are often mortal enemies. An appreciation of the basis and depth of the differences is essential to minimize hostile conflicts. The examination of the different views of the state attains a minimal threshold of success in developing an appreciation of the roots of disagreement.

Chapter 8

Ideologies

The four previous chapters with the three principal theories can be imagined as constituting three complete systems. The chapter headings of "nature," "authority," "origin," and "purpose" can be organized in the following manner: Theory one - Organismic, Absolute, Divine, and Collectivism; Theory two - Mechanistic, Relative, Social Contract, and Individualism; Theory three - Synergistic, Proper, Socio-logical, and Common Good. Such an imagined grid appears orderly and acceptable. When Theory one is related to Hitler's Nazism or Mussolini's Fascism or to Communism, as it easily can be, the simple linkage of nature, authority, origin, and purpose appear to work well. Each of those "isms" regards the political unit as larger than and having final say over the individual even though purporting to serve the best interests of humankind. Each views the state as originating in some force, historical, physical, or spiritual, over which individuals have no control.

Theory two works well when understood in terms of laissez faire liberalism where the political unit is viewed purely in terms of individual will, subject to the disposition of majoritarian change, originating in a contract, and serving the private individual. That configuration of elements is regarded as essentially selfish by some while revered by others. Its real-life representation is said to have occurred in various forms in the United States, England, and elsewhere during the nineteenth century. Some or all of the twentieth-century presidential administrations in the United States are castigated as consciously or unconsciously representing this approach.

Unless committed in some preset way to one of the first two systems most people prefer to believe that their government, in its best moments at least, reflects the third system. That is, most people like to view themselves, and correspondingly their governments, as neither selfish nor unwisely altruistic, as taking a proper and responsible position on issues, whether large or small, as acting in a manner ordained by nature, truth, and goodness, and as serving the common good. This preference, like those of the other respective systems, depends on the undemonstrated premises about man and reality.

To argue in favor of one system it is necessary first to argue a particular version of the nature of man. So, if individualism or collectivism is the goal, it is necessary to argue that human nature is aggressive, or selfish, or willful, or controlled by history or economic, biological, or spiritual forces. Depending on the premise the state's relationship to the individual is organismic or absolute, mechanistic or relative. The origin of the state is either completely uncontrollable or completely controllable. The system appears neat and uncomplicated.

The descriptions have been accurate to a point, but the appearance is deceptive. Complications arise when the systems are related to concrete political situations and programs. For example, it is convenient to refer to communism as fitting Theory One and having collectivism as its purpose. All historical communist states have been collectivist, although the reported personal enrichments within them and strong competition among the upper echelons somewhat belies the usual expectations. This view, however, runs into difficulty when reminded of "the withering away of the state" so that the "new man," the Marxian goal, may live unimpeded by any forces foreign and extraneous to himself. This unimpeded life suggests a radical, almost an anarchistic, individualism. With communism pointing to individuals as an ultimate goal the neat lines on the imagined grid begin to cross.

Additional line crossing occurs in probing laissez faire liberalism. For liberalism the goals as well as the premise appear to be unencumbered individualism. The means, however, are collective insofar as maintenance of the economic system is concerned. Likewise, the very mechanism for the operation of a system of laissez faire liberalism is majority rule, itself a collectivist principle. A minority of, say, forty-nine percent may have little practical or theoretical difficulty in reconciling both individualism and majority rule. A five percent minority does.

These anomalies and paradoxes unveil the complications of reality. The revelations should not give way to discouragement about the insights gained from understanding the different theories and aspects of the state; it should lead to an appreciation of the difficult practical efforts to explain the basis of politics on a popular level. Appreciation of the difficulties of theory is prerequisite to an understanding of ideology.

DEFINITION OF IDEOLOGY

Ideology is an attempt to describe the political world in an all-embracing way. There is an almost endless variety of books, definitions, and discussions of the term and its various forms. Leon Baradat (*Political Ideologies: Their Origin and Impact,* 304) described political ideologies as "action-oriented, materialistic, popular, and simplistic." His definition is especially useful because it focuses on the character of ideology, that of seeking to persuade large groups for specific purposes. The intention of mass appeal easily explains the simplistic aspect. If the daily news has to be presented on the level of mass appeal, then ideology would have to be similarly pitched. The materialistic aspect has root in making popular "accommodation to social and economic conditions."

Lists of Ideologies

There are so many definitions and discussions of ideology. Most works describe four or five ideologies. The prominent ones are: Democracy, Fascism, Marxism, and Nazism. Some lists would not include democracy, others omit Marxism and instead include communism. Some insist that the items be forms of socialism, capitalism, or totalitarianism. Others discuss liberalism versus conservatism. Some want to include nationalism, racism, humanism, and laissez faire individualism. A comprehensive list of basic ideologies, presented in alphabetic order with a brief description, follows.

Capitalism: an economic system based on nongovernmental ownership and direction of production and services and regulated by competitive activity among individuals and groups. Principally an economic doctrine it cannot be completely separated from a social and political context. It cannot be clear whether its successes or failure are purely economic or partly political.

Communism: an economic, social, and political system seeking government ownership of production and services directed by a process of scientific administration and universal assent. The process of administration and assent gives a theoretical utopian quality and an authoritarian practice. Historically, many religious and monastic communities are communistic in principle but they are also voluntary and they operate on a much smaller scale than the political versions. As with capitalism it is difficult to separate its economic and political roles.

Conservatism: a point of view that emphasizes tradition and established institutions and thereby appears to give greater attention to social entities than to individuals. Its first inclination is to oppose change. Although commonly associated with particular political parties, no exact relationship exists since political parties are generally pragmatic in their practices. In its more exact form, as represented by Edmund Burke, conservatism takes history and tradition as the measure of the true and the good.

Democracy: in its simplest form is understood as rule by the people (see Chapter 1). While at one point in the last two hundred years democracy was the dominant political and philosophical ideal, its implementation in many disparate settings reveals both its adaptability and its fragility.

Fascism: the system associated with Mussolini in Italy that emphasizes the authoritative direction of the leader and the following by the public in all things. No ruler proclaims the doctrine today since it is commonly used as a deprecatory term. Any leader, governmental feature, or practices with which the critic disagrees are accused of being fascist.

Humanism: a view that concentrates on human assets to the active exclusion of anything transcendent or spiritual in public affairs. Many different groups, ranging from quasi-religions, Marxists, and individualists, claim to be humanists. Some of the most strident are actively antireligious secularists. B. F. Skinner is an academic humanist.

Laissez Faire Individualism: an economic, social, and political view that emphasizes unregulated individual competition as the rule for social interaction on the assumption that a natural stratification and social improvement based on merit will result. It claims to focus on human strengths and abilities instead of frailties. It is associated with capitalism, nineteenth-century liberalism, as well as Marxism's new man.

Liberalism: a view that, although emphasizing individual goodness, sees more need for change and improvement in social relations requiring governmental involvement. In a nineteenth century mode it was more associated with laissez faire. In the twentieth century it is viewed as more on the side of state-interventionist socialism. It is always necessary to pause to figure out which meaning is intended.

Marxism: a particularly extreme form of communism, humanism, liberalism, economic determinism, and other ideologies calling for the ultimate elimination of the state and all other social institutions, to be accomplished by a transition that will itself wither in favor of radical individualism. It claims a large contemporary following but its success is debated as being more the result of unblemished power than the strength of an idea. Its doctrinaire supporters maintain that the fall of the Soviet Union demonstrates nothing about Marxism since it was not truly represented there.

Nationalism: a view which stresses loyalty and devotion to the nation-culture group as the greatest vehicle for self-realization and which has witnessed rapid growth in the number of nation-states in the last half century. It is not unreasonable to regard it as the most powerful simplified, unifying idea of the last two centuries. It continues to be the source of turbulence throughout the world. It claims success in the cohesive self-expression of previously repressed groups.

Nazism: Hitler's version of fascism, individualism, nationalism, socialism, and racism combined in a particularly virulent form claiming the superiority of some and the natural enslavement of others. The principal way it is distinguished from fascism is the claim that one race is superior to others. This claim is in its origin not so much directed against other races (although its effects are), as it is a concentration on innate, genetically, or statistically proclaimed data about one's own race. Such claims of exclusiveness are scientifically spurious and practically untenable.

Racism: a belief that race is the primary determinant of human abilities and action and that consequently social and political alignments are or ought to be consonant with ethnic stock. It is intrinsically an unprovable and hence irrational proposition, both logically and empirically. It is often present in the form of tribal and regional rivalry in multi-ethnic societies.

Religion: Religion is not an ideology although it may be perceived to behave as such. Robert Coles in *The Secular Mind* raises a disturbing point on how religion, detached from the transcendence, can misbehave. For non-believers religions fill all the components given above (action-oriented, materialistic, popular, and simplistic) for an ideology. It is the responsibility of believers and non-believers alike to recognize how they are perceived so that respectful non-belligerence may prevail.

Socialism: an economic and political doctrine which advocates governmental ownership and direction of production and services but which would retain existing institutions as the means for regulating them. Marxism advocates the abolition of existing institutions, but until that abolition is accomplished Marxism is a type of state-socialism. Socialism without Marxism has more of a majoritarian democratic dimension to it.

Totalitarianism: a system in which all individual, economic, social, and political actions are subject to the direction of the authoritarian ruling person or party. It is dependent on primitive or modern technology, especially the advance of communications, for both gathering and disseminating information. It has roots in Marx, Hegel, and Hobbes. Some regard Plato's carefully designed Republic, with everyone having an assigned place according to his or her inner composition and with a "clever fiction" for achieving harmony in the community, as being totalitarian. Order is the chief value in such regimes. Modern regimes are crude in accomplishing order in comparison to the elaborate sophistication of Plato's educational system and the role of ideas to achieve order.

Room exists for disagreement about the descriptions of the ideologies listed above. It may be maintained that items are missing, for example, "sexism", although the political and cultural context of that terms would need to be clarified. Some items might be excluded as merely an "*ism*." That reference does not improve the situation, for "ism" is for the most part synonymous with ideology. The distinction is in the understanding of ideology as a "systematic" body of concepts or as visionary theorizing as opposed to an "ism" as a distinctive theory. The systematic quality attributed to ideology does not reflect any objective character but only refers to the integration of concepts in a plausible theory. It may still be visionary or illusory even though systematic. (The Ptolemaic explanation of sun, moon, and planets rotating around the earth was systematic but illusory.)

Illusory Quality of Ideology

The illusory quality of ideology harks back to the origin of the word itself in the late eighteenth and early nineteenth centuries. A French philosopher and psychologist by the name of Destutt de Tracy is said to have first used the word in the mid-1790s. Tracy associates ideology to "the science of ideas" or to "the philosophy of mind." In his psychology he appears to use the term in the contemporary manner as a "philosophy of life." He is also said to be involved, possibly as a "speechwriter," with the government of Napoleon, who gave the term its political connotation. According to the Oxford English Dictionary, various sources such as John Adams, Sir Walter Scott, and the poet Shelley attribute to Napoleon the depreciatory sense of ideology as unpractical or visionary theorizing or speculation. Hence ideology, like ism, the older term, has a disparaging intention in its earliest usage.

It is the derogatory sense of ideology that Marx adopted in the mid-nineteenth century. Marx uses ideology to refer to what he regarded as illusory philosophies and doctrines current in Germany at the time of his writing. More specifically, though, he regards any false way of seeing the world, any way contrary to his way of seeing the world, as an ideology. For him only science can replace ideology, and science is equated with his own method. For Marx, ideologies are not simply the product of errors of thought but instead are rooted in the whole socioeconomic fabric that shapes a person's thinking, acting, work, indeed, whole personality. Religion and the state, for him, are ideologies in that they are illusory representations of one's true character suppressed by alienating material conditions. To change the illusions or ideology it is necessary, in Marx's view, to change the material conditions.

The change in the material conditions of which Marx speaks is a complete and total change in all institutions and relationships, from the family to the state and religion. It is for this reason that Marx is rightly regarded as radically revolutionary. For him anything standing in the way of a scientific understanding of the world should be unmercifully swept aside. For Marx, science equals Communism, which means a materialist and individualistic, radically new conception of reality. Scientific thinking, thinking which is not illusory, is based on sense-experience. People's actions can be observed, described, and interpreted without illusion. Everything is said to be empirically observable.

It is ironic that Marx on the one hand adopts the connotation of ideology as false and confused thinking and on the other hand uses science in the sense that Tracy originally did for ideology before it acquired its rhetorical connotation. Tracy, following Condillac, saw all ideas as derived from sensations and distinguished from "metaphysics," by which he meant traditional or speculative philosophy. Marx had the same intention with respect to science and distinguished it from metaphysics. This conjoining of opposites of science and ideology demonstrates that the contemporary confusion about the definition and agreed-upon list of ideologies has a basis in its own roots. Marx would have no sufferance of illusion. On the other hand, as each of the separate ideologies partakes of the original primacy of sensations, they are intolerant of anything claiming nonsensational verification or premises other than their own. That is to say, one ideology is as exclusive and intolerant as the next. For this reason ideology has an essentially rhetorical character.

Rhetoric is the art of using language to persuade. From early Greek times down to the present rhetoric has been a chief tool of political operatives. Presidents have seen their effectiveness wax and wane in direct proportion to their rhetorical skills. Ordinarily the difference between political rhetoric and ideology is a matter of scope and duration. Political rhetoric is mostly piecemeal commentary on current topics with a view toward eliciting popular support. The duration may be no greater than the length of an election campaign. Ideology on the other hand has a cynical quality to it, since it purports an integration of all aspects of the sociopolitical realm over an extensive span of time. Each of the ideologies claims that theirs is the best practical guide for political action. Tolerance between ideologies is low because they view their premises and goals as exclusive. One system accepts another only insofar as it sees the other as coming within the confines of its own structure.

Ideology may be described as a roadmap by which location or direction is known. A map is a simplification of the real road and it leaves out much detail. Maps can be drawn differently for truckers, tourists, and public transportation users, for the shortest route or the most scenic. Competing ideologies are the alternate maps of social and political experience. The difference between a map and an ideology is that a map's accuracy and validity can be easily tested. While an ideology may appear accurate from a few of its elementary signposts, its general validity must be judged by a much more encompassing logic. Because of the confused and inexact premises and applications of ideologies the test of validity ranges from the daunting, to the impractical, to the impossible. Ideology leaders proceed in a manner consistent with their premises, but that does not test their explanations against reality. The leaders and proponents of an ideology are not interested in whether their followers understand the answers, the premises, or reality. Their only interest is to persuade the followers to follow.

Is Democracy an Ideology?

At the outset of the chapter four ideologies were listed: democracy, fascism, Marxism, and Nazism. These few ideologies have had recent, clearly identifiable, political leaders who were spokesmen for their distinct ideological position. Democracy, however, does not have a distinctly identifiable spokesperson as much as it has had a long number of champions. There are reasons for not regarding it as an ideology at all.

Paradoxically, almost all ideologies want to present themselves as a form of democracy. Totalitarianism, Nazism, and Marxism claim in one way or another to truly represent the best sense of the people. The Shah of Iran and his successor Ayatollah Khomeini, for example, claim popular sanction even though they were never subject to a free election. Further democracy does not claim a solely materialistic or sensationalist base. Some of its modern advocates, from Locke to the present, and some of its critics, like Marx, may impute a limited empirical foundation to democracy, but its classical heritage will not allow it. Aristotle's democracy may have been "of the people" but this people had a "soul." That soul refers to a real, separable spiritual dimension, something better than humans in the universe, which keeps the political realm from being totalitarian. Marx and other modern commentators disagree with this classical heritage. It is precisely this point of disagreement that returns the discussion of the nature of ideology to the aspects of the state found in the previous four chapters.

Conclusion And Perspective

It is possible to examine in detail each of the isms or ideologies in terms of the specific elements of the state. Some ideologies may beg for more examination than others. The reader is encouraged to integrate the information gained from studying ideologies elsewhere with the imagined grid of aspects and theories suggested at the beginning of this chapter. The result will not be a foreordained set of conclusions, but an array of alternatives from which choices can be made. All alternatives should be considered so that judgment is on a reasoned argument. Freedom of choice based on the merits is the paramount value of an examination of the principles and foundations of politics.

Chapter 9

Subsidiarity And Justice

In moving from theoretical consideration of the state to practical considerations of government a bridge must be provided showing a juncture of the two, on one side an expansion of the purpose of the state and the sum of governmental activities on the other. The structure of the bridge is built from both sides and the bridge has a deep understructure that radiates from both regions. The link begins to emerge by examining the concept of the "general welfare."

The Preamble of the Constitution of the United States says that the government was formed to "promote the general welfare." Though this phrase and others in the preamble have wide locution they have no legal standing. The courts have never given the force of law to the preamble. Still, in ordinary usage "general welfare" is understood as a promotional activity of the state. It is a complement to the protective role of government, also mentioned in the preamble.

The preamble reads:

> We the People of the United States, in Order to form a more perfect Union, establish Justice, insure domestic Tranquility, provide for the common defence, promote the general Welfare, and secure the Blessings of Liberty to ourselves and our Posterity, do ordain and establish this Constitution for the United States of America.

The protective role is to defend against external attack and internal disorder. Though the protective and promotional roles appear to be concrete, disagreement exists over how much or how little is to be provided. Most especially disputes arise over the degree of support for the material, moral, and intellectual well-being of the people.

Different theoretical views exist on promoting the general welfare. Anarchism, for example, holds for no promotive role. Collectivism desires an extraordinary role for the state. In keeping with its theoretical position, it eventually sees the state assuming total responsibility for individual needs. Individualism, consistent with the proposition that the least government is best, seeks a minimal role. The common good, in the sense of the third theory, sees the general welfare as a difficult balance of individual and social interest.

GOVERNMENT MINI/MAX DECISIONS

Reflecting on the governmental budget can assist in understanding the notion of general welfare. The budget concretely summarizes governmental activities. It is the single most important policy statement of what the government at any level does. Although governments cannot be measured solely in terms of costs and expenditures, the budget reflects the overall dimensions of governmental activity. All the theoretical views of the purpose of the state, except for anarchism, agree that the state's purpose is reflected in the budget and the debate over the budget.

Of course, there is no formal discussion of the purpose of the state in the budgeting process. Nonetheless, to advocate the expansion of programs with corresponding costs or to call for the contraction of programs or balanced scrutiny roughly approximate collectivist, individualist, and common good positions. In other words, collectivists would like the government to do more by way of services and controls, individualists would like to see less, and the common good would, as explained before, be calling for "fair" or "just" policies. Whatever their diametrically opposed theoretical positions, the three theories always agree that for the present no sharp expansion or contraction can occur. Abrupt and sizeable changes are unacceptable because they do not work.

Budget changes rarely amount to anything close to five percent of the previous year. At the practical budget level each theoretical position is left to determine for the present the minimum necessary and the maximum possible in the next year. This practicality applies at all levels, national, state, and local. Although the protagonists hold to their original theoretical position and hope eventually to lead the other members and all society to their goal, practical politics persuade everyone, except the revolutionary, to make a decision along lines of maximum benefits and minimum costs.

In any budget process the deciding of priorities and price tags is a practical minimum/maximum decision. Revenues and expenditure limits are finite. Drastic proposals, no matter how desirable, are disruptive and, very likely, self-defeating. Therefore, changes are usually incremental. Theoretical disagreements do not appear except in the broadest rhetorical fashion in debates over expenditures or revenues, nonetheless, the liberal, the conservative, the centrist, the reactionary, and the radical serving on governmental bodies must each reconcile with practical necessities or become less a part of the actual policy process.

Since compromise occurs at all levels of government, the extent to which the theoretical and the practical are joined in daily governmental activity takes place more frequently than is generally imagined. Even people who serve at city and township levels of government have strongly held views about the theoretical role of government, and these views must be tempered for practical purposes.

Each responsible official or body makes the practical budget decisions in light of what other levels of government are doing. A state must consider what its cities are doing, what the national government is doing, and what other states are doing. All must consider minimum needs and costs and maximum expenses and benefits. For a state to provide total social security benefits for its citizens independent of the national program would be as impractical as providing the local police for every city and town. Local governments are circumscribed financially and practically in road maintenance, education, and other areas of traditional concern due to overriding state and national laws. And, even at the national level policy implementation is a severe problem. Working together is the only choice within and at all levels.

SUBSIDIARITY

Based on practical minimum/maximum considerations government, whether consciously or unconsciously, operates according to the "principle of subsidiarity." In its formal definition the principle states that the lowest unit of society that is able to accomplish a particular function adequately, efficiently, and with benefit to the welfare of the whole should be permitted to do so. It is unclear whether subsidiarity is a deductive or an empirical rule. Whatever its origin, subsidiarity is both a useful guide and a helpful description of governmental decision-making. E. F. Schumacher, the British economist and essayist, adopts its essential thought in his *Small Is Beautiful.*

Schumacher principally speaks of large-scale business operations. At one point, however, he refers to "a famous formulation" of the principle of subsidiarity which hold that it is an injustice and at the same time a grave evil and disturbance of right order to assign to a greater and higher association what lesser and subordinate organizations can do. This position holds that every social activity ought of its very nature to furnish help to the members of the body social and never destroy and absorb them. Schumacher adds that though the principle originally was meant to apply to society as a whole it can apply equally to the different levels within a large organization and that the higher level must not absorb the functions of the lower one, on the assumption that, being higher, it will automatically be wiser and fulfill them more efficiently. The burden of proof lies always on those who want to deprive a lower level of its function, and thereby of its freedom and responsibility in that respect. The higher must prove that the lower level is incapable of fulfilling its function satisfactorily and that the higher level can actually do much better.

In his economic writings Schumacher saw the principle applying to large businesses, pointing out that it is sound organizational, personnel, and economic policy. Until recently the principle was seldom mentioned with regard to society as a whole. Nonetheless, it well describes the pyramid of practical budget decisions. In recent years it has become a key element in debates concerning the role and range of responsibility in the European Union (EU). A literature on subsidiarity has developed among discussants of the EU constitution.

Subsidiarity is a description, almost an MRI or X-ray, of what government does and it is a guide to remind government of its practical limitations. It is at the same time a practical means for each of the theoretical approaches to the purpose of government to come to grips with immediate policy and budget issues. While no one rejects their theoretical goals, each must make incremental steps toward those goals if progress is to be made. Those individuals committed to socialism's growth must make practical or subsidiarity-type decisions about what control or program is most needed and what is most important to add next. On other hand, those who desire less government involvement in the economy must make similar subsidiarity-type decisions about which programs are least needed and can be first spun off.

At all levels of government decisions -to increase or decrease programs, to tax, to regulate, to intervene, to purchase, or to ignore- are made in terms of the minimum necessary and the maximum possible, the minimum costs and the maximum benefit. No government, no matter its determination, can make large-scale changes without disruptions, be they economic, social, psychological, or structural. Despite great revolutionary events, the perspective of time shows change to be incremental in the final analysis. In revolutions where there are immediate and total changes the price is great in terms of loss of life, often in the millions, and the disruptiveness that follows for decades before stability is restored. Examples are too numerous to mention.

The scope of these practical decisions shows that the principle of subsidiarity applies in matters of budgets and policy. The principle applies to the larger question of governmental organization, to revolution, and indeed to change as a general concept. The minimum/maximum principle of respecting the lowest unit and allowing for higher-level involvement where appropriate has a general usefulness that can be seen more broadly. A glimmer of that sweeping applicability is evident when subsidiarity helps explain the important but often confusing and neglected concept of justice. Later its applicability will be seen throughout governmental activity, from individual rights, to relation with groups, institutions, other states, and to governmental forms.

JUSTICE

It is an anomaly that college textbooks in "introduction to political science" do not consider "justice" or do so in a limited way. American Government textbooks deal with justice only as an administrative department and never as a general topic. This omission lends support to the postbehavioralists' complaint that much of political science is an apolitical or antipolitical treatment of methodologically limited topics to the neglect of questions of great concern. The reason for the void is that many shy from philosophical, or what is called "normative," considerations, as if there were no theoretical or normative underpinnings to their "more scientific" approach. If justice is not considered in political science then it is left by default to others like philosophers, sociologists, and religious scholars, who lack legitimating empirical knowledge of political science to come to grips with the practical complexity of situations that require justice. The avoidance of the study of justice leaves political science to a default justice of the status quo.

Two Contemporary Studies

Two contemporary studies in jurisprudence show the type of work possible in combining empirical knowledge and a profound concern with justice. John Rawls' *A Theory of Justice* and Ronald Dworkin's *Taking Rights Seriously* address the question of justice in the contemporary world. They treat current concerns while reflecting on the thought of Plato, Aristotle, Rousseau, Kant, Mill and others. Rawls created a great stir. Reviews of his work ranged from saying that he made effective use of the classics to saying that he misunderstood all of them. Dworkin takes a different tack. He examines Rawls and goes beyond the appearances of contract theory, utilitarianism, and game theory with which Rawls is associated. Dworkin finds a deep theory behind Rawls' original work based on a concept of rights that are natural. These contemporary discussants of justice get involved in some of the most classical questions in political philosophy. Rawls and Dworkin will only be touched upon below, but a description of the classical elements of justice will provide a foundation for independent study at a later time.

Classical Discussions of Justice

Justice is a structuring girder in the bridge between the theoretical and practical domains of politics. The girder must have substance in knowledge of facts and theory in order to support the superstructure of government and society. The classical foundations for the understanding of justice are found in Plato's *Republic* (I, 338). Three views of justice are given there. Thrasymachus, the Sophist, says that "just" or "right" means nothing except what is to the interest of the stronger party. Opposed to this is the view that justice is a compromise, the lesser evil between inflicting injustice without punishment and suffering injustice without the power of retaliation.

Neither of these first two views is satisfactory to Plato and yet they are often seen in later thinkers. Machiavelli adopted the view that justice is nothing more than the interest of the strong in *The Prince* at the beginning of the modern era. In Machiavelli's so-called pragmatic approach to the political world success alone is the measure of goodness. Under the criterion of success any means, even unjust ones, may be employed to accomplish a purpose. Hobbes's *Leviathan* took Machiavelli at his word by creating an absolute Prince whose goal was order but whose means was power. Lockean laissez faire individualism came to restore a more individual source of justice but its effect was to make everyone a little Prince. Marx saw this point and in his analysis rejected the "might makes right" of Locke's individualistic capitalism. Not too surprisingly, he provided the vehicle for the return of Machiavellian justice in oppressive totalitarian form in the leadership role assigned to the vanguard of the proletariat.

Rousseau, likewise mentioned in an earlier chapter, viewed justice ideally as a function of the vague general will of consensus. Rawls worked from a rationalized general will, which is proof that Rousseau's plan needed more concrete formulation. Utilitarianism, following Rousseau in the eighteenth and nineteenth centuries, saw weakness in his approach and attempted to give substance to justice by their famous formulation of "the greatest good to the greatest number." According to them a counting or calculating process determines justice. Strangely the power version of justice as well as the utilitarian are what Plato rejected. The utilitarians may not have intended a revival of what had been rejected, but in John Stuart Mill, for example, a surrogate, the wisest or most insightful interpreter, replaces the greatest number.

Plato proposed a third view, namely, that justice was "to render what is due." Plato's *Republic* was an elaboration of "what is due." He outlined a scheme of roles and functions within the state and a coordination of individuals who were fit for those tasks. Plato argued that as the individual has certain parts to the body that must work in harmony for well-being, so the state has similar parts that must be harmonized. For Plato the harmony of the parts is justice, a bond that holds a society together, a harmonious union of individuals, each of whom is fitted to an appointed task. The Republic, the imagined government created according to Plato's design, determined what the tasks were and who would best perform them: philosophers ought to be kings or kings ought to be philosophers, brave strong persons ought to be warriors, and persons of domestic skills ought to be artisans or tradesmen. Education provided the key to discernment of appropriate roles for individuals, much as education is understood to do today. Performance of tasks according to ability has an appearance of justice in contrast to the sophist's view that tasks and duties are performed according to force and domination. There is, however, a tyranny to the assignment of tasks and the rigid structure of the Republic in so far as the task once discerned was fixed. No room was left for late bloomers who did not score well on the Republic's version of today's SATs or LSAT so they could move to the warrior (officer's rank) or to the guardian (lawyer) role. Individuals were not so much free to choose and then to act, as they were instead compelled to perform within what the framework provided. This rigidity was a basis for Aristotle's criticism of his teacher's concept of justice.

Aristotle, like Plato, saw justice as a harmony within the community. The harmony had a natural part as well as a positive or humanly determined part. The distinction between the positive and the natural constitutes the difference between much of modern writing on justice, including that of Rawls and that of Dworkin. Instead of Plato's idealized form of justice, Aristotle explained kinds of justice in various relationships. For Aristotle the parts of the community and individual cannot have an order or relationship imposed upon then from the outside, although some read Plato as subtler in his design of justice through the use of education. Aristotle explains the community's parts and behavior and proposes improved relationships. He does not, as Plato does in his quest for justice, seek a stratified society. Nor does Aristotle, unlike Plato, seek the abolition of the family and the communism of wives and property in the name of greater harmony for the community. Book Two of Aristotle's *Politics* is a criticism of Plato's plan.

Contrary to Thrasymachus' justice of the strong, Plato offers a "rational" justice, but it is a hyper-reason of ideal forms. Rationally conceived forms stand in contrast to Aristotle's "natural" concepts, which are the product of an interaction of reason and reality. Although Plato's outcome is an improvement over force or chaos his structure is rigid. Aristotle offers structure and flexibility, principle and adaptability, a natural justice that is unchanging since that which is evil cannot be made good. Yet Aristotle's justice admits (*Ethics* 1134a, 25) a profound difference between the world of the "gods," of natural science, and the world of practical affairs where justice must be applied. What is unchangeable in one way in the realm of the gods is unchangeable in a different way in the realm of practical affairs. As the modern author Dworkin argues the critical difference is in a deep theory of natural rights (if he understands right to be objective instead of a function of will).

KINDS OF JUSTICE

In the essentially Aristotelian conception there are three kinds of justice: legal, distributive, and commutative. Each can be examined in terms of looking for what is natural or unchanging in them, that is, what is not subject to human control, and what is positive or civil, that is, what is subject to human control. For legal and commutative justice there is little disputing that something is naturally due in the relationship. What is due, the positive or civil part, may differ from place to place. That an obligation is owed stands uncontested. In this conception the existence of justice itself is unquestioned even though the particulars may be. For distributive justice, however, the concept itself is questioned as well as the particular determinations. For distributive justice, the principle of subsidiarity makes a singular contribution to both the concept and the determinations. The concept of subsidiarity contributes to the understanding of justice and demonstrates its own utility as a flexible but structuring principle in political relations. To appreciate subsidiarity's contribution the specific kinds of justice must be described.

Legal Justice

Legal justice concerns the individual's obligation to the state. If an individual does not feel satisfied with all aspects of the state, legal justice provides a base from which to seek improvements. But the individual has an obligation to obey the laws until they are changed. Without a minimum of order in which individuals obey the law it is not possible for improvements to occur. If each individual were free to choose which laws to obey there would be chaos.

The modern mass communication networks from which all benefit can be disrupted by a handful of agitators. Harassment of a single individual can send fear through an entire community. The order from which all benefit requires cooperative observance, otherwise the system breaks down with widespread consequences. So an individual owes the state more than just getting by, more than not breaking the law. Legal justice in its fullness means that one must observe the law in the sense of upholding the good of the community. Here is where the natural and civil parts of justice mix. Agitators may exercise their right to free speech but they are disrupting the right of many more. In particular instances harassment may not be technically illegal but it is nonetheless harmful to the individual and the community. The agitator may regard disruptiveness as serving the ultimate good of the community by forcing movement toward long needed change. Therefore the decision to disrupt is a grave responsibility and must be entered into with caution and in the spirit of respecting the law. Martin Luther King's *Letter From A Birmingham Jail* is a modern lesson in point.

The natural part of legal justice is the obligation to uphold the good of the community, to obey the law that upholds the state. The civil part of legal justice pertains to what the particular law is. In some countries the individual is obliged "under penalty of law" to tend to certain civic duties like voting or compulsory military service, while in others these practices are completely voluntary. The civil practices in themselves are indifferent. Alone they are neither just nor unjust. The system of military service before it becomes law is indifferent with respect to justice. It is only when the civil practices become a legal statute that they become a matter of legal justice. In the same way other matters such as jury service and the payment of income taxes are part of legal justice. They may seem relatively minor at the lowest level but as part of the cooperative functioning of the whole system individual acts of compliance assume a larger importance. It is in the context of the whole that the individual has obligations. These obligations are neither arbitrary nor misanthropic. The individual benefits from them.

The previous chapters on the philosophy of the state had clear implications for the relationship between the individual and the state, but it begs the question, does the individual have an obligation to the community? Must one serve on civic bodies or become a worker in political campaigns? There are no legal obligations in the sense of positive law for participation. There is, however, a larger sense of justice where one may be obliged to contribute in some way to the continued functioning of the community even though the exact actions may be unspecified. Passable but false excuses for avoiding jury duty is a test of a sense of legal justice.

The individual may be faithful in paying taxes and obeying the law generally. Some consideration must be given, however, to doing more, because otherwise the community itself is forced to operate on minimal standards. Analogously, the business that goes beyond the minimum, that offers better quality at competitive but still profitable cost excels and endures compared to the one getting by with minimum standards alone. Communities in which the individual does more than just get by are stronger and happier. Empirical evidence abounds that volunteer programs such as, the Red Cross's blood donor program, Little League sports programs, community orchestras, and planting flowers in the public square create a better community.

It is common to look at the legal system in terms of its rules and obligations. Legal justice accepts that some laws may seem excessive although they had some original merit. If that merit no longer obtains the laws then can be changed. The larger sense of justice accepts obligations while not letting them impede freedom, growth, and a positive outlook working for improvement.

Commutative Justice

Commutative justice concerns the relationship between two or more individuals. It, like the commutative property in mathematics, is an exchange. Here it is a matter of a fair day's work for a fair day's pay, a fair purchase for a fair price, a fair course for a fair tuition, a fair room for a fair rent. What is fair in work, pay, education, and tuition, may be subject to market factors. The point of commutative justice is that once the unit of fairness is agreed upon it cannot be unilaterally changed. The cashier in a restaurant cannot charge one patron a different price than another patron for the same meal. If someone borrows twenty-five dollars from you or carelessly causes twenty-five dollars worth of damage to your lawnmower then in commutative justice, that amount is owed. The natural part of justice, that an exchange is due, is clear. The positive part is determined by the factors of time and place and market.

Legal suits that involve property or contracts between individuals are often an acknowledgment of the natural part of justice, that something is due. The suit is over the positive part of justice, that is, what specifically is due. Commutative justice is a normal part, and a normally clear part, of the political order. Civil suits over property, damages, or divorce, are matters of commutative justice. Criminal matters, the other principal form of judicial proceedings, come out of legal justice and involve the actual breaking of the law.

That there are so many civil suits is not a sign of the lack of justice in the wider community of human relations since to draw that conclusion it would be necessary to consider how many suits were not entered. For the most part there is an ongoing agreement on exchange in the community where most relationships proceed smoothly. Commutative justice obtains. When relationships do not work smoothly, when a specific determination is necessary, the issues come before the courts and to public attention.

Distributive Justice

Distributive justice is an entirely different domain from legal and commutative justice. It is frequently called "social justice," which suggests that it has some special social character that the other forms of justice do not. That suggestion is misleading since all justice, as can be observed in the previous discussion, is social! Anything that involves two or more individuals is social.

Distributive justice is no more or less social than the other two. When the redundant phrase "social justice" is applied solely to distributive justice it is singled out and the impression is all too often taken that it alone is social. That impression is potentially harmful for the following reasons. Owing to the disagreements over the contents of distributive justice some people would like to disregard it and still assume that they are just. Furthermore to fail to regard commutative and legal justice as social puts them in a strictly contractual or positive light. This light ignores the broader natural dimensions that make community life successful. A strictly positive and contractual view of justice reduces all relations to tedious individualistic exchanges.

Distributive justice concerns the other side of the coin of legal justice; that is, as the individual is obliged to the state, so the state is bound to the individual. Distributive justice obliges the state with respect to the allocation of the benefits and burdens of society. This allocation is not wholly from quantitative equality. It looks to the needs, merits, and abilities of the individuals who compose society. In keeping with this mutual obligation between individual and society, each individual has the duty to contribute a just share to the common good, which share is determined in part by the ability of the individual. At the same time each individual has a claim to the advantages of society. The latter claim is measured to some extent by need.

Measurement by need and support by ability are challenging aspects of distributive justice especially when support is accomplished through a progressive income tax and distribution according to need is fulfilled through welfare programs. From these examples of tax and welfare distributive justice becomes controversial since contributing according to ability and sharing according to need sounds much like the slogan "from each according to ability, to each according to need." Because of its association with Marxism and communism it is easy to see why initially distributive justice does not get sympathetic attention.

Indeed, distributive justice says that the individual should contribute to the community to some extent according to ability and that the individual may also receive according to need. This is the natural part of distributive justice, that is, those in need should be helped, and those not in need should help. What must be determined is the positive part of distributive justice, that is, the content of what is due. Reflecting on the requirements reveals a two-way subsidiarity relationship.

Considering the infant born to an unwed mother living in poverty brings out the obvious requirements of need and support. Clearly the infant is in need while a child born into a wealthy family is not in need of public assistance. The poor child should not be denied help on the grounds that many other children do not require it. It may be said that the taxes to support the poor child come through the state from the wealthy parents of the other child. The redistribution of wealth at the expense of those who have no normal association with the poor unwed mother is viewed by many to be an offense in itself against justice. But, from where else is the help for the poor child to come? Is the poor child to suffer for not making a good choice of parents? (Care, of course, must be exercised that programs of aid are structured so that they do not encourage what they would hope to minimize.) The assistance cannot come from other poor people because they are, by definition, not in a position to help. In addition, if the help were to come from those just above the poverty level the results could enlarge the number of poor.

The only reasonable source for financing welfare services is those who are in a position to pay without being forced into economic hardships. The result is indeed one of paying according to ability and receiving according to need, but this result, contrary to possible first impression, does not have the character of leveling society. Leveling consists in taking the wealth of all and redistributing it on average to the entire population. Leveling or averaging is not involved in the aid to the poor child in need of aid. What is involved is some mechanism whereby the lowest unit of society, the poor child, can come to a point where it can operate adequately, efficiently, and with benefit to the welfare of the whole.

In this way need is functionally determined. It is not purely a matter of relative income comparisons. The ability to pay has a similar functional content with a progressive income tax system because the revenue is in inverse relation to need.

The two-sided subsidiarity relationship is such that the lowest unit of society is to operate adequately and the tax system sees to it that those marginally close to poverty are not brought into the lower level by paying what others can more easily afford. Subsidiarity makes understanding distributive justice easier. In a purely utilitarian sense, which is strictly speaking not just, those who are wealthy would want to see the poor come to a point of operating adequately because that point, by definition, is one at which there is no longer the need to "take from the rich to give to the poor." This utilitarian exchange concept is not strictly speaking just because its intention is selfish. It is a minimalist's position of saying, "Aid the oppressed, not because they are in need but to keep them away from the battlement."

In the theoretical question of what is truly just, the different theoretical positions about the purpose of the state and the role of government come to bear. Though disputes may occur about emphasis the practical subsidiarity position that something concrete must be done by way of distribution does not go away. There may be disagreement about the form of aid, of how much, and in what manner. There may be questions about the tax system and whether it is truly progressive or if some other revenue system might be more appropriate. Those questions about revenue, amounts, and forms of aid are the positive side of distributive justice. The natural side of distributive justice is that some assistance must be provided to those in need.

Conclusion And Perspective

Justice may say that a child born to a poor, unwed mother is entitled to aid. What does justice say about that mother continuing to have more children? Can the government take steps to prevent this from occurring? That is an issue of justice also which fits into a consideration of rights and the larger topic of the relationship of the individual to the state coming up next. The point of the above discussion of the poor child in the context of distributive justice was that the principle of subsidiarity can be helpful in understanding the usually troublesome concept of justice.

Subsidiarity does more than give insight into justice. It more broadly serves as a guide for what governments actually do and at the same time it serves as a norm for what policies might be considered. The example of the child describes what the government actually does and is a reminder of the importance of welfare policy at all levels of society. Because of its role of norm and analytic guide for understanding, subsidiarity has a potentially great role as an organizing concept for most relationships within the state. Schumacher used subsidiarity with respect to large business organizations but he indicated that in its origin the principle was intended for society as a whole. The next few chapters will make use of subsidiarity in discussing the relationships between the individual and the state, groups and the state, and of states to one another. Later its usefulness in understanding constitutionalism will be seen, and, perhaps obviously by this point, its special utility with respect to federalism in the United States will be described.

The disagreements over the purpose of the state are not forgotten and they will not fade from sight. Our attention shifts more and more to factual matters but subsidiarity provides a link to the important theoretical points that will appropriately surface from time to time. The structural underpinnings of the bridge between the theoretical and the practical constantly affect both sides. Subsidiarity is the fundamental girder linking the theoretical principles of politics with practical applications in government and society.

Chapter 10

The Individual And The State: A Focus On Rights

The individual is normally referred to as a "citizen" and a citizen is understood to be "one who possesses rights." This is the common framework for discussions ranging from the most minor role of the individual to the most fundamental matters of personal security. Everything important is encompassed in terms of the rights of the individual as a citizen. To be sure the focus on rights is legitimate, especially in the light of their denial in modern historical experience. Wholesale abuse of individuals by absolute monarchs, by revolutionary mobs, by twentieth century tyrants, and by oppressive legal systems makes abuse a constant concern.

Historical Perspective

Before undertaking the examination of the individual's relationship to the state in terms of rights it should be made clear that the consideration of rights is a relatively recent concern and it is important to see the larger context in which the relationship between the individual and the state can be viewed. Both with respect to the United States history and Western history in general, rights are a relatively recent concern. Although the Bill of Rights has been part of the Constitution of the United States for more than two hundred years, active legal recourse to its provisions is hardly seventy years old. Likewise, if Western history is dated from some point before Homer and the active concern with "rights" dates from the English lawyers of the late Elizabethan period, then on that scale also the topic is relatively recent.

By "a concern with rights" is meant a concentrated attention to limits on what may be done to the individual. Rights are understood to be "something the individual possesses as against the state," "what the individual has that the state may not take away," "what the individual possesses that may not be abridged." Those understandings imply an antagonism between individual and state that was not known in Greek or Roman times or during the medieval era. Although there was some political haggling over the inclusion of a Bill of Rights in the Constitution in the early American period the actual history of "rights" cases does not begin until well into the twentieth century.

The history of rights frequently begins with reference to the Magna Carta of 1215 in England. Examination reveals that barons and nobles were the principal beneficiaries of this early document. Its general applicability to individuals below those ranks did not come for another four hundred years. Only with the efforts of Edmund Coke and other English lawyers in the early seventeenth century did the slow process of making the concept of rights generally applicable to individuals in society at large begin. Similarly, at the time of the drafting of the American Constitution the concept of rights was current in learned circles. Some experience of the general abridgment of personal liberties had occurred under British rule, yet the practice of individuals needing protection from the state was not widespread. It is only since the 1930s that rights have assumed the prominence with which all history is myopically misjudged. So dominantly is the contemporary image projected onto the past that often nothing else can be imagined.

The notion that the individual possesses something that the state cannot take away suggests a negative relationship between the individual and the state. Although there are undeniable historical grounds for this suspicious view, the evidence is only partial. More importantly, that assumption of antagonism reflects the individualistic and anarchistic attitudes toward, or philosophies of, the state. It operates on an assumption of the primacy of the individual and of the state as a necessary evil. A balanced consideration of the relationship between the individual and the state cannot rest on the instances when there is abuse. The relationship needs to be judged more comprehensively.

PARTICIPATION

In classical Greece and in the prevailing philosophy of the state there was an assumption of cooperation between individual and community. The classical idea was that a citizen was "one who participates in the life of the community." For Aristotle the citizen was one who "shares" in the offices of the state and in the administration of justice. The citizen, for him, "should know how to govern like a freeman and how to obey like a freeman." The purpose of sharing was the betterment of both the individual and the community. He observed (*Politics* III, 1280b, 30-40) that the state is not a mere place for exchange and for the prevention of crime in a common location. These are the sine qua non of the state but they in themselves do not constitute the state since it is a community of families existing for the sake of a perfect and self-sufficing life. For him the end of the state is the good life, expressed in family and brotherhood, and exchange and the prevention of crime are merely the means toward it.

In Athens, participation was the greatest blessing and the greatest deprivation if lacking. There was no thought of rights as something possessed by the citizen against the state that wanted to take them away. Sharing and cooperative living was rich in early America as it had been in the ancient Greek setting. A very small portion of the rhetoric of constitution making involved the need for a bill of rights based on recent colonial experiences with England. The larger reality was sharing and growth in friendship. According to the historian Robert E. Brown (*Charles Beard and the Constitution*) who saw things more positively than did Charles Beard (*An Economic Interpretation of the Constitution of the United States*), the breadth of the country and its rich natural resources combined with a literal ocean of protection from foreign military and economic adversaries made it possible for the creation of a vast number of communities of like-minded individuals. America was more than an aggregation of individuals forced to live in a common place. People migrated because they could prosper and grow in a community that they themselves built.

In the American experience, as in ancient Greece, there was a slavery system that was a denial of rights. Slavery was a blind spot for both ancient and modern worlds. With minor exceptions, the question of slavery was not faced as an abstract issue of human rights. It is interesting, however, that Aristotle spoke of a "natural slave" as a way of showing how impossible it was. When the slavery issue was first faced politically in the United States during the drafting of the Constitution it was not as an issue of human rights but as a political issue of who could be counted in the community for purposes of apportionment of seats in Congress. Some early abolitionists spoke of the abstract rights of the person but those rights were only attended to in a practical way years later. It took a bloody civil war and another hundred years for them to begin to be fully implemented.

In such settings, participation was at the expense of others, even though slaves were only a small number of the total population. The participatory character of citizenship should not be diminished by the historic fault of slavery. Participation truly played a large role in nineteenth-century American growth. Because of that growth America took on a twentieth-century world role. Eventually the incongruity of legal membership of the former slaves and actual exclusion gave way to change. Emancipation in itself did not accomplish an immediate realization of personal rights. The civil rights movement of the 1950s in the United States gave impetus to full realization to the unfortunately gradual but nonetheless steady emancipation.

It is only with the experience of individual rights in community situations and in a participatory setting that the abstract adherence to rights becomes something more than words. Although people of late nineteenth-century and early twentieth-century America thought of themselves as respecting the rights of citizens, it was only with the spread of those former slaves and their descendants throughout the country as a result of industrial growth and World War II that the reality of nonparticipation challenged the verbal assumptions. Western frontiers, the clarion call to participation by migration in the nineteenth century, were replaced with urban and personal frontiers of real participation. Frontier homesteading became urban development. The enjoyment of rights followed this growth rather than preceded it.

Today rights are emphasized and participation is given scant attention, which may explain why apathy is a greater phenomenon than voting and why legal justice is often viewed in a minimal sense. Citizenship should be appreciated in the dual sense of both possessing rights and participating in the community. One problem with the participatory aspect of citizenship is that the opportunities for involvement often seem limited to either voting or being a candidate. Participation in the life of the community should not be limited to such disparate alternatives. It involves more than the biannual election ceremony. People are participating when they give blood, or help out at the young girls' softball league, or serve a volunteer fire department, or drop money in the Salvation Army canister at holiday time. This involvement in the community restores that classical sense of citizen as a participant and represents a fuller sense of Cicero's notion of the state as "a public thing, a thing of the people."

Studies of various national political cultures show a gradation of participation. Judging participation primarily on the basis of voting should be challenged. Voting and nonvoting are important and easily countable factors, but other factors are also important though difficult to tabulate. A correlation between all levels of participation and the actual enjoyment of rights in various countries would tell more, though such a study might be impossible to undertake.

Origin Of Rights And Are They Absolute Or Relative?

Do rights come from the state or some other source? Are they unchanging? Are they relatively durable but not absolute preferences? Are they true in one place or one part of the country or in one nation and not in others? Who decides what a right is and what is not? Do they apply to non-citizens? Such questions quickly erode our normally assumed knowledge of rights. If rights come from some external source then individuals are in a dependent position. If they come from some constitutional majority, individuals may be only slightly better off since the majority may change. If rights are relative they lack security; if they are absolute they are unrealistic since it cannot change anywhere or anytime. If absolute "rights" existed there would be a problem of deciding which is more absolute. If the only alternative to "absolute" is "relative" and relative means subject to time and circumstance, rights do not have a very stable base. These observations show the shortcomings of the commonplace sense of rights.

The alternative to understanding rights as either absolute or relative is to say that rights are "principles." A principle is something that carries with it the importance and respect that the word "absolute" attempts to convey. At the same time "principle" suggests the need for understanding, application, and interpretation while not implying the fluidity of being relative. Rights as principles are held most dear, they are fundamental and comprehensive but not dogmatical. A right taken as an absolute would condemn any abridgment of it, whether in self-defense or by accident. All infractions would fall before the sweeping indictment of violators of the absolute. Understood as a principle to be respected and applied, rights do not have the problem of absolutes, nor do they have the problem of the ephemeralness of being relative.

Rights are not usually described as principles. Nonetheless it is a clearer way to understand the relationship of government and state to the individual. There are so many cases about rights that the common practice of memorizing passages and cases becomes increasingly impossible. The confusion becomes more manageable when rights are understood in terms of the principle of subsidiarity. The understanding is both efficient and accurate.

Subsidiarity means that the lowest unit of society that can perform a function adequately, efficiently, and to the welfare of the whole should do so. In the instance of rights, the lowest unit is the individual or the activity of the individual and the individual's integrity or activity is to be assumed. If the lower unit cannot perform the necessary function or if its improper performance is of serious concern to society, then in some way the unit or activity can be interfered with. Subsidiarity favors decentralization yet within it is a centralizing corollary. This means non-performing necessary activity can be overcome. In application to rights, if an individual acts in a manner harmful to society then some appropriate level of society can intervene in an orderly way.

To appreciate subsidiarity's contribution to the understanding of rights, an overview of several rights and their related problems follows. The rights are in the general grouping of life, liberty, and property. Subsidiarity serves as a tool for understanding and as a normative reminder of the respect expected.

LIFE AND CAPITAL PUNISHMENT

Before all other rights there must be life. Special ceremonies marking the commencement of life and its ending are found in all communities. Likewise, there is a common horror at the artificial termination of life in large calamities or individual accidents. Murder as a crime against life is subject to a harsh response in organized or unorganized communities. A significant test of a community's respect for life comes in circumstances when a murderer is found guilty. Should capital punishment be exercised? Can life be respected in that instance?

There is no question that capital punishment can be invoked when society cannot be secured in any other way from future harm by the convicted murderer. A crucial question comes when society's security is not in jeopardy and yet the convicted murderer is guilty of heinous actions. It is a question of the severity of the legal response that is central to the controversy about capital punishment. If life were an absolute then there would be no question that capital punishment could not be used. But this also challenges all past taking of life whether in military or in criminal procedures. To condemn capital punishment outright suggests that all past use was wrong and indicts all future use without consideration of circumstance. While a sweeping position assumes too much it may be just as unreasonable to continue to use this form of punishment. Given contemporary conditions, at least so far as the United States goes, it is entirely possible to secure society through adequate prison systems. When prisons were less secure than today, execution of the guilty was necessary in order to protect society. The principle of respect applies differently in less secure conditions.

Many arguments are raised in capital punishment debates. It is argued that the murderer did not respect the right of the victim and therefore surrendered the right to life. Other arguments are: the punishment should suit the crime, life in prison is cruel and inhumane and execution is more humane, life imprisonment is too costly to the community which must support the guilty murderer, and capital punishment is a deterrent. These arguments lack respect for life, though some argue that the punishment is needed as a symbol of concern for life and safety. The symbol for life argument is strange because while it may be a symbol of safety it is hard to imagine how it is a symbol for life. The guillotine would be a surreal symbol for life. Killing to prove that it is wrong to kill inconsistently accepts the premise of the murderer. Trading one life for another is a vengeful brutalization of society and contradicts pretensions of respect.

Capital punishment's reinforcement of *dis*respect for life is evident in a press release that opposed a mandatory national highway speed limit by the Independent Truckers Association at the time of severe fuel saving efforts: "If Gary Gilmore [a convicted and executed murderer] can be allowed to kill himself, or be sentenced to death, then the nation's speeding motorists should have the same right." Gilmore, whose brutal murders made headlines (similar to the recent "BTK" murderer in Kansas), got even more attention when he insisted that the state carry out his death sentence. Norman Mailer subsequently wrote a book about Gilmore and a movie gave further publicity to this despicable individual. Instead of contributing to all this attention when Gilmore was making his noise in the court he should have been told to return to his cell and the media's requests for information about him should have been ignored thereafter. If that had been done Gilmore could possibly still be sitting in his cell and the writers could have waxed on about how horrible it is to sit in prison for the rest of one's life. Any merit to the deterrence argument for capital punishment might be tried in the ordeal of imprisonment for life.

Former Senator James Buckley argued that capital punishment is "the ultimate deterrent" and he said that it is "cruel and inhuman to allow a person to linger in prison for long periods of time awaiting death." That same Senator Buckley had argued against legalized abortion as a new medical ethic in which the dignity and sanctity of the person is sacrificed upon the altar of social utility. His reasoning suggests that it is okay to sacrifice the dignity and sanctity of the person on the altar of social utility if it is a deterrent to crime. Sociological studies about the deterrent effect of capital punishment go in every possible direction. The only thing that can be agreed upon is that the executed murderer is deterred from further crime. A secure prison can achieve the same effect.

Should the murderer's life, as life, be respected? It is a question of whose premises are to prevail, society's or the murderer's. Life imprisonment is properly a symbol of life and safety. If the prison guards or other prisoners are not safe from some murderers, the answer can be to lock the prisoner up and, literally, throw away the key. Society should insist on its principles and not be talked into lesser ones. More should be written about prisons, not as a way of minimizing justified punishment but as a way of convincing people that they do not want to go there. Depictions of individuals serving their well-deserved sentences should be instructive.

One concern with keeping individuals in prison for life is the amount of tax money that pays for it. Expenses for running prisons are begrudged and would be even more so if needed improvements were made. Warren Burger, before he became Chief Justice, acknowledged the dilemma of the criminal justice system when he argued that in part the terrible price we are paying in crime is because we have tended, once the drama of the trial is over, to regard all criminals as human rubbish. He commented that it would make more sense, from a coldly logical viewpoint, to put all this rubbish into a vast incinerator than simply to store it in warehouses for a period of time, only to have most of the subjects come out of prison and return to their old ways. Burger continued somewhat of a crusade for more adequately dealing with prisons and criminal justice practices when he was on the Court. His is not a proposal to mollify criminals. Nor would he mitigate criminal responsibility by blaming society's environment for the acts of crime. Burger was not proposing a system of incinerators to deal with convicted criminals. The savings realized by executing all those currently on death row is marginal compared to total prison costs and the amounts needed to rectify inadequacies. The criminal is to be neither coddled nor abused. What is needed is a tough, adequate, and fair system where overcrowding, homosexual rape, drug abuse, and other abuses do not occur. To provide this more money needs to be spent on the prison system.

Each year more money is spent separately on liquor, beer, cigarettes, cosmetics, luxury cars, electronic games, and designer swimwear than on the prison system. Although these personal items are manifestation of individual free choice, they should be weighed against the value of supporting life, even of the undeserving. Personal comfort is desirable in moderation, measured in part by the context of society and its values. If respect for life is an intended societal value, then it must be consistently held. Viewing life as a right in light of subsidiarity holds that life is to be respected, even the life of the convicted murderer, *unless* there is no other way to secure society from future harm from that murderer. (The hanging of Saddam Hussein would have to be debated in this context and in the context of a war torn society.) War is expected to be the last resort, police are expected to resort to force and weapons only when there is no other course of action, truckers and all drivers are expected to manage their vehicles so as not to endanger others, and individuals are expected to be nonviolent in personal disagreements. These are ways to respect the life of others. Avoiding capital punishment is consistent with these values.

Still, police use force, wars occur, and individuals come to blows, and all these come about, or so we hope, when the action is necessary, when there is no other recourse. Those expectations and events are in keeping with the principle of assuming individual integrity. The individual or individual right is not an absolute. At the same time, principle is not based on majority preference. The right starts with the assumption of individual integrity but when it is demonstrated, as in a legal system of jury trials and appeals, that the action or person lacks integrity, then intervention may occur. The burden of proof for interference is on society.

In *Furman v. Georgia* (1972), the Supreme Court ruled against capital punishment on the grounds that procedures were arbitrary and capricious, with some individuals receiving the death penalty for crimes for which others received much lighter sentences. A few years later, after many states adjusted their sentencing procedures, the Court in a series of cases (chiefly *Gregg v. Georgia*,

1976) found the death penalty statutes acceptable and not a violation of the cruel and unusual punishment provisions of the Eighth and Fourteenth Amendments. The Court took note that some thirty-five states had enacted death penalty statutes since its 1972 decision, and the Court seemed to defer to popular sentiment supporting capital punishment. The Court said "a large proportion of American society continues to regard it as an appropriate and necessary criminal sanction." The Supreme Court is not usually so cravenly political in its decisions. The Court may have been caught in the logic of its own Furman decision. When the states enacted less arbitrary and capricious procedures, the Court either had to accept them or ban capital punishment outright on the grounds of violating cruel and unusual punishment prohibitions or on other grounds. From the point of view of federalism it may be better that the Court not be the instrument to ban capital punishment and instead the respective state legislatures should address it. State legislatures and politicians by their inaction will eventually force the Supreme Court back into the arena.

If conditions in American prisons continue as they have, the Court in coming years will be handing down a large number of widely publicized decisions in the area of sentencing and capital punishment. The current examination is not about which level of the legal system should decide, the concern is respect for life and how long it will be before the Court finds itself unable to let state legislatures continue to ignore it. Eventually capital punishment will be banned once again. Probably, and unfortunately, it will be the Court and not the legislatures making the public policy.

THE RIGHT TO PERSONAL LIBERTY

Besides the usual rights of speech, press, and fair trial, personal liberty involves the extensions of life itself, which include physical and mental attributes possessed by human beings. The latter means that an individual may not be deprived of limbs, eyes, brain, reproductive power, or other attributes without just cause. Decisions on these items concern personal integrity, not community preferences. Troublesome cases arise often about mentally handicapped individuals, abortion in the instance of rape, and refusal of medical treatment for minor children. Abortion in itself provides occasion for soul searching in the application of subsidiarity to fundamental matters of life and other rights, like that of choice, its timing, versus the life of the child. Subsidiarity provides the framework for personal reflection. Though all the extensions of life might be profitably explored, the capital punishment consideration above has shown how the examination of rights as principles could be undertaken. The approach, referred to as the principle approach or as the subsidiarity approach, will be applied below to specific liberties to further suggest application to all rights. A depiction of the approach is found in *Appendix D*. It shows the assumption of integrity and the corollary of what occurs when integrity is lacking.

Free Speech

Freedom of speech is especially good in supporting and explaining the principle approach to rights. The Courts pay great deference to freedom of speech. As established in the *Schenck Case* (1919), if the speech constitutes a clear and present danger it can be lawfully suppressed. The case questioned a law passed by Congress prohibiting certain types of actions disruptive of the Conscription Act. Schenck, as general secretary of the Socialist Party, had sent out leaflets to men who had been called to military service, urging them to oppose the draft. When he was arrested and tried, Schenck argued that he was protected in his actions by the First Amendment guarantee of freedom of speech and press.

While making clear in its decision the privileged position of free expression the Court added that an act must be judged in the circumstances in which it occurs. Justice Holmes maintained that when a nation is at war many things that might be said in time of peace are such a hindrance to its effort that their utterance will not be endured so long as men fight and that no Court could regard them as protected by any constitutional right. In other words, the character of an act depends upon the circumstances in which it is done. The most stringent protection of free speech would not protect a man in falsely shouting fire in a theatre and causing panic. The Court ruled that if the circumstances "create a clear and present danger" which would bring about "substantive evils that Congress has a right to prevent," then the action of Schenck is not protected. Thus the Court upheld the protected position of speech and expression while making clear legal standards for determining circumstances warranting interference. The lack of integrity of the action or speech must be demonstrated and the burden of proof is on the state. The Court felt in this instance these requirements had been met.

There is immediacy to the circumstances in the *Schenck* case that would not apply in other freedom of expression situations. During World War II, after the development of the Communist cell movement in the 1920s and 1930s, Congress passed the Smith Act (1940), which outlawed teaching and advocating the overthrow and destruction of the United States by force and violence. Eleven leaders of the Communist Party were arrested and convicted under authority of the Smith Act. In the trial and appeal, as the *Dennis* Case (1951), the eleven argued that their arrest and conviction was unconstitutional since unlike the Schenck situation there was no immediacy involved. Once again the Court decision spoke at length on the merits of First Amendment, which holds that the wisest governmental policies are the product of the free debate of idea, the free and unfettered interplay where speech rebuts speech, propaganda answers propaganda.

The Court acknowledged that the societal value of speech must, on occasion, be subordinated to other values and considerations. It noted the distinction between discussion and advocacy. The intention of the Smith Act, it said, was to protect government from change by violence, revolution, and terrorism, not from change by peaceful, lawful, and constitutional means. To the heart of the difference between peaceful change and the advocacy of violence the court observed that whatever theoretical merit there may be to the argument that there is a "right" to rebellion against dictatorial governments it is without force where the existing structure of the government provides for peaceful and orderly change. The Court noted that, carried to its logical conclusion, any principle of governmental helplessness in the face of preparation for revolution must lead to anarchy. It later observed that overthrow of the government by force and violence is a substantial enough interest for the Government to limit speech and that if society cannot protect its very structure from armed internal attack, it must follow that no subordinate value can be protected.

In *Dennis* the "clear and present danger" rule of the *Schenck* case was altered to what might be called the "grave and probable danger" rule. Quoting from Judge Learned Hand of the appeals court from which the case had come, the Supreme Court stated that "in each case [courts] must ask whether the gravity of the 'evil,' discounted by its improbability, justifies such invasion of free speech as is necessary to avoid the danger." Here was a new though reasonable modification of when the assumed integrity of speech can be abridged. The court's lengthy argument indicated that it was concerned about safeguarding First Amendment freedoms, but it acknowledged at the same time that the very integrity of the constitutional government that guaranteed the freedoms had to be maintained. In the Court's view the government could not be forced to wait until the "putsch" was on the courthouse steps before it could take action to defend itself.

In *Schenck* and *Dennis* the court took great pains to spell out the unusual circumstances when the assumed integrity of speech could be abridged. That the court was concerned about maintaining the assumption of free expression can be seen six years later when in the *Yates* case (1957) it refined its notion of "advocacy." There it distinguished between advocacy "to do something, now or in the future, rather than merely to believe in something." In *Dennis* there was advocacy and preparations to do something while in *Yates* it was "too remote from concrete action to be regarded as the kind of indoctrination preparatory to action which was condemned in Dennis." By making a distinction between action and belief the Court found that the lower court judge had not sufficiently instructed the jury in these matters. The Court reversed some of the convictions and remanded others for retrial.

Later cases reinforced *Yates* consistent with the principle approach. To be noted is that by the time of the *Yates* decision the domestic situation had changed to the point where the Communist Party members, whatever its doctrine, were no longer regarded as threats to the nation. The danger or perceived danger of a few years earlier could no longer sway a jury. The ruling is not ground for arguing that the right is relative, however. The pains with which the assumption of integrity was always insisted upon supports the substance of the principle approach. Applications to post 9/11 terrorist activities present new challenges both in the United States and in other countries.

Freedom of the Press

Freedom of the press and other forms of expression also benefit from the principle approach. The integrity of what is written, printed, produced, staged, performed, is assumed. Legal action can only be taken in the absence of integrity after the performance or distribution of the material. In other words, prior censorship is not allowed. Libel laws and obscenity laws apply to actions that have already occurred and not to anticipated actions. An author or a director is not required to obtain prior approval for the presentation of his or her work. The law does not protect them, however, from penalties if the work is later ruled libelous or obscene.

An ironic example of prior censorship was found in the Greek censorship law of May 30, 1967. There the government, while acknowledging the country's historic place as the "cradle" of art and while insisting that it did "not intend to impose any restrictions," declared that it would not tolerate anyone "undermining healthy Greek habits and customs and corrupting Greek people, especially Greek youth." The law obliged all theatre directors to submit for approval an application and a copy of their proposed productions. The directors were especially reminded of their responsibility for any alterations made after the approval of the text. The law forbade all theatrical pieces, or musicals and public shows which: "1. disturb or could disturb public order; 2. propagate subversive theories; 3. defame our country nationally or touristically; 4. undermine the healthy social traditions of the Greek people and their ancestral habits and customs; 5. touch on Christian religion; 6. attack the person of the King, the members of the Royal Family, and the government; 7. exercise a noxious influence on youth; or 8. exercise a distorting influence on the aesthetic evolution of the people."

These criteria stand in contrast to the great Greek literature of the golden age and the phrasing of corrupting the youth is reminiscent of the charges brought against Socrates some twenty-three hundred years earlier. The previous discussion about Supreme Court decisions and internal disruptions legitimize governmental concern about internal order and self-defense. However, the provisions of Greek law point out the particular difficulty of attempting to define and monitor the things outlawed. Some of the terms left undefined and hence subject to the unchecked discretion of lower level enforcement authorities are "disturb," "subversive," "defame," "healthy," "noxious," "distorting influence," and "aesthetic." The ambiguity of the such terms would result in arbitrary enforcement, which would leave the government itself the most conspicuous violator of provision number three about defaming the country nationally and touristically (sic).

Obscenity

The Greek law has a flaw common with all attempts at defining and enforcing restrictions on artistic activity. In the United States obscenity laws are minimally enforced because of problems with definitions. The prevailing definition of the obscene is "whether to the average person, applying contemporary community standards, the dominant theme of the material taken as a whole appeals to prurient interests." Although the definition appears to say much, there are huge gaps in it. Left undefined are "community standards," "dominant theme," and "material as a whole." Gaps lead to problems when there is an attempt to enforce the law. Legal scholars, literary critics, religious and educational professionals abhor pornography but find it difficult to agree on the definitions by which they would attempt to fight it.

In making decisions regarding obscenity, many echo Justice Potter Stewart in saying that they cannot define pornography but they know it when they see it. Without intention the obscene becomes an example of the mathematician's "null set," the set that has no elements. The mercurial property of the subject makes it void as public policy in that everyone knows what is obscene but there are no winnable cases curtailing it. The problem expands with technological innovation while the sophistication of controlling it does not keep pace. The only area in which restrictions have been somewhat effective concerns child pornography insofar as an age limit of subjects can be more easily enforced. Yet it is increasingly known that the globalization of pornography has added to the challenge of finding some principled way of protecting children from predators.

The principle approach insists that the integrity of actions be assumed but that there are circumstances when that integrity may be lacking and the assumption can be suspended. Integrity is lacking with obscenity but there is an impaired ability to curtail it, which leaves the impression that community standards are low. The situation may not be so bleak because the mere acknowledgment that artistic work may lack integrity and should be curbed is more positive than a nihilistic assumption that there are no standards.

Community standards do not automatically rise and fall by the dictates of the legal system. Although the Court may rule on a legal definition, there are many other actions that establish a community's standards. The number of museums, orchestras, and performing arts groups that are available and the amount of financial support given to them as well as to the local library also set community standards as do the admission price to an art museum versus other forms of entertainment. Standards are set by community sponsored summer orchestra and jazz concerts, by art programs promoted in the schools, by teachers references to good literature, and by the number of summer educational programs in a community. A balance of athletics, arts, education, and civility have as much to do with the denominator of public morality as any Supreme Court decision. Standards are set by what people choose to express and not just by legal proceedings.

Exhibits or special exhibits at museums have been subject to controversy. For the sake of possibly getting attention some museums have chosen to display works that raise public ire often on religious or ethnic grounds. Though the selections are defended on free expression and artistic merit the very selectivity of offending some religions or ethnic groups and not others leaves the merit open to question. Academics and literary people frequently are aghast at the suggestion of curtailing artistic expression even though they find situations in which excess is obvious. Inconsistent support for and then rejection of the criticism should lead to reflection on the principles in use. The public has a larger role than participating in debates about limiting offensive forms of expression. That role is in the choices it makes about what it will patronize, what it promotes, what programs it watches or will attend, what books and magazines it purchases, what internet sites it supports.

Keeping perspective is important. Subsidiarity does not impose the Court rulings on all members of the community. The rulings are for the individuals in the case. The vast majority of the community has their own integrity that they can continue to maintain; the ruling does not mean that everyone must stand in line to buy unsavory movies, magazines, or videos. Rulings stand as a challenge to the educational system and community organizations for creative responses. Subsidiarity maintains that if a necessary function does not perform adequately others must see to proper performance. Thus subsidiarity serves as a challenge to society to respond in unrelenting creative ways to obscenity rather than letting court cases alone determine norms.

John Stuart Mill and Personal Liberty

Some argue that First Amendment freedoms are absolute. Justices Black and Douglas in some of their dissents seemed to argue that the First Amendment provision "Congress shall make no law . . ." meant precisely that *no* law should limit or regulate religion, speech, press, and assembly. It is often maintained that this provision of "no law" is supported by the sound theoretical position of John Stuart Mill who, in his *On Liberty*, is thought to have favored absolute freedom of opinion and sentiment. William Ebenstein (*Great Political Thinkers*) said that Mill's work is, together with Milton's *Areopagitica*, the finest and most moving essay on liberty in English, perhaps in any language. Mill had said (*On Liberty,* Chapter 2, Paragraph 1) that if all mankind minus one, were of one opinion, and only one person were of the contrary opinion, mankind would be no more justified in silencing that one person, than he, if he had the power, would be justified in silencing mankind. From this observation Mill gained the reputation as the defender of absolute freedom.

Mill receives almost universal approbation and his view is held as a standard for society to emulate. Overlooked are his thoughts a little later in the same work (ibid, Chapter 3, paragraph 2) where Mill, more realistically perhaps than some of his disciples, admits of circumstances that curtail free expression. He held that even opinions lose their immunity, when the circumstances in which they are expressed are such as to constitute their expression a positive instigation to some mischievous act. The two positions show Mill as consistent, unknowingly, with the subsidiarity position as he holds the right of free expression most dear while he acknowledges circumstances when its immunity is lost. Similar to the later Supreme Court cases Mill observes that an opinion that corndealers are starvers of the poor, or that private property is robbery, ought to be unmolested when simply circulated through the press, but may justly incur punishment when delivered orally to an excited mob assembled before the house of a corndealer. The admission of the role of circumstance foreshadows the clear and present danger doctrine. Grave and probable danger would only be a slight modification, as the Supreme Court found in *Dennis*. Most defenders of Mill and of free expression are not aware of his second statement or of subsidiarity itself. Joining Mill with subsidiarity shows the usually unrecognized power of the principle.

Students' Rights as an Example

The subsidiarity approach can be applied to and found in many other areas of the relationship between the individual and the state. The approach can even be used as a guide in matters that are not yet fully developed litigiously. In an area that may be called "students' rights" the Court ruled in *Tinker v. Des Moines* "school officials do not possess absolute authority over their students . . .. In our system, students may not be regarded as closed-circuit recipients of only that which the state chooses to communicate." The *Tinker* case involved the appeal of students who had been suspended from public school for wearing black armbands as an expression of opposition to the Vietnam War. The Court ruling acknowledged that students are "persons" "possessed of fundamental rights" and held that only when it is demonstrated that the forbidden "activities would materially and substantially disrupt the work and discipline of the school" could the circumstances justify the prohibition. (The attention and examples in this book are primarily focused on the United States. The wider applicability of the principle is suggested by reflecting on the Tinker issues and the possible parallel with respect to the recent French Government's rule about the wearing of scarfs by Muslim students.)

There have been cases where courts have placed the burden of proof on the plaintiff in school discipline cases. In Arkansas (*Pubsley v. Sellmeyer*, 1923) the state court pronounced the commonly accepted rule that it would not annul a rule adopted by a locally elected board unless it is demonstrated that the rule was *not* "reasonably calculated to effect . . . promoting discipline in the school." This had been the prevailing standard until *Tinker*, which changed that earlier state court position and made it clear that when fundamental rights are involved the burden belongs to the school board. A 1985 Supreme Court decision, known as the "*Piscataway* case" for the name of the school district in New Jersey where the action occurred, on the constitutionality of searching students in school maintains the *Tinker* principle. The court, while sanctioning the particular search in question, held school officials to a "reasonableness" test. The test, according to the court, is different in the school setting, but it nonetheless intended to protect the "interests of students." The court was once again acknowledging a protected right that could be circumscribed while pointing out that circumstances are different in a school setting than for searches that would be less reasonable in non-school settings.

Two of the above three examples of students' rights involved what the institution can or may not do to the student. The *Tinker* case concerned what the student may do in a public high school setting. What the student may do in a high school versus in a university raises interests because of the age of the students and because of the public funding in both instances. Inviting speakers or using student newspapers and other institutional media for the airing of opinions are areas of concern. The age factor in the high school setting and the learning dimension in both are sighted as restricting the full application of rights. It is maintained that complete freedom, as in the normal community, ought to apply so that there is every opportunity to learn even by mistakes. The other side is that education precisely needs leadership so that directed learning can occur. Also, the public funding of education and the non-representativeness of freely distributed media in the schools and universities there ought to be stricter limits than apply in the larger public world of competitive sharing of opinions. Student newspapers subsidized by the required fees from all students are not subject to the pressure of subscribers or advertisers who can choose to no longer subscribe or advertise. Application of these principles in the private high school or university presents an additional dimension of challenge. Proprietorship versus public control involves responsibilities of ownership in itself that will be discussed later. What factors control in the private educational setting is not immediately clear either in fact or in law since practice varies and litigation is sparse partly due to the assumed non-commercial nature of education. The topic invites clarification by sorting out the principles involved.

Fair Trial

Attention should be paid to the cardinal element of the entire criminal justice system. "Innocent until proven guilty" proclaims the assumption of the integrity of the accused until it is proven "beyond a reasonable doubt" that the person is guilty. All the specifics of indictment, due process, fair trial, grand jury, petit jury, sentencing, and appeal are expressions of the fundamental principle. The precise application of these specifics in particular circumstances is what much of the criminal procedure case law is about. Still, everything revolves around the assumed integrity and understanding the circumstances when integrity is lacking.

Individuals dispute the fairness of their particular case and as a consequence a separate case is made of their claim. The separate claim on procedure is what occurred in the famous *Escobedo*, *Gideon*, and *Miranda* cases. In these cases, about the right to counsel and the reading of constitutional rights, it was not and is not, contrary to some popular rhetoric, the criminal who is being protected, it is the innocent. It is always hoped that the criminal will be properly apprehended and convicted. Nonetheless, the motto of fair procedure stands as, "Better the guilty go free, than one innocent person be found guilty." A criminal justice system founded on the assumption of innocence serves all. While society does not want the guilty to go free, it wants even less that non-guilty persons be unprotected. Recently there have been a number of instances where modern technologies such as DNA tests have shown that innocent persons were imprisoned. There can be legitimate sadness at the mistakes, but celebration at their rectification.

Affirmative Action

The policy of "affirmative action" seems to contradict the assumed basic integrity or innocence of the individual, the unit, or the function. The policy involves the requirement that some owners and administrators of businesses and other institutions demonstrate that they are not practicing discrimination in hiring and personnel procedures. The premise is, in effect, that innocence must be proved rather than assumed. If charges of noncompliance are brought the burden of proof is not that of the accuser but of the accused. This policy squares with subsidiarity on the grounds that the policy was established to protect the integrity of individuals who, by reason of being female, black, or some other minority, had been discriminated against in the past. Patterns of discrimination, not always consciously practiced but nonetheless true, have been established and so the burden of proof is rightfully shifted to the institutions. The policy furthers the principle since the basic unit of society, the individual, is promoted.

President Lyndon Johnson articulated the principle of affirmative action in a commencement address at Howard University in 1965. Johnson stated, "You do not take a person who for years has been hobbled by chains and liberate him, bring him up to the starting line of a race and say, 'You are free to compete with all the others' and still justly believe that you have been completely fair . . .. Thus it is not enough to open the gates to opportunity. All our citizens must have the ability to walk through those gates . . .. This is the next and most profound state of the battle for civil rights . . . the task is to give twenty million Negroes the same choice as every other American to learn, to work, and share in society, to develop their abilities -physical, mental, and spiritual- and to pursue their individual happiness." Johnson recognized the enormity of the task. He believed it imperative that individuals who had been discriminated against in the past must be helped so that they might function adequately, efficiently, and with benefit to the welfare of the whole.

Affirmative action policy is not easy for many to accept. It has a salutary effect of stirring thinking about matters of principle. An additional benefit is that it is an excellent example of where subsidiarity's assumptions of integrity cannot be applied easily and that the principle approach is not simple and automatic.

In another expression of affirmative action, colleges, universities, law schools and similar institutions give consideration to race in admission practices in a way that racial neutral standards would not allow. In a recent (2003) Supreme Court decision involving the University of Michigan law school, in the 5/4 decision, the Court found justified the use of race in admissions practices. The majority supported the school and upheld the position of Justice Lewis Powell from the 1978 *Bakke* case that there was a compelling state interest in racial diversity. In the Michigan case Justice Sandra Day O'Connor stated for the majority that "the law school's educational judgment that such diversity is essential to its educational mission is one to which we defer." On the same day the Court found against the University in its undergraduate admissions for giving too much weight to race in a formula used in the admission process itself. Thus while the law school decision was celebrated the overall picture was not entirely clear.

Justice Clarence Thomas dissented from the majority in the law school case, arguing that the preference given to race was an insult that casts a cloud over achievements. Ward Connerly expresses similar sentiments in his *Creating Equal: My Fight Against Race Preferences*. Connerly, a black, had experienced negative aspects of race in his own life yet he argues forcefully against preferences. As a member of the University of California Board of Regents he was instrumental in ending affirmative action in that system. Nonetheless, the debate continues. Those supporting the Michigan law school decision argue for the positive effect of affirmative action and the diversity gained by the community. One defender quoted Emerson, "I pay the schoolmaster but 'tis the schoolboys that educate my son." The implication is that the diversity of the classroom is as much of the educational process as the content of the courses. In all the strong feelings over the policy notice should be taken of the future looking aspect of President Johnson's advocacy and of the comments in the Michigan cases that looked to a day when affirmative action would not be needed, fulfilling the "dream" of Rev. Martin Luther King, Jr.

Privacy and Personal Liberty

There is little statutory or case law setting forth the precise character of privacy. It is an area of discussion reflected in congressional hearings, books, articles, and some lawsuits. Great concern is expressed about data banks, electronic bugs, the ubiquitous Internet, credit fraud, undesired publicity, and heightened ability for snooping into personal matters. There is no agreed-upon position on the issue of privacy, and if society is to await the excretions of case law before having a standard the exudations of technologies will have all but inundated privacy in the meantime.

Alternatives to personal privacy are not appealing. They range from a return to exaggerated individualism or a move toward statism. In most dichotomies the more likely outcome is "neither" since the concern may be warranted but not be as grave as feared. Post 9/11 legislation and enforcement has heightened attention to the issues, however. The need for a standard by which to measure personal privacy once again calls attention to subsidiarity. Proceeding by way of the assumption of the integrity of the personal domain and the inviolability of records, domicile, and possessions as extensions of the individual is the appropriate starting point with the burden of proof placed on any abridgement effort. While there are serious concerns that in the effort to thwart terrorist activities the assumption of integrity is being eroded, there are equally legitimate concerns that the failure to act effectively will cause irreparable harm to organized society. A careful combination of principles and facts is needed to unravel the new mysteries in the area of privacy rights.

Privacy's assumption of individual integrity is not an impenetrable shield against determined violators. Inviolable privacy is not absolute, nor should it be, since it can be used as an expedient to bring harm to others. Therefore for justified reasons privacy can be abridged through proper court orders, personal property can be searched, mail opened, telephones tapped, computers seized, and Internet communications traced. That this invasion can only occur legally through a court order with stated objectives, times, and reasons is a solid indication that the defense of privacy is sound. Further refinement based on principle is in order.

THE RIGHT TO PRIVATE PROPERTY

Life and liberty are only two of the many rights in the individual's relationship to the state. Many other separate or related rights could be examined such as free movement, free assembly, religious freedom, employment rights, and the right to the products of one's labor. Some will be taken up later; others must be left for application through the general principle that has been outlined. The right to private property is the only other personal right to receive separate treatment here and only systems of ownership will be discussed. Sufficient application of the principle will be evident to encourage further exploration on one's own.

Universal Ownership

There are four basic systems of ownership: individual, corporate, public, and universal. Universal ownership is a somewhat vague concept that relates to items like the oceans, the resources below them, and the air space above them. Universal or communal ownership frequently goes by the phrase like "freedom of the seas." Custom and treaties acknowledge freedom based on universal ownership, yet historical reality suggests that it does not work as easily as theory imagines.

It may be argued that no nation may claim sovereignty (exclusive jurisdiction) over a part of the ocean or the air lanes above it. Past experience suggests, however, that those who have the technical ability to develop a new enterprise and the power to defend it basically establish the rules for continued use. Many maintain that the laws of the seas are a product of international law yet this international law may first have been the product of the practices of those who use the high seas. Landlocked nations did not have a sizeable input into the formulation of sea law even though the international commerce that results affects them as well. This calls attention to the ambiguity and complexity of the relation between states.

Problems related to the inexactness of universal ownership are not limited to the international scene. On the domestic level the difficulty can be appreciated as the high seas creep up to the shore. Ownership of the shoreline becomes an issue. Of the thousands and thousands of miles of shoreline in the United States, only a small percentage is open to the general public even though more than half the population lives within an hour's drive from the water. Most beachfront is privately owned. Where there are municipal, state, or national parks, frequently a fee must be paid for access to that which universal ownership says all people own.

Reasons for private ownership of seafront property and for beach fees for public parks are understandable in their given context. For example, who will pay to pick up the debris or pay the lifeguards in a "the public owns everything" environment? Nonetheless, it is disconcerting that the alleged universal heritage is not freely available to all. The usefulness of the concept of universal ownership may therefore be questioned. While song and verse say that "the moon belongs to everyone" and that "the best things in life are free," when it comes to booking passage on a lunar flight, preserving the environment, and maintaining clean air, reality intrudes forcefully. The concept of universal ownership should not be completely dismissed, however, since it at least is a reminder that there may be aspects of ownership not completely subsumed by the other three forms of ownership.

Individual, Corporate, and Public Ownership

Individual ownership is the starting point in discussing ownership because the individual is the "lowest unit" and because individual ownership is the place where the Western and American economic system begins. The theoretical merits of the economic system and comparative economic systems will not be examined and must be found elsewhere. The operations of the system are discussed in the light of the principle of the assumed right of ownership.

Individual ownership is taken to be about those things, business things in particular, which the individual alone can manage and develop. Individual ownership is sometimes equated with private ownership but it is not the sole form of private ownership. ***Corporate ownership*** is also a form of private ownership since it is a combination of private owners. The system of private property operates on the assumption that if the lower unit can perform adequately, efficiently, and with benefit to the whole, it is permitted to do so. The corollary, though, applies when individuals join together in a corporation on the basis that in combination they can perform necessary functions better than solitary individuals. There are many corporations. While attention is normally focused on the large corporation there are actually other intermediate combinations of individuals such as partnerships and, what is known as an "S corporations," which are between individual and corporate ownership.

Individual and corporate ownership are "private" as opposed to "public." ***Public ownership*** means government ownership or, as it is otherwise called, socialism. The word socialism colors the discussion for those who react without reflection. Arguments offered against public ownership are thought by its opponents to be irrefutable. Similarly, the citing of one or a few cases of successful public ownership is thought by others to establish its universal merit in all things.

Neither unqualified rejection nor unreserved acceptance of public ownership is warranted. Rules of logic require that a universal rule be not established by a few particulars. Furthermore, the very logic of the corollary that moved ownership from individual to corporate would move it from corporate to public. That is, when corporate ownership cannot perform a particular and necessary function adequately, efficiently, and with benefit to the welfare of the whole, then something above that must see that the function is performed.

There are intermediate combinations or forms of ownership between individual and corporate. Likewise there are intermediate steps between corporate and public ownership. The exact nature and kind of intermediate steps does not disturb the logic that leads to the justification of public ownership. There may be cooperative efforts, regulations, subsidies, receiverships, bail-outs, publicly sanctioned trusts, or public corporations. No matter how many intermediate steps there may be, public ownership is not precluded by some doctrinaire concept. The logic of subsidiarity says that if a function is a necessary function and it is not being performed adequately at a lower level, then some next higher level of activity must become involved so that the function can be performed. The next higher level may be a coordination of units at the original level. It may be a temporary subsidy or it may be trade protection until adjustments and normalization occurs. If the intermediate steps will not work then public ownership may be necessary. Which step is appropriate depends on the circumstances. What is important is that no single solution is mandated and no particular step is prohibited. It is important that the function under discussion is a necessary one for society.

Arguments advanced against public ownership are that it promotes waste, inefficiency, and maladministration. Due to the lack of a profit motive it weakens or eliminates competition, lessening incentive and efficiency, and brings politics into the economic sphere leading to favoritism, mismanagement, and corruption. Further, it is argued that political power in the economic sphere will eventually lead to totalitarianism. Each of these objections has some merit and for each historical examples may be cited. Taken as a whole, however, the objections give a distorted picture. For years the Tennessee Valley Authority (T.V.A.), a government operation set up in the 1930s, has been a model of efficiency for public and private corporations alike. T.V.A. has provided effective service to the people of the region it serves with no suggestion of the maladies said to afflict public ownership.

Except for ownership, there is no difference between the actual operations of the T.V.A. and the many utility companies and other similar monopolies throughout most of the United States. Competition, as in the auto industry or the computer industry, does not serve as an incentive for efficiency in the energy field even though efforts at instituting competition have occurred in recent years. The profit motive serves no more as an incentive for the worker at Hewlett-Packard, Boeing, Chevron-Texaco, or Wal-Mart than it does for the worker at T.V.A. The secretary, the welder, the bundle sorter, the retail clerk, and the vast bulk of workers in any corporation are paid fixed wages or salaries. Although some workers may know the relation between their income and profits, it rarely serves as a personal incentive. Incentives, such as bonuses and penalties, are employed equally by publicly owned corporations as by businesses, thus showing the lack of difference in their operations.

In an effort to respond to foreign competition the American auto industry introduced programs to instill greater worker awareness of individual impact on overall efficiency and competitiveness. Still, the competitive advantage or disadvantage of an industry is less the result of the profit incentive of production workers than it is the result of employee working conditions and the production systems introduced by management. Focusing discussion on wage earners misdirects attention away from the high-salaried decision makers who have a greater immediate affect on general efficiency and product success. Since the highly paid management individuals easily switch from one company to another within the private sector or even to and from the public sector, the assumed effect of the profit motive on the efficiency and effectiveness of private business in contrast to government ownership appears to work at their level without consideration of the worker. The ripple effect of the profit motive within a corporation appears exaggerated. It was inverted in the Enron scandal where executives appear to have sought personal profit at the expense of the corporation and especially the simple employee who lost not only a livelihood but also assumed accumulated pensions. The profit motive should therefore not serve as the major point of contrast between public and private ownership. Ownership should be examined in terms of the functions performed, their necessity, and the ability to perform these functions.

As with the efficiency argument, the contention against public ownership on the grounds of waste, favoritism, mismanagement, and corruption has a partial basis in reality. Such defects are seen in many government operations at national, state, and local levels. These deficiencies exist in some, though not all, government operations. Of equal importance, their occurrence is not limited to government. Recent scandals in the business fields of energy and finance serve as examples in the private sphere that are worse than those of public ownership. Whether legal convictions ever occur in some of the cases, the charges against Enron, Martha Stewart, and other corporations have cast a pall over the business world that government has not had for a long time. For perspective, however, it must be remembered that all the examples of deficiencies, whether private or public, are a small percentage of the domain of either field. The mismanaged corporation is as much the statistical bad sample that gets all the media attention as the bungled government operation. The well-run operation or industry is about as much headline worthy as the six o'clock news reporting that all commuters arrived home safely and everything is peaceful and quiet.

Public ownership fits into the systems of ownership in a functional way. If a lower level cannot perform a necessary function adequately, then some next higher unit must come into play to see that it is performed. If the next higher level happens to be the government, action is not precluded. Emphasis is still on the lowest unit. Accordingly, if public ownership exists but a condition is reached when the activity might be performed adequately at a lower level, then the government might divest the activity. Subsidiarity maintains that what goes up the ladder of ownership can come down. The experience of changing the Post Office Department from a cabinet level agency to the quasi-governmental Postal Service represents the semblance of a divestiture. The efforts to run the postal system on a pay-for-itself basis resulted in greatly increased postal fees. These increases have had the effect, whether intended or not, of reducing the scale of activity and encouraging competing and alternate delivery systems. While the reduction of activity is as it should be, it could only come about when alternate communication systems were available. The postal department for almost two centuries had provided the only long-range societal communication system for and with individuals and businesses. Through electronic and other media the function can now be satisfied by many other means.

Other public activities can be looked at as candidates for divestiture. In determining the adequate performance of a task, business and economic factors should not be the exclusive concern. With the postal service, for example, costs and revenue were not the sole concern. For many years the government subsidized the postal service as a means of ensuring reliable and low-cost communications between all parties within the country. That knitting of the country together by the postal system through the pony express and the tradition of "through rain, sleet, and snow" was a service that could not otherwise be provided at the time. Now that the postal service's role in the earlier knitting function is no long needed divestiture can be afforded.

When the T.V.A. was created it was not, as some argued at the time, a form of creeping socialism. The need to aid the development of a neglected region could not have been accomplished by other means. The Tennessee Valley area was economically and technically deprived, needing rural electrification and flood control projects. The creation of T.V.A. brought economic development as well as social, political, and cultural enrichment to the region. Neglected since the Civil War, the region took on new life. Here an unequivocal example of public ownership enhanced individual freedom and initiative rather than diminished them as is often erroneously alleged. The essential point in T.V.A. was whether the units of the region could function at a lower level. Since they could not the government stepped in. Thus subsidiarity, applied to the forms of ownership, becomes a wholly integrated social, political, and economic principle, based on reasonable judgments of what constitutes adequate, efficient, and sound levels of activity. Responsible levels of government, from local to national, working in cooperation, make these judgments.

Conclusion And Perspective

The fundamental concerns of life, speech, assembly, and property can neither tolerate absolutes nor afford to be decided on a majoritarian basis. Absolutes are attractive but unrealistic, assuming a simpler world than experience shows. This is not to say that there are no absolutes. Absolute values such as the sacredness of life, the importance of truth, justice, and goodness, exist. If "man is the measure of all things," as some philosophies have taught, where humans alone determine value, rights would have little meaning as they become subject to the final human interpreter. They would become at one and the same time absolute and nothing.

Rights, taken as principles, are sacred while at the same time their application is not automatic. Rights require study, reflection, debate, patience, and humility. Only by a spirit of respect and tolerance can rights exist that do not produce their own downfall. It is not an easy task. For this reason it is important to understand their elementary principles and not pretend to reduce them to simple rules.

Chapter 11

The State And Groups

In the previous chapter the relationship between the individual and the state was discussed in light of subsidiarity (also called the principle approach). The principle starts with the assumption of the right of the individual and then acknowledges that circumstances may exist where that assumption of integrity is not warranted. The approach gave an accurate, structured, and systematic way of looking at all rights, not just the few specifically examined. Ownership of property was discussed as an extension of the individual. Corporate and public ownership were viewed as parts of an integrated system flowing from and directed to the welfare of the individual. Because businesses are groups, that is, combinations of two or more individuals, some of the state's relationship to "groups" is implicit in that discussion of systems of ownership.

There are many groups other than businesses and some of them, like the family or the church, are of primary importance. It is necessary, therefore, to formally address the relationship of the state to groups and to develop in some detail how subsidiarity is helpful in understanding the relationship. This relationship can be looked at in terms of subsidiarity or there is a descriptive approach of classifying and measuring groups by using empirical means to possibly gauge their effectiveness within the state. This "group model," with merits of its own, is a return to political scientist's empirical methods discussed in earlier chapters. It is useful to experience the range of what political science can do in studying groups so as to appreciate, in contrast, the subsidiarity perspective that will follow. It is not that one approach is good or bad, it is a matter, as indicated in the chapter on methodology, that they do different things and complement understanding.

The Group Model

Groups are of different types and sizes and can be classified in a variety of ways. Political scientists call attention to the role that groups play in the political process and then they attempt to measure and predict the effect of groups in the process. Since all groups do not have the same characteristics, what is identified and the precise role played within the system differs considerably. Types of groups will be described and then the efforts to measure them and their impact will be explained.

Spontaneous or temporary groups arise over particular events or issues. They take the form of a riot or demonstration and normally have only a short-term impact. Such groups do not ordinarily last beyond the event that brought them into existence. During the demonstration the assembled individuals behave as a group, perhaps even eliciting some governmental response. They most likely would never assemble again and so their role as a group is different from those with greater duration. Other groups have greater permanence than these ephemeral groups but also lack an organized character. Referred to as *nonassociational interest groups*, they are based on ethnic, kinship, regional, status, or class factors. Such groups have a potential for mobilization but the individuals within them usually go their separate ways; only special circumstances or extraordinary effort over a long period of time overcomes the prevailing inertia. For example, in most American communities individuals of Irish descent usually come together and act like an organized group only once a year (March 17th) yet for the rest of the year they do not have the same interests.

If the ethnic or other nonassociational interest group comes together on a more permanent basis and begins to regularly assert its identity, then the group would take on the characteristics of the more familiar interest groups. The more commonly recognized interest groups are referred to as *institutional and associational groups*. These are combinations within the general public or within institutions designed to represent and reflect the interests of members. Since such groups can be blocs within institutions or organizations as well as separate entities, they have a more easily identifiable role and so assume a greater importance. They can range in interest from a faction within a major political party to a business-supported think tank. As such they receive the attention of political scientists.

Political scientists do not simply consider groups with obvious political roles. It is the interplay of all permanently organized groups, even those with no ostensible political role, that interest political scientists. The model, or group theory, maintains that all meaningful political activity is to be understood in its terms. Sometimes the activity of the group is one of struggle; other times it is the quiet satisfaction of dominant interests. Policy makers are viewed as constantly responding to group pressures and public policy is regarded as a function of the group process alone. Struggle between groups is the normal political reality. Politicians are seen as forming coalitions of groups in order to mount successful election campaigns. Public policy enactments represent the supposed temporal equilibrium reached in the group struggle.

Not all political scientists subscribe to the group model. When discussing the political system it was pointed out that some political scientists see the systems model as singular in understanding the political world, while in the chapter on methodology many other models for capturing the secrets of the political world were suggested. The institutional model gives emphasis to the dominant force of established institutions in the making of policy. The elite model sees a few select individuals in society as controlling its direction and character. An incremental or evolutionary model sees political life explained by slow and almost inevitable steps determined by past practice. Some other models are game theory, power, role, communications, rational, and individual-psychological. Sometimes these models are in combination, as are the game and rational, whereas at other times the particular political scientist proponent holds them to be unquestionably separate.

Each model claims that its technique is a better way to capture reality than the others. It is not unusual then that political scientists disagree on the dimensions and the significance of the group model. A respected feature of political science is that it acknowledges the complexity of the political world and offers a variety of ways to understand it. Some do not regard politics as a struggle of groups but instead view groups as contributing input into decisions that are then independently arrived at by policy makers.

A special feature of the group approach is its identification and measurement of groups in terms of their possession of certain characteristics. This feature has the appearance of offering some practical utility. The characteristics of leadership, size, cohesion, status, wealth, doctrine, and organization help capture the strength of groups. The positive possession of these primary characteristics together with the absence of certain adverse factors, such as dilution by overlap and latent groups, combined with a positive effect of the multiplier of time, marks a group for success. The American Red Cross and the American Cancer Society are prime examples since both possess the primary characteristics in a positive way and are not adversely affected by overlapping appeal to each other or other health groups. Neither do new groups that would weaken the older group's popular appeal threaten them.

Positive possession of the group characteristics means that the group has effective or dynamic leadership, good size, cohesive membership, well-developed organizational structure, a sound doctrine, is well received by the public, and has a solvent treasury supported by a self-sustaining membership. Organizations and interest groups possess these characteristics in varying degrees. Some may lack leadership or size; others may be weak on cohesion or wealth. Size, always a nebulous quality, means neither too large nor too small for strategic purposes. Positive possession of all the characteristics means greater access to the public and to public officials and a correspondingly greater chance of success when requests are made in the policy arena.

New groups, like an environmental awareness organization, whatever the merits of their particular doctrine, will have reduced chances of success unless their relative newness is offset by overwhelming popular and financial support. A group seeking handgun control may feel it surpasses the National Rifle Association (NRA) in doctrine with the contention that the Second Amendment ties the right to keep and bear arms to the existence of a "well-regulated militia" which is accomplished through the National Guard. The NRA does not accept that proposition and with its membership size, national leadership, local chapters, communication networks, and experience, it usually prevails. Legislators approach with caution any proposal that might incur NRA opposition.

Assessing the likely success of the NRA against competing groups shows the practical potential of the group model. Applying the model to the American Association of Retired People (AARP) or the trial lawyers association further illustrates the utility of the model. AARP is a fascinating phenomenon in application of the model since everyone over the age of fifty is claimed to be in the population represented. Even though the AARP does have a large subscription membership the sweep of the organization's claim on many issues encompasses members and non-members alike. By their doctrine and organization strengths they appear recently to assume the role of super representatives of everything affecting "seniors." Their ability to influence the public would constitute an intriguing challenge for the pros and cons of the group model.

It would be valuable to know for certain whether one group instead of another is most responsible for a particular policy. This desire reveals the principal weakness of the model in that it has the appearance of working well in obvious cases and poorly in most others. In obvious cases the positive possession of characteristics is easy to gauge while in the non-obvious ones measurability is problematic and the model is not particularly explanatory. There are too many factors in closely fought policy issues for strengths and weaknesses to be reduced to known numbers. Furthermore, if there were a secret formula for success using the model, if one group found the key to dominant influence, others would quickly discover the same formula and no one would be any better off than before. It must be concluded that the model has descriptive merits in revealing the importance of knowing more about the size and strength of competing interests yet the model cannot go much beyond that. It is especially limited on prescriptive tasks.

The group model, with its descriptive rendering of the political world, is a prominent feature of contemporary political science but it is not a new concept. Plato and Aristotle each spoke of the competition among groups within Athenian society. And, long before the formal model was a major feature in political science, American historians were speaking of the struggle between the Tidewater, the Piedmont, and the frontier interests in early American society revealing group competition without calling it an analytical model. A century ago Beard explained the American constitutional origins in terms of the struggle of economic groups. Though this reading of Marxist economic interpretation backwards into the founding period may be invalid, the discernment of the role of group interests is longstanding. Similar descriptions of competition and rivalry as found in developed countries are often applied to developing countries even when they have a paucity of formally organized interest groups and strong cultural inertia to withstand them.

It is to be recognized that the group model has descriptive merits even with its analytical weaknesses. The model can help evaluate the strength of various interests even though it cannot fully access responsibility or predict outcomes. The group model cannot draw a practical distinction between formally organized groups and all formal interests nor can it show when a group accurately represents an interest. The classification scheme, though conceptually neat, ultimately collapses when put to harsh practical tests. Though the model may ultimately fail in a strictly scientific and logical sense before judging everything in that final light the richness of the descriptive insights should be appreciated for what they are. Both elected representatives and the public are better served by knowing the contending factors in decisions even when neither can point to specific final determinants of policy. Representatives are given to justifying their decisions in terms of what sits well with the electorate while they may in fact have voted by way of an agonizing hunch that they were doing the "right" thing. Votes on declarations of war, treaties, social security policy, bankruptcy procedures, and budgets are conveniently explained as the product of a calculus of interests. The actual decision may not be explained by what is said.

Subsidiarity And Groups

From the group model attention now shifts to the subsidiarity relationship of groups to the state. Subsidiarity does not involve the measuring aspects of the group model. It takes units as givens and explains their respective autonomy, their integrity, and how they can be affected by the state. Four representative groups to be considered are the family, voluntary associations, the church, and other states at the international level. They are singled out because they have special challenges, the examination of which will lead to a fuller understanding of both the principle and the groups themselves.

The Family

The consideration of the family basically assumes its integrity or the integrity of the activity associated with it. Subsidiarity acknowledges circumstances when intervention is necessary. In the corollary situation, once again, the lack of integrity that justifies interference must be demonstrated. The family, the primary association which most persons form, is considered under three topics of interest to the state: formation, size, and development.

Formation: The individual may marry whomever he or she prefers without prohibition or directive from the state. This understanding is the basic assumption about the *formation* of the family. Freedom of choice for the individual was not always the practice. In earlier centuries planned or arranged marriage was the regular practice and it continues to exist in some societies. The state's role in this situation is one of sanctioning societal and religious practice. In those circumstances there is little interference in what families or kinship groups have already decided. There are some rules against certain types of marriages but these mostly reflect societal or religious agreements.

Today individual choice of spouse is the prevailing practice. The state only regulates in those areas where it is demonstrated that the assumption of integrity of individual choice is lacking. The state sets minimum age limits, prohibits marriage between persons within certain degrees of blood relationship, sometimes requires blood tests (required well before the HIV crisis), refuses to issue licenses to those with certain contagious diseases, requires some capacity for consent, and prohibits plural marriages. These regulations are designed to protect innocent parties. The innocent party may be one of the partners or the children who would result from such a union. The requirement of obtaining a marriage license is not a matter of the individuals' obtaining permission to exercise their choice; it is a means of enforcing the other legitimate concerns. The actual role of the state in this area is still passive although it may change in light of new issues concerning the cohabitation of same-sex individuals and granting them legal marital status.

Size: On the matter of family *size* it may appear that the individual family units may choose to be of whatever size they desire, that they may have as many children as they please. That is not true since in many places today family size rightly or wrongly raises the issue of overpopulation. Some countries speak of limiting, or actually do limit in some way, the number of children in a family. Many view country and world overpopulation as a problem. That position is counter posed by denial of the population claims and by appeal to the personal rights and integrity of individuals and families, which are violated by countries that interfere. Added to the personal and family side of the issue is a religious dimension that makes the issue all the more troublesome.

Underpopulation was a concern in the past. Then states encouraged population growth through immigration policy, homestead acts, tax exemptions, and family allotments. When the state encouraged population growth it was not neutral and there was general support for the policy. If the state could encourage growth, those who object to discouraging growth must be fully aware of the subtleties of their possible inconsistency. Yesterday's tax encouragement can be turned into today's discouragement. The question becomes, therefore, what is the "limit," if any, to the state's role on family size?

Can the state require an individual family to obtain permission by taking out a license in order to have children or to have more than a fixed number of children? This is but one of many proposals raised for limiting population growth. It is not just a theoretical issue since it is reported to be a practice in China. From other countries there have been reports of required sterilization or instances of sterilization in exchange for a free transistor radio worth a couple of dollars. Other less severe proposals for population management exist in various countries. Among measures proposed is the postponement of the legal age of marriage, thus reducing the childbearing years, while maintaining current proscriptions against illegitimate birth. The problem of teenage pregnancy in premature parents reveals how unrealistic such a simple legal measure would be. Other proposals are for even lower taxes for single persons than for married ones, the end of the tax exemption for children, government funding of birth control supplies and abortions, and even the establishment of a child tax. Another proposal is that women should be given equality in educational and employment opportunities so that they could develop alternative interests to the family.

Many of the proposals are in effect to some degree, but most have no more chance of success than the one on raising the legal age for marriage. The proposal about giving women an alternate interest to the family presumes that it is only women's interest in children that has been the cause of large families. Women receive more equal treatment today in many areas. To say that fairer treatment is deliberately planned for population control purposes confuses many issues and suggests that fairness is not a value in itself. The tax situations, which discourage large families already, exist in varying degrees but most have not come about deliberately. Decades of inflation and income tax practices have converted the former exemption incentives into disincentives. Sorting out incentives and disincentives in American tax law is not easy. While the deduction per exemption has increased the cost of living has gone up too and other factors have been added to the tax code such as child tax credit and child and dependent care credits, all of which make it difficult to judge whether the changes are disproportionate or not. Proposals for more direct incentives or discouragements are precisely issues that are difficult to determine.

Subsidiarity has been helpful thus far in giving an idea of how to view any problem. It creates an understanding of what should receive preferential treatment and it shows on what grounds intervention may occur. In regard to population and family size, a simple answer is not possible, but the principle gives a structure to priorities. Subsidiarity holds that the individual family should be assumed to have integrity, that any lack must be demonstrated, and the need for intervention for the public good must also be demonstrated. Yet, so great is the population in some countries, and the projected world population for just a few decades from now is so large, that attention is being given to some of the more drastic proposals.

Concrete figures should be given to appreciate the context of the problem. World population, which took about nineteen hundred years since the time of Christ to quadruple, has quadrupled again in the last one hundred years. It is expected to grow by more than fifty percent, from the present six billion plus to more that nine billion, in the next fifty years. Subsidiarity in urging respect for the integrity of the individual family would seek some moderate measure to induce responsible growth. A problem exists with inducements in that they do not work with some and they work too well with others such that at some point inducements give way to more direct measures and difficult problems of coercion arise. In light of highly populated countries it is hard to imagine grounds for opposition to efforts to limit growth although predicted economic decline of countries that have had population-limiting practices for many decades should give pause. Western European countries as well as Japan, for example, of late have had to consider increasing legal retirement ages and other measures in light of pension fund shortfalls that have resulted from decreased numbers of workers and increased numbers of pensioners. Countries with a shortfall in natural replenishing populations turn to migrant workers which creates problems as have arisen recently in all of Europe. Indonesia has reportedly been encouraging growth through family incentives.

Simple answers like the absolute rights of individual families or the preference of the existing majority within a state begin to appear attractive. Unfortunately these alternatives do not solve problems as much as they hide them and create others. Subsidiarity, although not providing direct answers, urges that principles be involved in the painstaking process which tries to see that "solutions" to "problems" do not create new problems. "Principled" answers are not dramatic. They require making distinctions, delving into the firmly held views of others, being patient, and minimizing tension. Such actions are hardly perceptible. They are sounder, however, and have a greater chance for eventual success than the more dramatic answers.

Development: As there are more governmental activities regarding the size of the family than about its formation, so there is an even greater amount of activity in the area of family *development*, that is, if development is taken principally to be education. Since the time of the one-room schoolhouse education has been a concern of the state. It is recognized, as was expressed by the Supreme Court in the *Pierce* case (1925) that "the child is not the mere creature of the state." Even though the state may require education the court recognized the right of parents to send their children to private and parochial schools. Still the adequate performance of the task is assumed to be the responsibility of the state, and parents who would home school their children or privately school their children must demonstrate that the task of education is adequately performed.

There have been instances where, under special circumstances, parents have not had to comply with state requirements. This has occurred with the Amish or in instances where gifted parents instruct their own gifted children. The assumption today in favor of the state instead of the family seems a reversal of subsidiarity according integrity to the lowest unit. However, the assumption in favor of the state looks toward protecting the integrity of the child and that person's opportunity for an adequate education. Parental abuse of children in not providing an education is still in evidence. In cities as well as in rural areas cases of neglected truancy manifest delinquency on the part of parents and children. Often the pressures of competing concerns leads to inadequate attention to this most basic need. Subsidiarity insists that the problem must be addressed on behalf of child, parent, and state.

The state's role in education should not give the impression that the state is absorbing the areas of responsibility previously reserved to the family. Focus on education ignores other complex dynamics of family development. Mark Twain once commented, partly in jest, "Education ain't what it used to be, and never was!" That insight can just as easily be applied to the family, "it ain't what it used to be, and never was." There are many and subtler aspects of family development from which government is far removed. To say that the family is in decline because of some perceived factors gives into a tendency to simplify the past and correspondingly to misunderstand the present. The extent to which different families emphasize homework, prayer, acquisitiveness, sports, music, orderliness, travel, history, fellowship, neighborliness, community service, and cleanliness are a few examples where development is far from the purview of the state. These many and varied areas of family responsibility create the great symphony that is society. Each family is a section of the orchestra developing separate musical instruments of different sound and perfection. Without the autonomy of families monotonic uniformity would prevail to the dismay of all. The state has an appropriate role but society celebrates the family's freedom of making its own harmony and dissonance, its own particular music.

Voluntary Associations

Voluntary associations are generally understood to be any combination of two or more individuals. They are encompassed in the groups and interests mentioned above in discussion of the group model. The family can be considered a voluntary association, although it is usually singled out as a separate primary association. In this same respect the church can be regarded as simply a voluntary association but, as will be explained below, it also receives separate attention because of special considerations associated with it. Voluntary associations encompass business, labor, professions, political organizations, social and fraternal interests, athletics, theater, etc. People voluntarily form these associations, hence the title, "voluntary." They, like the family, play an important role in expressing the freedom within the community and they perform tasks that the government might otherwise need to do.

Once again the relationship is one of assuming the integrity of the group and recognizing that there may be circumstances where state action is required. To put the relationship in slightly different words, there is a twofold relationship of these groups to the state, one positive and the other negative. On the positive side, the state encourages and fosters the existence of voluntary associations in recognition of the principle of their assumed integrity and their benefit to society. On the negative side, it can be said that the state refrains from interfering or that there should be the least interference possible. This twofold relationship acknowledges that the state may intervene either by assisting or restricting when the lower unit does not perform its function adequately, efficiently, or with benefit to the welfare of the whole. The principle is also saying that there should be as little intervention as possible.

Many voluntary groups perform functions that are helpful to the community but which the state would not undertake if the organization failed. Such organizations are engaged in community activities that are important but not imperative. Little League baseball and soccer are examples. The local government would not step in if fathers and mothers no longer contributed their time in these youth activities. The Red Cross, on the other hand, is so important that if it failed as a continuing voluntary organization the government would have to intervene immediately. It is instructive to reflect on which of many organizations are essential and would need to be assumed by government if they failed and which are expendable though not superfluous.

Any group is normally assumed to have integrity. Permission is not needed to form a group whether motorcyclists, singers, knitters, or collectors. However, if the organization consisted of radicals building bombs responsible for acts of violence or if they were a group preparing a storehouse of ammunitions to allegedly defend the country as vigilantes, their integrity certainly may be questioned. In both instances the groups are a threat to the safety of the community, even though they may claim to be concerned with its true interests. It would be entirely unsafe to live in the house next to either of them with their basement or attic full of munitions. Governmental intervention for the safety of the community would be expected.

Intervention must follow established legal processes. Standard rules of evidence are expected and the burden of proof is on the state. The assumption of innocent applies in dealing with groups as much as when dealing with individuals. Recent measures taken with regard to terrorists and the passage of the Homeland Security Act put the established principles to new tests. There are more groups that operate with integrity than groups that lack it. Nonetheless, the few who can cause irreparable harm force traditional standards to be reexamined and applied to changing circumstances.

THE CHURCH AND THE STATE

The state's relationships to voluntary associations also apply to the church. In treating the church as no different from other voluntary associations, the state would encourage and foster its existence and would refrain from interfering in the same way as with other associations. Yet, the church is discussed separately from the other voluntary associations. In a certain respect the church is no different from a country club in that some individuals go religiously, and voluntarily, to the country club every Sunday to play golf while others go to church. Today when the role of religion is discussed so widely in elections and in the media it is instructive to examine in a formal way the church–state relationship.

Church as *Not Different* from Voluntary Associations

Churches and believers maintain that the church is different from other groups and that this difference imposes a unique relationship with the state. The claimed differences and the ramifications must be explained, but proof of the religious claims will not be explored here. The relationship is examined because of its historic and continuing political importance and also because delineation of the place of the church and its relationship to state helps clarify the range and limit of both institutions. The relationship will be considered first as if there is no difference between the church and other groups and then as if there is.

The first consideration is relatively easy and has already been sketched. If the church is no different, then the state would encourage and foster the same as any other voluntary association and there would be the least interference possible. On such terms the barring the practice of polygamy, or barring the use of poisonous snakes in religious ceremonies, or forcing compulsory inoculation upon those who refuse on religious grounds, or inducting into military service those who have conscientious objections is merely a secular matter. Each of these measures is, in the words of the Supreme Court in an 1890 polygamy case (*Davis v. Beason*), "actions regarded by general consent as properly the subjects of punitive legislation."

The justification of the government's action against polygamy is the general grounds for state action involving fringe religious practices. On the assumption, for the time being, that there are no truly separate religious principles to be followed, little problem would exist if the state interfered with the use of poisonous snakes by a private club or the refusal of inoculation by an individual family or the practice of plural marriage by any private person or simple refusal to comply with the military draft. All these can be interfered with on the purely secular grounds of being regarded as properly the subject of punitive legislation. There are, however, some problems.

In the polygamy cases, where the court set forth the rationale for action in religious cases, the settlement was in fact purely secular and not religious. The cases falsely serve as examples of the way in which the state may interfere in religious practices. This normally cited legal precedent was not a First Amendment religious freedom case at all. So the lesson to be learned from the polygamy cases about the treatment of voluntary and religious groups is not apt. The Court construed *Davis v. Beason* as a clash between the legitimate criminal laws of the state and the practice of religion saying that however free the exercise of religion may be, it must be subordinated to the criminal laws of the country. The Court acknowledged that "with man's relations to his Maker and the obligations he may think they may impose, and the manner in which an expression shall be made by him of his beliefs on those subjects, no interference can be permitted. . . ." The Court immediately added that this was so, "provided always the laws of society, designed to secure its peace and prosperity, and the morals of its people, are not interfered with." The Court set the case in the framework of a dispute over a religious practice and the First Amendment.

The polygamy case was not decided on a First Amendment basis but on the constitutional grounds of Idaho's territorial status. Idaho, like Utah in similar cases, was a territory at the time and subject to the absolute jurisdiction of Congress. In other-than-religious cases the principle of Congress's jurisdiction over territories have been tested and all decided on the side of Congress. The only provision of the Constitution applying to territories is the one giving Congress jurisdiction. Congress can change the territories' tax system, their court system, set conditions for admission as states, and deny the application of the Bill of Rights. Congress had proscribed the practice of polygamy in Idaho and Utah and this was the technical ground for the Court's decision. By the time the Idaho and Utah territories were admitted to the Union as states, the religion involved had changed its doctrine on polygamy. If the doctrine had not changed the legal situation would be entirely different because with statehood the First Amendment would be applicable and a true constitutional religious freedom conflict would have arisen. The confrontation on First Amendment grounds never occurred in the courts. The territorial basis of the decisions is never fully acknowledged. The assumed First Amendment justification for the government action in the polygamy cases has been used in other cases, which compounds the misunderstanding of an important issue.

Government actions limiting polygamy, the use of poisonous snakes, and other "bizarre" or unusual religious practices are of limited public concern. "General consent" would regard these as "properly the subjects of punitive legislation," as matters to which "the law of society, designed to secure its peace and prosperity" should apply. However, the reaction would be less sanguine if it was decided that practices of majority religions were prohibited. There would be an uproar if some jurisdiction decided that for the sake of health drinking from a common cup or many hands breaking bread from a common loaf should be prohibited. And there would be little equanimity if legislation prohibiting the glorification and display of violence applied to the crucifix. Then the view would be that "genuine" religious issues were under attack and the reaction would be broad-based. Those who use poisonous snakes or refuse inoculations would like the same serious attention given to their religious practices.

This discussion of interference and of court cases may create the impression that the relationship between church and state is chiefly negative. Instead there are many positive things that the state does. It does encourages and fosters the existence of religious groups by their tax exempt status, by the public sanction given to religious holidays and days of worship, by the chaplaincy service in the military, by the prayer services which are part of official ceremonies, and by the respect generally accorded religions and religious officials. The positive aspects of the relationship are of benefit to the religions, to the state, and all its individuals. The state is therefore not indifferent toward religion.

Church *as Different* from Voluntary Associations

The dimension that distinguishes the church from nonreligious group is crucial. The church regards itself not only as different from other voluntary associations; it regards itself truly as bigger, better, and greater than the state. The state is viewed as originating in human nature and natural law where, by contrast, the church views itself as instituted by a direct act of creation, as originating in divine law, receiving its authority directly from God. The claimed differences are significant in themselves and they have a political significance because of what appears to be a challenge to the authority of the state. They also have a political significance in another sense in that many people who are citizens believe the religious claims and can be mobilized as an interest group. Therefore whether true or not the claim becomes a political concern.

The phrase "the church" has been and will continue to be used here. It is an ambiguous phrase since a particular church has not been specified. Reference will frequently be made to the Catholic Church because it is well known, it has a long history, there are instances of it bullying the state and others, there are instances of it being persecuted by others and the state, its pronouncements are similar to those of other churches if abstracted from local particulars, and reference to it is more common. However, the Catholic Church is not "the church." "The church" is "*your*" church and *you* may well be a Catholic, a Baptist, a Jew, a Muslim, a Mormon, a whatever, and the reference applies. The validity of the claims of religion is not the point. The political implications are the point.

A whole new set of questions arises with "the church" viewed as superior to other voluntary associations and to the state itself. Is there any need now for encouragement and fostering from the state? Does the state, as a lower unit, have any right to intervene in the affairs of the church, as a higher unit? In answer to such questions, it may be that precisely "no" interference and "no" encouraging and fostering should exist. There are, however, some problematic consequences to such an absolutist position.

If there were to be no encouragement and fostering then the church would in effect be discriminated against, because it would receive less regard than other nonreligious voluntary associations. If, in the second instance, there were to be no interference whatsoever, then the evidently fraudulent and harmful pretenders at religion could literally get away with murder under protection of a claimed religious origin. Little harm may flow from certain unusual religious practices or from the use of poisonous snakes in religious ceremonies, as long as children are not involved. Practitioners of the latter may take their inspiration from Mark 16, "In my name they will cast out demons, they will pick up serpents, and if they drink any deadly thing it will not hurt them," and an occasional death of someone being struck in the temple, pun intended, by a poisonous snake may be explained by "divine will." However, the same tolerance may not be extended to instances of strychnine used as a communal drink.

Fraud in religion is difficult to detect because the distinctions between sincere belief, harmful intent, and insanity are difficult. Respect for genuine religious belief requires the state to tolerate more than it would for a nonreligious group but there is a limit to such tolerance. It is the method and criteria for setting these limits that test both church and state. If religion truly comes from God (again, the term "God" will not be defined here), then who is the state to tell God what the definition of religion should be? The state in effect would be putting words in God's mouth. On the other hand, if those who bring harm can get away with fraud in the name of religion, the internal protective role of the state for its members is undermined.

There have been small town efforts in some places to have every homeowner in the community claim to be a minister and to have the home proclaimed a church in order to avoid local and other taxes. In such instances the state is forced to get into the business of defining legitimate religions. Established churches and the state like to avoid conflicts of this nature, yet they will never be completely absent. All that can be reasonably asked for is that there be deference and respect greater than that paid to nonreligious voluntary associations. Where and how to draw the line is a test of fairness, tolerance, and wisdom.

THE CHURCH OVER THE STATE?

What follows in the next few pages is an extended example of church-state as an issue in politics where the question is one of the church interfering in state affairs. It is offered as a model by which many, and what appears to be an increasing number of, specific issues of a church-state nature can be understood. The broad range of particular issues will become evident as the discussion develops. What also will become clear is that this is not a parochial issue. It is one that involves all of politics, at all levels, and in almost all states mentioned at the end of this section. To establish the model, the relationship first will be discussed primarily in terms of one church.

The relationship between church and the state may be viewed as no different from other voluntary associations, or church and state separated by a wall, or the church as higher than the state. These three approaches are depicted in *Appendix E.* The first relationship was examined in the previous section. The next task is to examine the logical and practical consequences of the church as the higher unit. Is there or should there be a wall separating church and state and consequently should there be no practical contact between the two beyond the earlier caveats?

Instances where the church might act in a manner lacking integrity were discussed a few paragraphs ago. Normally the principle of subsidiarity would have the assumed (for the sake of discussion) lower unit not interfere in the assumed higher one, but cases of fraudulent churches necessitate a change. Now where the state engages in activities that in its judgment are necessary for the welfare of the community, yet the state's actions lack integrity from the church's point of view, may the church intervene or interfere in such state affairs?

The question may at first appear to be only of historical interest. In medieval and early modern times the church was involved in state affairs to the point of deposing heretical monarchs, settling territorial disputes and property lines, and interdicting various state policies. With the level of state activity today church involvement in state affairs is not that complicit. Still there are occasions when the mixing of religion in politics occurs. Abortion, pornography, textbook censorship, prayer and bible reading, teaching creationism, religious displays at Christmas time, restrictions on religious expression, faith-based federal programs, the morality of economic systems, war, Jihad, and militarization's impact on society are examples of contemporary issues that have been the objects of lively church-state debates. Are the disputes academic, imaginary displays of power, or genuine instances of church interference in state affairs? The question requires clarification both for the state and for the church.

For centuries there has been some overlap in the claimed jurisdiction of both institutions. When the church regards a state action as improper, can the church intervene to bring about a reversal? The issue is not one of the church acting as an interest group. The issue is one of sectarian belief or practice being imposed on all. The issue is of worldwide applicability. Events in Iran, Afghanistan, the Middle East in general, Northern Ireland, northern India, many African countries, Latin America, and specific issues in the United States show the relevance of the topic. In this context it is instructive to consider briefly the theoretical positions on church-state relations in the history of Catholic thought. There a straightforward documentary record is available that continues to be relevant. Other religions have such a record also, but lack of familiarity makes it less useful for most readers. Used as a model, the long experience of the Catholic Church can help identify theoretical principles related to all religions that give insights to current and future conflicts.

Theories On Church-State Relations

Discussion of church-state relations dates back at least to the Catholic writing of Augustine in the early fifth century and Pope Gelasius in the late fifth century. Three theories have evolved, namely, the direct theory, the disjunctive theory, and the indirect or unitary theory. *Appendix F* depicts these theories. A fourth theory will be examined because of incompleteness of the three. The positions will be briefly described to give a historical perspective. It will become evident that contemporary experiences are not as new as imagined.

Direct Theory: This position holds that the church may directly or unilaterally intervene in the affairs of the state because the state is a mere creature of the church. As expressed by Pope Boniface VIII in 1303, in the church document entitled *Unam Sanctam*, the relationship of the church to the state is like the relation of the sun to the moon. As the moon receives only the reflective light of the sun, so the state receives only the authority that the church chooses to give it. The argument was in terms of the ultimate worth of the two domains and that the lesser domain could not possibly outshine the greater. Even though Thomas Aquinas had earlier argued that the state preceded the church in temporal existence and therefore could not have the reflective power of the church, many found it appealing.

It may appear that the direct theory became obsolete, for practical purposes at least, when the thirteenth-century situation of one dominant religion no longer held. Still, the argument of practical obsolescence begs the theoretical question, and, the position is not practically obsolete. While the Catholic Church is no longer in the dominant historical position it was during part of the Middle Ages, small groups in almost all religions continue to hold this theoretical sun/moon theory. A prominent practical example is the Iranian Islamic Republic where religion is the directing force of the state. The Iranian experience is not isolated. Many others in the Middle East, and indeed in all parts of the world, have similar views. Shiite Muslims in Iraq, Muslims in Indonesia, Hindus in India are other examples. To outsiders the position may be disliked and it does not represent the Catholic Church, nonetheless it must be understood since it gives insight into historic and contemporary political matters. Today there are about 50 countries in the world with established (state sanctioned) religions: 25 Islam, 12 Roman Catholic, 6 Lutheran, 1 Greek Orthodox, 1 Judaism, 4 Buddhism, 1 Hinduism, 1 Pancasila. There is little discussion of countries with established religions changing that status. There are, however, other countries that talk about going in the direction of firmer establishment than what they currently maintain.

Disjunctive Theory: The disjunctive theory holds that the Catholic Church ought to be the established church with overarching authority if it is the predominant religion in society. This position appears opportunistic and it enkindles fear because it seems to say that the church is opposed to "establishment" unless the Catholic Church is in the majority. This proposition is specious since it appears religious while in reality it is political in that it is based on numbers of citizens belonging to a specific church. Most instances of church establishment have such a circumstantial base. In France, Italy, England, Scandinavia, Iran, or Israel a religion is not "established" unless it reflects a substantial number of the population. The positions of the "Moral Majority" in the United States is a variation on the disjunctive theme, although a clear distinction exists between legal "establishment" and impact on policy because of societal influence. The growing Muslim population in countries in Europe and other places in the world raises concerns resulting from this theory.

The size factor in the disjunctive position is important in contemporary experience. Although there are many states, for example in Protestant Europe, that still have "established" or official religions, in most of those occurrences they are experienced mostly in a ceremonial sense. The critical concern is the "establishment" of the practices and proscriptions from that religion on all the state. It is that establishment of beliefs and practices that arouses nonmembers against the "Moral Majority," the "Muslims," the "Catholics," or whatever group appears to be advocating a particular position. The disjunctive theory certainly provokes concern as it speaks of a majority and it implies a minority. The discomfort leads to the attractiveness of a more comfortable "indirect" position.

Unitary or Indirect Theory: The unitary or indirect position maintains that the two spheres of church and state are and ought to remain distinct. It claims that only when spiritual matters become involved has the church the right and duty to denounce the law that endangers souls. In such cases the church touches the temporal order but only "indirectly" through the individual church members who as citizens use the available political means. This is said to be a pluralistic position particularly well adapted to the realities of American and democratic society. The unitary position maintains that since there are many different religions in the United States, the church demands no dominant position and only acts through its members instead of through the institution's leaders.

The indirect position is initially appealing yet it contains hidden problems. On the one hand it hides from the hierarchical or central direction of church affairs. On the other hand it surprisingly turns doctrinal decisions over to the laity, something that the Catholic Church at least does not accept. Either the church members are presented all sides of an issue, such as abortion or capital punishment, and told to make up their own minds as citizens, or they are told the position of the church as determined by its leaders and are expected to support and carry out this position. Neither alternative is indirect. Both are direct, either with the citizen as member determining doctrine or the member as citizen implementing doctrine. The indirect/unitary theory is prominent because on first impression it satisfies both religious and societal needs. Upon closer examination it is not consistent with either. A fourth theory is needed.

Subsidiarity Position: All three theories, direct, disjunctive, and indirect, are unrealistic. Politics may be temporarily satisfied with the unitary pluralistic position, as has been the case in the United States for many years. When religion starts operating according to the terms of this position, however, those opposed to religious or church involvement in state affairs become concerned and yet they have no theoretical position to cite. If the Catholic Church, the Moral Majority, or Muslims operates through citizen majorities, they utilize both the unitary position and they become disjunctive. Anti-abortion religious groups and others operate in the same way and those who oppose their involvement must take a position that is repressive or intolerant. The theoretical alternatives to church intervention in state affairs all run into the problem of repression/intolerance on the one side or on the other lack of full respect for the integrity of the state, or other churches, or of individuals either within their own church or other churches or with no church. Subsidiarity provides a way out of the dilemma.

Subsidiarity would say, "Yes," to the question of intervention of the higher unit in the affairs of the lower unit. That may sound like the direct sun/moon position but it is not. Implicit in any application of subsidiarity is the expectation of respect for the integrity of the lower units. The higher unit would take over a task only if it is demonstrated that it is necessary and there is no other way to preserve society from harm. For church-state relations, the lower units involved, whose integrity must be respected, are not only the state but also all units of society, including other churches and all individuals.

Every church regards itself, and properly so, as "the church." Catholics, Baptists, Jews, Lutherans, Methodists, Muslims, Episcopalians, and Mormons each regard theirs as the one true church. Individual members of each religion regard it as something special, determined not so much by them as by God. For one church to intervene in the affairs of the state by imposing its views on public policy is to tamper with the integrity of everyone else. Subsidiarity resolves the issue without undermining religion, or the state, or individuals.

Subsidiarity gives a more precise answer to the relations of church and state. The Catholic Church, whatever the earlier impression, appears to subscribe to this fourth position. In both Vatican II and in the *Catechism of the Catholic Church* religious freedom is explained to mean that all men are to be immune from coercion on the part of individuals or of social groups and of any human power, in such wise that in matters of religion no one is to be forced to act in a manner contrary to his own beliefs. Again in both sources it is stated that nobody may be forced to act against his convictions, nor is anyone to be restrained from acting in accordance with his beliefs, whether privately or publicly, whether alone or in association with others, within due limits. The statements are clear and specific. The respect for the integrity of individual belief seems unequivocal. The phrase "within due limits" appears not so much a limitation on integrity as a recognition, as discussed earlier, of those situations of the extremely fraudulent type where integrity is completely lacking.

This position of Vatican II and the *Catechism* may appear not wholly consistent with church history and stories about the treatment of individuals like Galileo and victims of the Inquisition. Those historical circumstances are acknowledged in the same document of Vatican II where the synod spoke of religious freedom having its foundation in the dignity of the person and that the requirements of this dignity have come to be more adequately known to human reason through centuries of experience. Whatever is read into that statement about the past, the expectation of respect for freedom and integrity of other churches and of individuals is clear.

The respect also seems to encompass the freedom of some individuals to have no religion. The statements speak of "all men" being free from coercion and of "no one" being forced to act in a manner contrary to his or her own beliefs. Some belief may indeed be "no belief" and though that may be in error, from the view of the church, individuals who take that position are not to be coerced. This respect is not to be taken as indifference toward belief since that would be contradictory to religion itself and to the principle of subsidiarity. Though religion says that belief is important, it also says that faith is a gift. "Gift" precisely explains both the variety and absence of belief. The importance of religion would justify neither indifference to the concerns of the world nor accept harm to itself. Accordingly, religion can neither accept a wall of separation nor impose its beliefs on others who freely do not believe.

"Wall of separation" suggests that religion and politics or church and state have nothing to do with one another. While the notion of a wall of separation has been cited in Supreme Court cases it does not appear in the Constitution and is the product of historical circumstance. The theoretical, not the legal, idea that church and state ought to be separate is the present focus. Many would like to understand the separation of church and state as a matter of the church staying out of state affairs and the state staying out of church affairs, that the one should not get involved in the jurisdiction of the other. If that is all that is meant nearly everyone would agree. The point, however, is what happens when the two spheres do in fact overlap?

Institutional overlap occurs when church and state claim jurisdiction over a common area such as abortion, cloning, war, educational issues, public prayer, or public decency. A wall of separation would have the two spheres separated such that religion would be, as expressed in the surprising commentary of Marx on the First Amendment to the United States Constitution, relegated to the refuse heap of arbitrary private whim. Marx in this comment was not defending religion. He was objecting that the First Amendment protected religious individualism and thereby supported laissez faire economics. Laissez faire was antisocial and he maintained that a wall separating religion and politics would in effect endorse, if not reflect, it. A recent thoughtful study by Philip Hamburger, *Separation of Church and State*, shows that religious feelings in nineteenth century America were well within the individualism framework. (Hamburger also shows how separation of church and state in American law was accomplished not through formal amendment, which was attempted, but evolved from nineteenth and twentieth century individualism and prejudice.)

The practical church-state question must be conceived in a way that does not endorse laissez faire individualism, church dominance, or state dominance. The difficulty with the church-state issue is that it seems impossible to see a role for religion or the church without reverting to some of the past practices that unduly interfered with the integrity of others. Those difficulties can be avoided and a solution consistent with subsidiarity is possible.

One of the documents from the Catholic Vatican II, *The Church in the Modern World*, stated that it is always and everywhere legitimate for the Church to preach the faith with true freedom, to teach her social doctrine, and to discharge her duty among men without hindrance. She also has the right to pass moral judgments, even on matters touching the political order, whenever basic personal rights or the salvation of souls make such judgments necessary. (The same position is found in the *Catechism*.) This is to say, any church can teach, preach, and pass moral judgments on abortion, on the conduct of war, or capital punishment, or on any social issue, but in doing so it would not, consistent with the respect for religious freedom, impose its belief on others who are not of that same faith. The solution pieces together all the ingredients of subsidiarity and respects all the parties involved. (This relationship is depicted in *Appendix G*.)

Teaching, preaching, and passing moral judgment appear politically inert. Efforts on a constitutional amendment to overturn the Supreme Court's abortion decision, protest marches on train tracks scheduled to transport war materials, sanctuary movements in behalf of refugees from political and social strife, and pastoral letters on other social issues show the suspected passivity as dynamic. In doing these things no belief or practice is imposed on anyone. The officials, demonstrators, and speakers are acting according to their beliefs. What they advocate will not be accepted as policy unless it is agreed to in the normal policy-making manner. Unless other groups, including other religions, indeed a constitutional majority, become persuaded to support the policy it will not become law. If it does become law it is no different, except perhaps in origin, from any other public policy. All policy, whether wise or unwise, has the support and opposition of an amalgam of the community. If there are officials or members of the Catholic Church who have taken a leadership role on the issue of abortion or other social issues, there are others in the Church who, although not disagreeing on the doctrine, see the policy option differently. If the policy advocated were enacted it would be as public policy and not church policy.

The job of the churches as well as of the state does not end with an official pronouncement or policy decision. Poverty, war, abortion, oppression, all bring severe mental and physical anguish. Religion and churches have a continuing role to heal the wounds of society and to aid those who anguish over troubling issues. Religion's task, by definition, is much larger than momentary acts or particular legislation. It deals with that part of human beings that cannot be defined in the law and that cannot be limited by time. It calls all persons to a life and a practice of which they prove themselves incapable from time to time. Religious inspiration and content is said to come from a source beyond the human.

Subsidiarity provides a way in which the respective roles of church and state can be viewed in an orderly and understandable manner. If the topic were neglected because it is unfamiliar and complex, religion would be relegated to the refuse heap of arbitrary private whim.

THE STATE'S RELATION TO OTHER STATES

One final relationship is to be considered, that of the state to other states. This involves among other topics, international relations, international law, the sources of law, international organizations, regional organizations, commerce and economics, war, the settlement of disputes, and diplomacy. This broad topic is included in this chapter to suggest that the relation of the states to one another can be understood effectively and efficiently in the framework of subsidiarity.

The basic concern in the relation of states to one another is what happens when they do not get along adequately, efficiently, and with benefit to the welfare of the community of nations. The most familiar manifestation of not getting along is some form of invasion. Invasion, often thought of only in military terms, has many forms. It can be economic and it can be cultural, where in seemingly benign ways the invaded country loses control of its resources and heritage. Although investments from abroad and enrichments from new cultures are normally welcomed, they can overtake a culture to where the results are no longer beneficial. A few examples can illustrate the nonmilitary forms of invasion.

Japan accepted the American military occupation, which lasted about seven years, after World War II as the price of war. The effect of American cultural practices that accompanied and followed the occupation was more enduring and is still being felt. In another example, for a couple hundred years the United States has had a friendly relationship with its neighbors to the north, but Canada has at times expressed a concern for its separate identity. Recently it has deliberately begun to forge a divergent path in tolerating some nonprescription drug use that is illegal in the United States and it has adopted other highly controversial social policies. It attempts to maintain the difference between the two countries by way of different magazines, newspapers, television, and even Canadian rules for football. A third example is the concern for the threat of petro-dollar invasion and other investment invasion felt in recent decades by many in the United States. Investments both within and outside the United States are not unwelcome. It is the extent of the investments that contributes to a concern that outsiders will have a larger say in one's domestic affairs and that sovereignty could be lost. Economic, cultural, as well as military invasion are similar in that one nation does not respect the integrity of another when unilaterally entering into the other's affairs.

The greatest continuing concern in the relation of states to one another is the threat of war. Closely related to the threat of war is the concern for economic deprivation, which frequently leads to war. When these conditions exist, the relations between states are, by definition, not adequate, efficient, and beneficial. In this situation the essential subsidiarity question is whether some higher level of government is necessary to establish order. When the lowest unit, which happens to be the highest available unit, cannot perform its function adequately, does subsidiarity require the creation of a new higher unit in the form of world government? Subsidiarity up to this point has moved from the lowest unit of society through various steps along the way up to the state at the top of the ladder. The question is whether there is an appropriate next step beyond the state in the form of world government?

World Government

The proposal of world government is centuries old. Dante, the poet famous for *The Divine Comedy*, advocated a single world government in his work entitled *De Monarchia*. He argued that the human potential for growth is best carried out only when human beings enjoy the quiet and tranquility of universal peace. Such peace cannot exist, he contended, when states are in conflict with one another; it can only be brought about under a single world government with universal law. Many others have argued the same point and have invoked Aristotle, Cicero, Augustine, Aquinas, various Popes, and other authorities for support. The general contention is that the present international system of independent states without a common authority is tantamount to anarchy and should be replaced by a world government of some sort.

A drawing of the relation of states to one another (see *Appendix H*) depicts various states of differing sizes, each with a ladder of subsidiarity within it. As drawn there are a few states not on the line of equality, which is a matter not of size but of worth, integrity. Equality and independence are theoretically assumed in the relationship of states to one another. On the practical level that assumption does not always hold. When the relationship between states breaks down in war or other forms of invasion does subsidiarity lead to world government as a next appropriate step? To ensure the tranquility necessary for the growth that Dante spoke of is some step beyond current arrangements needed or appropriate to accord all states equal respect?

Some, like the World Federalists, answer the two previous questions in the affirmative and seek to bring about a common world authority. They seek to achieve a governed world by changing the present United Nations organization from its confederate form to something they call "world federalism." Federalism itself and the contention that it is merely a fiction used rhetorically for political purposes will be examined in a later chapter. Here, in discussing the world order, it is not necessary to enter into the theoretical questions; it is enough to consider what the World Federalists seek in the light of subsidiarity.

Running through the literature of the World Federalist Association is the theme that a strengthened United Nations will be given "power to . . . prohibit any nation from using force or threats of force," that the strengthened United Nations have power to "govern" the seabed, that it have "taxing power," that the expanded United Nations judiciary have "final authority," and that there be universal membership without the right of secession. The United Nations' Charter should be changed in their view to handle any problem not adequately dealt with by the individual state relations.

The proposals by the World Federalists and the theme enunciated by Dante appear consistent with the principle of subsidiarity where the nonperformance of a necessary function by the lower unit gives way to the next higher unit. World government would handle only those problems of war, disarmament, nuclear weaponry, the seabed, trade, or human rights that cannot be adequately solved at the present national level. It is therefore expected that the world government would be established on a "federated" basis with the constituent members and lesser groups retaining their original autonomy over matters properly within their respective spheres. In this way, as in the theory of federalism as it is applied within particular countries, world level diversity will be retained in unity, pluralism will be maintained in common purpose, and harmony will be achieved in contrariety as it occurs musically in the case of the bow and a stringed instrument.

Diversity in unity, pluralism in common purpose, harmony in contrariety show the poetic character of the discussion. Problems, complexities, and painful situations of international conflict lead to a desire for dramatic solutions. The proposals are inadequate. Situations where states do not perform their functions adequately do not lend themselves to nations being disposed to favor establishing world government. Nor does subsidiarity lead to such a conclusion.

Subsidiarity emphasizes that a unit perform its function. In discussing individual rights, private property, groups, and religion, the assumptions of integrity primarily focused on each unit coming to perform its function and if it could not, other units were expected to assist or to assume the task as a last resort if necessary. The point was that a unit perform its function, that it give according to ability, and if it cannot function it was to receive aid according to need. The downward focus existed until there was no other way for a necessary function to be performed. The responsibility of the next higher unit aiding the lower was emphasized in, but not limited to, the consideration of corporate and public ownership of property. And, there was always a next higher unit in existence when it was needed. These points are crucial. The argument in favor of world government overlooks the fact that it does not now exist and that it would have to be created. Unfortunately, the process of awaiting the creation of this imagined higher government becomes a way for existing states to neglect their current obligations.

Currently the United Nations is a confederacy, by definition a loose union of independent states legally free to reject proposed rules and free to withdraw at will. While corrective actions against invasions and other irresponsible activities are desirable it is important that the creation of world government does not result in more harm than what is to be prevented. Furthermore, the "creation" or "origin" of the world state presents problems that are both practical and theoretical. On the theoretical side, the issue of the origin of the state was not settled in the chapter of that title. Whether the state originates in a social contract, is the product of the socio-logical origin, or comes about by "divine" origin is not settled. Leaders do not debate the theoretical justifications when states are formed. When world government is discussed, such theoretical issues are debated. Practical justifications are important but in this instance the theoretical differences play a larger role. Because the consequences are so great and because of intense divisions between existing states, the justification for a world mechanism is of enormous importance.

Separate from the theoretical and philosophical divisions that cloud the discussion of world government, practical consideration complicated the issue. Nationalism, the emphasis on one's own nation to the exclusion and sometimes the harm of other states, is a practical and not just a theoretical problem in international affairs. Irresponsible and violent displays of nationalism have been exhibited throughout modern history. Since the end of World War II almost 150 countries have been added to the list of nations. This new membership of the United Nations has changed the organization from one of broad discussion and exchange to one looking at detail in international as well as national life. Though created to remedy the evils of nationalism the UN seems to have exacerbated it. Unsatisfied nationalism continues in Europe, Africa, the Middle East, and Asia. The success or failure of the UN is still imponderable, especially as the divisions over the Iraq war have exasperated them.

There are other practical problems and caveats in strengthening the United Nations. Some concerns are the seemingly minor details of its structure. Questioned are whether the United Nations' governing body should be bicameral or unicameral, what type of equitable financing should be arranged, and how the management of its administrative should function. The current arrangement has problems enough of this nature as seen dramatically in the oil-for-food investigation related to pre-war Iraq. The United States, Japan, and a few other may pay a disproportionate amount of the United Nations' costs (although this greater payment may be as distributive justice requires) yet, in the face of the hostile stance encountered within the United Nations by the United States, it seems impractical to expect enthusiastic American support for an expanded United Nations let alone increased financial support.

The details of structure and organization may be potentially more divisive than the general ideal of improving world order. Disagreement on theoretical issues may inhibit and delay action, while disagreement on practical matters such as financing or the implementation of resolutions can lead to strife. Resistance occurs in the United States when there is mention of a United Nations' sponsored peacekeeping mission where US soldiers would be under United Nations' command. In a redesigned and strengthened organization the tensions within and about the United Nations as currently constituted could give way to greater conflict. The semantic and rhetorical differences of the present would become seismographic if decisions of the world body were seen as interfering in the sovereignty of particular states. The diplomatically patched over disagreements on the Iraq war could portend graver consequences if opposing sides in debate were to become warring sides.

To question or oppose world government is not to give in to present injustices or to the forces of laissez faire in international relations. In the contemporary world many states do not function properly in their relations to one another and many are unable to do so. It is important in terms of their own needs and in the terms of the principle of subsidiarity that they function adequately, efficiently, and with benefit to all. If world government is not deemed the appropriate step to ensure that level of performance, other means must be considered.

Practical Alternatives

Laissez faire and world government are dramatic alternatives. Progress seldom comes in that form. Even modest proposals reveal the intricate complexity from which improvement must be wrought. Furtherance of free trade, the development and expansion of arrangements for international banking, coordinated international assistance programs on health and social issues, and the regulation of multinational corporations seek to improve the relations between states without resorting to world government. These proposals have the advantage of building from the present international system. They accept the current world framework, accentuating aspects that can build relations and improve conditions and seek to advance the integrity of existing individual states.

Respecting integrity is the cornerstone of subsidiarity. It is lacking in trade barriers, tariffs, quotas, and strings-attached bilateral foreign aid linking international charity and coercion. Likewise multinational corporations often treat the countries in which they do business in a subservient manner because there is a third country to welcome them if the second does not comply. These practices are a breakdown in the presumed integrity and theoretical equality of states.

Counterpoints to the above practices are free trade, international banking, and regulation of multinationals, using the existing framework of states to enhance the respect for all. *Free trade* starts with the assumption that the parties engaged are equal at the minimum in statehood. Free trade—fair trade might be a better description—fosters equality by eliminating artificial barriers. There is a fear that free trade supports harmful unregulated international competition injurious to all parties, but that concern must be judged in light of its alternatives of massive political manipulations. The challenge is to break formal trade barriers in the form of tariffs as well as indirect barriers of national subsidies that promote selected economic sectors. Subsidies, both hidden and overt, are a major contention in trade conflicts between the United States, Europe, Africa, and, indeed, all nations. Each country for objective or for internal political reasons views its position on trade and subsidies as fair and reasonable. Solutions to inequities will come about through a combination of bi-lateral, multi-national and international efforts.

Whatever the form, barriers erected to the free and fair flow of commerce will not disappear quickly. The European Economic Community of the European Union is in part an effort to overcome trade inequities, though their success leaves much to be desired including their relations with the international community. The same can be said about other economic communities founded to reduce regional barriers while extending them elsewhere. Nonetheless, efforts to bring about improvements are at least a concrete step to better the relations among nations. Also it is to lessen inequities that the GATT (General Agreements on Tariffs and Trade), the WTO (World Trade Organization), and other trade conferences are dedicated. These efforts are the hard realities of international politics. They make positive contributions to the relations among nations without awaiting the dramatic formation of a world legislature.

In similar fashion *international banking* arrangements improve the ability of states to function adequately. Some international banking efforts already exist, such as the World Bank (properly called the International Bank for Reconstruction and Development) and some regional banks like the Asian and other regional development banks. The International Monetary Fund and affiliates of the World Bank, such as the International Development Association and the International Finance Corporation, also serve in the same capacity in seeking to aid needy nations through loans and various forms of development assistance. All programs need added resources. Reluctance caused both by economic strain and philosophical outlook keeps developed nations from being entirely forthcoming with investment funds. Progress is also impeded by uncertainties flowing from political instability in the needy nations. In addition, recipient countries resist stipulations of the IMF and lending organizations as impinging on local sovereignty, which resistance should be read as either a bargaining ploy or the necessary response to internal political pressures.

The traditional mode of economic assistance on the international level was in the past a system of bilateral loans and grants from wealthy nations to nations they chose to help. Along with the personalized selection process there is a factor, as in all personalized lending arrangements, that economic aid brings a political price. Thus with economic aid came implicit, and frequently explicit, strings that prescribed political expectations. Even where not intended in the beginning, the strings are added in time, often because of new political realities. Where pure beneficence exists there comes in time a perception of dependence. Resentment and hostilities often followed.

In defense of the practice of tying strings to aid it is argued that if others want a wealthy nation's assistance they ought to be grateful, that political support to the helping country and to the system that made the aid possible is not too much to ask, that resources are limited for even the wealthy and it is only reasonable for them to aid those who would not abuse the benefactor, and that it is not as if the wealthy need to "buy" friends as much as a matter of giving aid to those who would be friendly. This defense is argued in both domestic and international politics despite the fact that in private personal lending practices it has long since been realized, in the words of the adage, that "If you want to keep a friend, don't lend him money." The adage is based on the experience that suspicions and resentments crop up even among the best of associates. As the practice of private lending is fraught with danger, most reasonable individuals invest in banking institutions from which others borrow. The borrower pays a reasonable interest for the use of the investor's funds. On this analogy international banking is proposed. The banking arrangement depersonalizes the contacts between nations and lets aid be accomplished through formal business channels as it is in domestic banking practices.

International lending sees that loans are secure, are made for legitimate purposes, and have sound financial bases. Concern for repayments, extending credits, refinancing, credit limits, and all other arrangements are handled so that the political or personal dimensions does not get in the way of development. Political and personal considerations are important in international dealings, yet they sometimes interfere with other sound political principles and impede progress. When temporary political concerns get in the way of respecting the integrity of other states short-term interests adversely affect long-term goals to the injury of all parties. The application of the broader principle of subsidiarity in this area of the relation among nations guides the users to focus on the long-term goals.

Integrity and equality of all states are principles that the advocates of an improved world order espouse even though they seek a larger and more dramatic change. Efforts in behalf of the immediate concerns of integrity and equality should have general support rather than be looked upon as something that delays major change for the well-being of free nations. The rapacity of *multinational corporations* is another factor that brings about the subordination of nations to an external force. Although abuses are universally condemned, precise measures for mitigating the harm and restricting the practices are noticeable chiefly by their absence. "Invaded" countries are in no position to fend off corporations. The recipient countries benefit economically through the investments and the resulting jobs. Unfortunately they are also harmed through the inability to regulate working conditions or products and through corruption that often accompanies large business contacts.

The countries that spawned the multinationals are themselves not in an altogether good position to regulate their overseas activities either since they fear that the businesses could slip away to another country (like auto plants have moved to Mexico and textile plants to the Far East) with resulting loss of jobs, and lessened ability to influence offensive practices. Since nations share this problem but face it from different perspectives, the likely solution will come from the economically and politically powerful nations joining together on restrictions that will benefit large and small nations alike. Such an approach will not come about easily and the lack of universal acceptance will leave loopholes unless addressed forcefully. Nevertheless, delayed solutions that satisfy the interests of the powerful countries as well as the wealthy corporations harm the common good, which is one's own good as well as the good of the community. A narrow perspective argues for selfish self-interest. The occasional disaster at the facility of a multinational quickens concern. It would be better if improvements, along with corporate and political accountability, came without a crisis.

There are already several international organizations that regulate or facilitate commercial contacts between nations. Although the regulation of multinationals is much more complex than the commercial activities currently encompassed by these bodies, they do offer a precedent and design for more extensive efforts. The International Postal Union, the International Civil Aviation Organization, the World Intellectual Property Organization, the International Telecommunication Union, the World Meteorological Organization, and the International Labor Organization are a few of the organizations established in the twentieth century to promote or facilitate a particular aspect of the interaction among nations and their peoples. More dramatic, of course, but also much more overtly political is the International Atomic Energy Agency (IAEA) which must deal with governments as it attempts to deal with corporations. The efforts of the IAEA to deal with nuclear power projects in Iraq, Iran, North Korea, and other countries in the early years of the new century manifest the difficulties of any international regulation of a commercial enterprise deemed to be in the national interest of a host country.

Failure of adequate regulation will continue to plague international commerce. Nonetheless the current efforts are superior to what would occur without existing organizations. Necessity was at the origin of current regulatory organizations. Similar needs may produce regulation of multinationals. International organizations function today without complaint of their interfering in the rights and autonomy of the participating states and they enable all the states to conduct their own affairs more smoothly. Such results are as is to be expected with subsidiarity. They give hope that in time more arrangements will be found that will apply effectively to business.

DISCUSSION

It may be argued that goals of world government are improved free trade practices, enhanced international banking, and regulation of multinationals. The legal means by which the changes occur are crucial, however. Retaining state autonomy may mean that some may still be free to act irresponsibly. Yet that behavior would not be precluded even in a world government. With autonomy all will continue to exercise that pluralism of choice requiring cooperation that makes politics at every level both challenging and beneficial. With world government massive planning and coordination would be necessary when these abilities are not even proven on the domestic level.

It is true of international politics, as Aristotle had said regarding domestic politics, that the recognition of the differences in humankind is of the essence. Accepting differences is the chief factor that distinguishes a political development of forced unity from one of freedom. The goals of world government are a subtle and seductive distraction from doing effectively the hard work necessary on a practical level. Realistic goals will better serve the future peace of the world than idealistic dreams upon which there is great disagreement. The modest proposals of free trade, international banks, and the regulation of multinationals clearly do not constitute surrender to the continuation of laissez faire on the world scene. Instead they are means to practice distributive justice in the relation among nations. Implemented more fully they will make it possible for the lowliest nation-state to come to function adequately, efficiently, and with benefit to the welfare of humankind.

It may be asked why one nation that is prosperous should have to help another that is poor. There is an inclination to answer that question in utilitarian terms, that if the wealthy do not aid the poor there will be economic disruptions. This utilitarian sense of justice sees the deprived as eventually revolting or causing some disorder that the wealthy will have to pay to rectify. Ghetto conflagrations, riots, labor union unrest, and domestic revolutions are offered as evidence of the advisability of the utilitarian thesis. The logic of utilitarian response calls for some efforts in behalf of the deprived but their satisfaction requires nothing more than the minimum. Utilitarian answers are alleviative instead of curative or preventative.

The difference between the minimalist utilitarian response and one out of a fuller sense of justice is illustrated in a story about an earthquake in Guatemala some years ago. When an American relief team began setting up camp on its own at a local village after deplaning and driving to an obviously devastated site, residents came running to ask what they were doing. The Americans explained that they were there to aid the quake victims. The surprised Americans were told by the villagers that the quake area was actually a number of miles further up the road, that the condition in the village was the way people normally live. Distributive justice requires preventative and corrective measures for the "normal" but neglected village. Assistance should come because the village is "in need" and for no other reason.

The efforts of the United States government, other governments, and the world community to assist those countries afflicted with HIV/AIDS are an example of non-utilitarian compassion. (Showing the depth of the problem is the report that more than thirty percent of the populations of some countries in Africa test positive for HIV/AIDS and that fifty percent of the farm land is going uncultivated because farmers are debilitated due to AIDS infection.) Nothing is to be gained for the United States from those unfortunately destined for premature death resulting from their illness. Assistance may only alleviate human suffering. A "political" angle may be suspected for the relief efforts without actually knowing the motivation of the benefactor. It may merely be out of a sense of humanitarian justice.

Justice on the international or domestic level does not mean the leveling of all societies, all men, and all nations. It means at a minimum that all persons should be able to operate in a manner that is adequate, efficient, and beneficial to humankind. The common good within states is the common good among states. Subsidiarity in the relation of states to one another is intended to bring about that common good.

Chapter 12

Constitutionalism

The indignant cry, "It's unconstitutional!" or the proud assertion, "It's constitutional!" reecho throughout American history and politics. In spite of the ease with which constitutionalism is cited, it is not well understood. Confident individuals explain it as "rule according to law and not men," but that confidence fades when reminded that "men make the law" or that "not all rule according to law is good since the law itself might be bad law." Constitutionalism's unchanging fundamental character and its dynamic qualities can be appreciated by reviewing the classical roots, the modern dimensions, and a classification scheme for constitutional government, its growth characteristics, and its elusive "spirit."

The Roots of Classical Constitutionalism

"Constitutionalism" has an ancient/classical meaning and a modern meaning; each has a special type of constitutional "root." To most Americans the term refers to a written document setting forth the structure of the government and specifying the power of those who serve in governmental offices. This view emphasizes limits. Furthermore, government should be conducted in accordance with fixed written rules as opposed to operating according to the convenience of a particular regime. In England, on the other hand, constitutionalism denotes not a single document or few closely related documents, instead it denotes the body of laws and customs that make up the character of the government and that have been formed over centuries of experience. The English broad classical sense of constitutionalism has as the basic reference not a particular written legal document to which lesser legislation must conform, but the whole life and scheme of living of the community. Aristotle refers to constitution in this broad way as "the way of life of a people." It is, for him, comparable to the constitution of a human being who is his or her "disposition." In this broad sense the constitution is basically a moral force that guides government while lacking specific legal or political techniques for ensuring compliance.

The Roots of Modern Constitutionalism

The positive roots of classical constitutionalism were seen in a different light when modern times produced a break with the previous conception of moral and political life. Modern times witnessed the quicker and more immediate impact of governmental actions on private individuals. In this milieu more concrete means of checking unacceptable governmental practices were needed. The historic model for this transition was the break between America and England in the seventeenth and eighteenth centuries.

The development of legal and institutional means of restraining arbitrary rule thus characterizes modern constitutionalism and is commonly identified with the American view of written limits specified in a document carefully laid down in advance. Basic is the element of a "written" fundamental document. Often, though mistakenly, modern constitutionalism is associated with the English "Glorious" Revolution and parliamentary supremacy principle of 1688. The English constitution remained unwritten. More accurately the tradition of a written constitution is traced to the Mayflower Compact of 1620, the Fundamental Orders of Connecticut of 1637, and the many other charters, compacts, and agreements that coexisted with the beginning of American "colonies." The practice of working with and beginning with a written document was so ingrained that when the Americans in the 1770s found themselves moving toward independence from England, one of the first thing done was the drafting of the "Declaration of Independence" and simultaneously the drafting of a common constitution, the Articles of Confederation.

When it was quickly discovered that the Articles were not well formed, they were altered in the Constitution of 1787, the present Constitution. The American practice became the model of constitutionalism when it was copied in the efforts at written documents in France in their revolutionary era. The practice spread in the succeeding decades in other European countries and more tellingly in their newly independent colonies particularly in Latin America. Today written "constitutional" restraints exists in most major states in the world except England and Israel, Saudi Arabia, New Zealand, and about four other countries. Even those without written or codified documents follow some formal procedure or consensus process in major rule making.

Classification Of Constitutions

There is a classification scheme of governments distinguishing between legally limited and legally unlimited government and actually limited and actually unlimited governments. In this scheme a legally limited regime is one in which rules of conduct are carefully laid down in advance. An actually limited government is one where the regime conducts itself according to expected standards of behavior whether written down or not. Thus England would fit as actually limited even though not "legally" limited. For reasons that will become clear it is useful to understand the classifications as used in the past and to understand why the scheme does not have the same utility now as it once had. It does give useful insights though.

In the scheme the United States is classified as legally limited and actually limited. The old Soviet Union, which had a written constitution very much like that of the United States, and indeed even more detailed, was said to be legally limited but actually unlimited since it was regarded as not living in conformity with constitutionalism and its own constitution. England is classified as legally unlimited since it acts in accordance with constitutional expectations, customs, and traditions. While the category legally unlimited and actually unlimited fulfills the four-part scheme, examples are difficult to specify since most states now find a claim to legitimacy in having a written constitution even if it is violated with impunity. Of the eight or so states currently without a written constitution none is blatantly capricious or tyrannically arbitrary so as to fit into the fourth category.

The constitution of present day Russia (called the "Russian Federation") is like that of the former Soviet Union in detail although it clearly dropped the language and rhetoric of the Communist Party. While still a statement of broad principles and declaration of rights it has become in detail much more than the outline found in the United States Constitution. In contrast to the Soviet constitution the new Russian constitution prohibits state sponsored or mandated ideology. There is also the contrast between the established socialist economic system of the old and the freedom of entrepreneurial private ownership of the new. The old, in the would-be workers' paradise, spoke of "the reduction and, eventually the complete elimination of arduous *physical* [manual] labor." There is no such panacea in the new constitution and instead it seems to fully grasp reality in stating, "everyone shall pay lawful taxes and fees."

Although the wording differs modestly there are similarities in the old Soviet and new Russian constitutions in many of the detail that contrast with the United States constitution. For example, both the old and the new speak of a "right to rest," a right to privacy in the family, in correspondence, telephone, and mail, a right to education and to higher education, a right to cultural accomplishments, protection of motherhood, childhood, and family, and a right to medical assistance and health care. In another provision the newer constitution makes clear that "children who have reached 18 years old shall care for their non-employable parents." A similar provision in the old had children "obliged to show concern for their parents and to help them" which sounded as if they had a duty to do assigned house chores. The two constitutions speak of guaranteed "social security in old age, in case of disease, invalidity." In the United States these latter guarantees are found in legislation rather than in the constitution.

Both the old Soviet and the new Russian constitutions spoke of freedom of conscience to express any religion or none. Also, the newer constitution speaks of a right to a favorable environment, which had been implied in the older constitution although not explicitly stated. Likewise a right to work under safe and hygienic conditions is stated in the new and implied in the old. Both refer to the equality of women. The older one went further to say that "the spouses are completely equal in family relations." What so many of these statements do is raise questions about what was stated solely for propaganda purposes and what had a real possibility for implementation. When in the United States there was a debate and ultimate defeat of an "equal rights" (for women) amendment it was easy for the Soviet Union to put such a provision in its constitution because both men and women were equal in poor treatment. Laws can lead a culture, and rightly so, but they can lead only so far. An examination of the reality of Soviet (and current Russian) culture and the American with respect to the equal treatment of men and women would bear out the utility or facetiousness of constitutional formulation.

What is strikingly new in the Russian constitution is in the area of a right to association where it is specifically stated that this includes "trade unions." While the Soviet Union was in theory one big ruling trade union the reality was that efforts of workers to organize were viewed as a conspiracy against the state and the reigning ideology. The impact of reality on theory is an issue, indeed, in all constitutions. The very lofty provisions of any modern constitution have to be put in the context of what reality can afford, especially economic and political reality. This is particularly true of the constitutions like the Russian that have considerably more detail than the simpler outline as in the United States. A little later in this chapter there will be a brief examination of the current Philippine constitution that likewise has statements of goals, which no matter how desirable are unattainable. The Philippine constitution states that a goal is to "free the people from poverty through policies that provide adequate social services, promote full employment, a rising standard of living, and an improved quality of life for all." Though no one could disagree with the goal its accomplishment would be many decades in the making.

The sighted provisions in the Philippine and Russian constitutions raise serious questions about constitutions and constitutionalism. The classification scheme of legally limited and unlimited and actually limited and unlimited constitutions falls apart when nearly everyone has a legally limited, that is, written, constitution yet many are in no position to fulfill the provisions in the areas of rights and services that are most directly meaningful to the ordinary citizen. When it comes to the areas of the constitutions dealing with the structure of the government there is a cynical expectation that powerful interests will prevail no matter what the stated provisions of a written document. That statement raises the profound constitutional issue that it is the institutions of government, their specified powers, and the ability to check and restrain them that mark a truly constitutional government with the ability to deliver the promised services and protections. Goals and rights may have the appearance of importance but if the structure of the regime precludes their implementation then constitutionalism is little more than rhetoric.

The Spirit Of Constitutionalism and Literal Constitutionalism

England and the United States are understood to be actually limited and are generally classified as "constitutional" regimes. Other regimes although having similar, written constitutions stand in sharp contrast in their compliance with the spirit of constitutional rule. Implied in such a contrast is that one adheres to the intention of its constitution and the other does not. One acts according to the letter but not in the spirit of constitutionalism. Though literal constitutionalism versus the "spirit of constitutionalism" seems an obvious distinction its specificity remains a challenge.

For legally constituted legislative bodies, whether a town council or a national legislature, to perfunctorily approve what was already decided by a closed private decision process may preserve the appearance of constitutionalism and legality but not its spirit. In the United States it is understood that all policy and especially constitutional change are enacted by following the prescriptions of the Constitution and using the legal bodies of the government as intended. In following this process the United States acts in a manner consistent with "the spirit of constitutionalism." Many countries follow that same model while other regimes are thought not to act so. Extralegal means of policy making or the overriding of the legal machinery by political dictates are not used in the United States while they are viewed as common practice in authoritarian regimes whether historical or contemporary. Communist regimes and contemporary authoritarian regimes are viewed as acting in the literal manner, that is, according to the letter of the law, and not in the true spirit of constitutionalism. This commonly agreed upon favorable contrast of compliance with the "spirit of constitutionalism" undergoes a severe test, however, when looked at in the light of constitutional growth in the United States.

CONSTITUTIONAL GROWTH IN THE UNITED STATES

Constitutions grow in two ways, formal and informal. ***Formal growth*** is the process provided in the constitution itself for amending the original document. In the United States, Article V of the Constitution specifies this formal process, providing that two thirds of both houses of the Congress shall propose or two thirds of the states shall petition Congress to call a convention for proposing amendments, and following the proposal process three fourths of the state legislatures or special conventions within the states ratify the proposed amendments. England, even though it has an unwritten constitution, has a formal amending process according to which, by generally accepted convention, no fundamental change will be made without an express mandate from the electorate. Proposals for major changes such as the nationalization or denationalization of industry or the possible elimination of the House of Lords follow an agreed upon procedure. Such proposals considered by one membership of Parliament cannot be enacted until another membership was chosen at an intervening election.

Other countries that lack a written constitution follow a similar convention to England in undertaking significant regime change. New Zealand follows England, Saudi Arabia maintains a consensus of the royal family and conforms to the expectations of Sharia, the law of Islam, Israel follows a constitution of time and regards the Torah as a source of its authority. Variations on the formal and informal amending process are found in all countries and constitutions. According to its formal process, the United States Constitution has been amended eighteen times with twenty-seven amendments. In contrast to this small number of amendments some individual states in the United States, all of which states have written constitutions, have had more than 500 amendments. Thus the formal amending process can be employed sparingly or extensively, depending on varying circumstances in different jurisdictions.

The process of ***informal growth*** involves procedures that differ significantly from the formal. There are four methods of informal change: judicial interpretation, congressional or legislative enactments, presidential or executive initiatives, and custom, convention, or usage. An examination of each will show that all are equally interpretative even though the interpretative character is usually only ascribed to the judicial.

Judicial Review: Judicial interpretation refers to the process whereby the courts in the course of ordinary decisions expand, limit, or otherwise alter the previous understanding of part of the constitution. In any legal system, even those with lengthy constitutions, the exact meaning and application of a law is often not explicitly or perfectly detailed in the constitution or statute. The refinement or detail of the application of the law is worked out in what is known as case law, which, as the name implies, is law as the product of decisions in particular controversies or disputes. Judges normally attempt to apply the laws and precedents of earlier decisions to the case before them. Where the ruling of the court deviates from what the legislature originally had in mind, the interpretation given by the court can be reversed, but usually is not, by new correcting legislation. When the law that the court interprets in a particular case is the basic law of the constitution, then the court in its decision is expanding the constitution. If the court broadens or limits the content of specific provisions of the constitution as understood, it has amended the constitution in a way other than through the formal amending process.

In the United States judicial interpretation is especially understood to be, but is not limited to, judicial review where the court, particularly the Supreme Court, can declare actions of the Congress or the President unconstitutional. The basis of the court's interpretative power is its ability to say that the legislation or action in question is not consistent with a provision of the Constitution. The provision happens to be what the court's interpretation of it is. Since the Supreme Court's pronouncements provide the norm for all lower courts it, rather than the legislature, has "made the law" for the society. It is commonly expected that the only way to reverse such a decision of the Court is to take extraordinary measures, such as passing a formal constitutional amendment. That understanding is inaccurate since it is possible for the Congress to alter the Court's jurisdiction or to alter the Court's membership. Since these congressional measures are marked by disuse, the perception of Court preeminence becomes the reality.

It is instructive to note that the courts in the United States acquired the power of judicial review not by some particular provision of the constitution explicitly giving them the authority but by a decision in a case, *Marbury v. Madison*, 1803. In other words the Court acquired the power of definitive legal interpretation of the Constitution by a case in which they gave a definitive legal interpretation of the Constitution. The case was a classic in political and legal skill. The court ruled on something it was not asked to do and avoided what had been asked because it was unenforceable. The rule that it established, that it could declare an act of Congress unconstitutional, was used sparingly and so in time it became an accepted practice raised to the level of a doctrine. Even though the second time the Court declared an act of Congress unconstitutional, *Dred Scott* (1857), was unsuccessful in its final effect, the Court's measured usage in the following decades was skillful enough that judicial review became a well-established element of the American constitutional system. It helped that in the intervening years between *Marbury* and *Dred Scott* the Court used judicial review to declare acts of the states unconstitutional in a variety of cases such that its power was established without always attacking Congress or attacking all the states at one time.

The practice of judicial review is not limited to the United States. It is also found in quasi-similar form in West Germany, Italy, Japan, and many other countries. Its historical origins have some roots in English practices even before Edmund Coke at the opening of the seventeenth century. Judicial review is a soundly logical practice given certain basic assumptions such as the equality of the various branches of the government and the sacredness of the language of the original constitution. On the other hand it is fundamentally unsound from the perspective of democracy and parliamentary supremacy. Court primacy is unacceptable from the view that the body elected by the people has the ultimate determination of what is law.

In the United States while the impartiality of the judiciary still stands in public imagery the process of Senate confirmation and Presidential nomination in recent decades has possibly skewed appointment eligibility. The Court itself seems to contribute to this phenomenon by decisions that turn on psychological and sociological grounds more than on solely legal and constitutional arguments. For example, the 2003 affirmative action case involving the University of Michigan was argued by the Justice presenting the majority opinion to be needed for only an additional twenty-five years. A decision, as was that one, looking to an historical past and an anticipated future, which are normal legislative criteria, stands in contrast to a decision focused solely on the meaning of the words of the constitution. Likewise development by the Court in cases involving abortion and sexual orientation of a "right of privacy," which is not found in the constitution itself, has given substance to its challenge on political grounds. Thus, that the United States Senate is divided over the confirmation of judicial nominees seems to be occasioned in part by the courts entering the political arena. Historical reflection would show that all the great controversies concerning the courts were because of the political dimension of their rulings.

Whether judicial review is to be preferred or not depends on premises about the forms of government that precede the examination of judicial review itself. Judicial review does not exist by definition in final lawmaking character in the parliamentary system. While it exists in some of those systems in a partial way, it is the legislative body that makes ultimate constitutional determinations. A more careful examination of the premises of the forms of government will come later when the parliamentary and presidential (separation of powers) systems are examined. In the meantime it is not incorrect to look at judicial review as being for the most part uniquely American.

Congressional Enactments: Despite the attention that judicial interpretation gets, other methods of informal growth are equally interpretative and equally important. Legislative change involves enactments that significantly expand, limit, or otherwise alter the arrangements specified in the original Constitution. An example of such changes can be found in the creation of the independent regulatory agencies, which add a structure to the government not mentioned in the Constitution. There are now many commissions, starting with the Interstate Commerce Commission in 1887 and extending to the Securities and Exchange Commission, Federal Reserve Board, National Labor Relations Board, Federal Communications Commission, Civil Aeronautics Board, to name only a few of about fifty. Each such agency exercises independent legislative, judicial, and executive powers in their area of responsibility. Each has been created by Congress precisely to be independent of Congress, the President, and the courts in order that they make decision on purely administrative and technical grounds.

Since the time of their original creation, the independent agencies have become so powerful that they are referred to collectively as "the fourth branch of government." The appellation is not inappropriate and special studies from time to time have advocated that they be placed under presidential direction more consistent with the constitutional outline of the three branches. The original intention in creating these agencies was to remove them and their area of jurisdiction from the ebb and flow of partisan politics. That extraction from election politics sustains their continued independence. In the creation of the fourth branch, Congress expanded the Constitution beyond its original design without a formal amendment. It is small consolation to constitutional purists that the legislative expansion received the approbation of the courts and of the president. In other words, interpretation by one branch is reinforced by the other two, which makes the first act appear savory.

Often cited as an example of judicial interpretation and lawmaking is the 1824 case of *Gibbons v. Ogden* in which the Supreme Court gave the first authoritative interpretation of the meaning of the commerce clause. The case also sustained the national government's jurisdiction over the jurisdiction of the states. What happened is that the Court overturned a navigation act of the state in favor of a navigation-licensing act established earlier by Congress. Referred to for the interpretative role of the Court in giving meaning to the commerce clause, the interpretation was first that of Congress which in 1793 had decided to enact the licensing law. The Gibbons case is indeed important because it makes clear the jurisdiction of the national government in the vital area of commerce and it is legally the constitutional basis for the later actions establishing the regulatory commissions. It is another example of an interpretation by one branch reinforced by another, though in this instance Congress was the first interpreter.

Presidential Initiatives: Presidential interpretations are exemplified in executive agreements ranging from the Louisiana Purchase in 1803, the controversial lend-lease initiative in 1940, and the diplomatic and war powers of the contemporary era. Each exercise of presidential initiative is entirely reasonable in the context of its particular exigencies. Jefferson could not have waited for formal congressional and constitutional debate before purchasing the Louisiana territory because the opportunity may easily have slipped away once notice was given of the prospect. Presidents today, in carrying out foreign policy, need flexibility beyond the treaty making power and other limited provisions of the Constitution. Crises in the foreign policy area are not arranged to occur during the time when Congress is in session. Making the President subject to Congressional approval on the exercise of broad authority could be contrary to the interests of the Constitution.

Both Presidents Lincoln and Franklin Roosevelt went beyond accepted constitutional practice during wartime and they defended their action on the grounds of preserving the very Constitution. Roosevelt was not known for justifying his actions in other than broad terms of "war power" or "the statutes." He did not cite chapter and verse. Congressional backlash to Roosevelt and to undeclared war activities under Truman, Kennedy, and Lyndon Johnson resulted in the "War Powers Resolution" (1973) restricting the authority of the President in committing troops without congressional approval. Though the resolution satisfied criticism of an "imperial" presidency and seemed to require the involvement of the President with Congress to a greater extent it was done without drastically limiting executive prerogative. (Further attention to these issues will come up later in the context of comparative forms of government along with further consideration of the final character of judicial review.) In the case of a surprise attack in the middle of the night during a congressional recess, the ability of the President to act seems mandated rather than precluded by the Constitution. What is clear is that the debate on war powers involves competing interpretations of the Constitution. It is noteworthy that no one is talking seriously about a formal amendment to the Constitution as a resolution to the issue.

It is convenient and appropriate for congressional hearings to question the exercise of presidential war power. Serious questions have been raised by what appeared to be misleading representations of war justification by President Johnson and by President George W. Bush that provoked congressional scrutiny. Hearings that examine the actions of the president usually occur after the fact since an attempt to question the action during wartime could adversely affect the troops. To conduct military operations "by committee" would be disastrous for both the committee and the military. George Washington made it clear during the Revolutionary War that as far as he was concerned Congress could not run the military aspect of the war. That has been the position of all Presidents and for the most part it has been respected. In most litigious challenges the courts have upheld the executive showing once again where interpretation reinforces interpretation. (The debate continues with the recent revelations concerning the use of the National Security Agency for some forms of domestic "spying.")

Custom and Usage - Political Parties: The last examples of informal change, "custom, usage, and convention," get closer to the concept of an unwritten constitutional "way of life" and as a consequence its illustrations are easier to picture as applying to other than American settings. To start with though, the chief example of the custom and usage is the American political party system. It is important because it points to a part of the American political system that defies constitutional formulation. The party system is universally recognized as part of the political system yet it cannot be put into constitutional language.

The American party system historically has several components: two major parties, tolerance of minor and third parties, and the possibility that over time smaller parties will grow to replace one or both major parties. The system evolved from a one party arrangement at the time of President Washington through the flux of parties in the nineteenth century to a relatively stable arrangement of the Democratic Party and the Republican Party from the late nineteenth century into the twenty-first century. The two current parties appear to be permanently fixed in the system. Occasionally there is anguish over the future of one party or the other as election fortunes change. Though parties are the operative reality, technically and legally only candidates run for office and all candidates are treated equally. Over time party groupings came to be recognized in the passage of state election laws. This recognition gave greater prominence to party candidates, which contributes to the permanence of the party. In recent decades some limited national party rules have been supported in the courts, which contributes further to strengthening the existing parties. The full implications of the rulings will take years to evaluate.

The political party system is important because it is only through the major parties that the presidential election system in particular and all elections generally function effectively and it is the party competition that gives the public a framework for selecting between candidates. Further, it is through party cohesiveness that the constitutionally separated branches of government become fluid and less rigidly dysfunctional. The congressional and executive branches could insist on formal constitutional ceremony, which would cause the system to break down. Instead the parties serve as a lubricant that makes the wheels of government run smoothly; they bridge the relationship between the two separately empowered bodies. Despite the usefulness of the party system and the seeming permanence of the present parties, they lack constitutional standing. Many of the laws that are thought to regulate parties actually regulate elections and the parties are involved only by implication.

Attempts to regulate the parties as such, particularly in the area of campaign finance, have failed when challenged on the grounds of constitutional fairness. It is the case, however, that much of the regulation fails due to lack of sufficient will in the very design of the legislation. In addition inadequate enforcement procedures have doomed well-intended reforms. The test of fairness is a large stumbling block. Fairness is a three-part dilemma: (1) to freeze into law the current two major parties would be unfair to the minor and third parties and deprive them of the historic role of potentially replacing the major parties; (2) to give equal treatment to the minor and third parties along with the major parties would be harmful to the major party component of the system and their contributions to the political system; (3) to do nothing leaves the system to the voraciousness of unregulated competition for votes, money, and mass media attention. In the future additional legal regulations beyond the campaign finance laws can be expected. In the meantime, the serious considerations of fairness and constitutional formulation prove the importance of informal constitutional growth.

Time and experience play a large role in giving flesh to the bare bones of a constitution. The political party system in the United States has added more than flesh. By the process of informal growth it has added muscle and agility to the political system. And, the United States is not alone in experiencing such informal change. By definition countries without a written constitution constantly grow in this manner, albeit, as mentioned before, in measured and respected ways, but it is useful to observe that even they do so within a durable framework. In England it is the practice, understood to be "constitutionally" expected, of the Prime Minister stepping down and calling new elections after failure on a vote of confidence in the House of Commons. Similar observance occurs in other parliamentary systems even though the law does not mandate it. Another example of change with time is the evolution of the relationship between the monarchy and the elected government. In some countries the written constitution suffices, in others the change is informal but equally acceptable.

Discussion of Informal Constitutional Change

Informal changes have played a large role in altering the original constitution of the United States. Some observers are inclined to oppose this process of change and prefer that all growth be authorized through use of the formal amending process. Those who object are particularly upset by the not unwarranted idea that the informal changes have played a larger role in altering the original constitution than have formal amendments. The matter of comparison between formal and informal change will be examined in a moment. First, the justification of informal change should be addressed directly and it can be done with a question: Should the President in a time of emergency be permitted as "Commander-in-Chief" to direct the Air Force to evacuate Americans from or to introduce troops to a crisis spot in some distant location? While the obvious answer is "Yes!" it is incorrect on the score that the President is not Commander-in-Chief of the Air Force or of the Armed Forces in general. The President is Commander-in-Chief of "the Army and Navy." The Constitution was never formally amended to include the "Air Force" or the other armed forces. Added to this annoying constitutional caveat might be one about the legal status of the FBI as, in effect, a national police force. In reality the FBI was created by interpretation, not by any explicit provision of the Constitution.

The above observations might be dismissed as nit-picking about matters that are clearly intended or justly implied by the Constitution. The comment of being "justly implied" in the Constitution is reminiscent of the position of former President and later Chief Justice William Howard Taft who observed that the true view of the executive function is that the President can exercise no power which cannot be reasonably and fairly traced to some specific grant of power or justly implied or included within such express grant as necessary and proper to its exercise. He maintained that such specific grant must be either in the Constitution or in an act of Congress passed in pursuance thereof and that there is no undefined residuum of power which he can exercise because it seems to him to be in the public interest. Taft was a "strict constructionist" and his rhetoric intends to convey the sense of limited constitutional powers. He actually says something quite different. "Reasonably," "fairly," "justly," "necessary and proper," and "in pursuance thereof" amount to loophole after loophole that can legitimize all the informal changes mentioned above. Taft's statement might have been effective rhetoric for whatever purposes he had at the time. Technically all that his statement does is point out that informal constitutional growth must be judged and decided upon through the limits of reason and not by some automatically operative legal yardstick.

The critical role for reason in providing the limit to constitutional interpretation is supported by the fact that it is chiefly through interpretative reasoning that the formal amendments have come to have their primary importance. Examination of the twenty-seven amendments in the Constitution reveals that they fall into just a few groupings: those clarifying some chiefly mechanical detail in the original document, those that were foregone conclusions before they were passed, and those that did not assume the importance now given to them until they became subject to the interpretative process. By way of a lengthy parenthetical illustration, a review of the amendments shows their role as responding to interpretation instead of setting in place unequivocal constitutional dictates.

The first ten amendments were enacted among much clamor following the ratification of the Constitution. Proponents insisted that a bill of rights was imperative while others said that it was not necessary. In retrospect the latter position was borne out because there was no major protective application of the Bill of Rights until twentieth-century 1st Amendment cases. It was interpretation by the Court that delayed the application in the first place (Barron v. Baltimore, 1833), and it was later interpretation that gave a large role to them later. The 12th, 20th, 22nd, and 25th, Amendments were designed to clarify or rectify detail provisions in the Constitution about the election, term, and succession of the President and, to a lesser degree, of the Congress. The limit on the number of terms for a president is probably very significant. The direction of the significance, however, is not completely clear. For example, the two-term limit for Presidents may be consistent with the democratic principle of rule in turns, but it may be contrary to principles like the effectiveness of policy leadership and popular control.

To continue, the 11th Amendment proclaiming states immunity from suits was easily circumvented by the Supreme Court when it very quickly allowed the states to be brought to court on appeal of actions which they initiated and when the Court did not exempt the officers of the states from suit. The 13th Amendment was important, but it was enacted almost three years after the presidential Emancipation Proclamation had already abolished slavery in reality. The reality of the full abolition of slavery and all of its secondary forms did not come about without nine or ten or more decades of interpretative implementation. The 14th Amendment is of great significance, probably more so than any other amendment, and came to be so only through interpretation. The Court initially, in the Slaughterhouse and Civil Rights cases of the 1870s, made it little more than a battlefield monument. The "life, liberty, and property" guarantees of the amendment were gradually applied by the Court in reverse fashion, first to business, then to individual liberty, and then only later to the former slave population for whom it was originally intended. The 15th Amendment, prohibiting racial discrimination in voting, is like the previous one in that it was not implemented according to its literal intention until a half to three-quarters of a century later.

The 16th and 17th Amendments were foregone conclusions at the time they were formally proposed for ratification. They were much debated and discussed twenty years prior to their enactments making their later passage easy. Congress had enacted an income tax before the passage of the Sixteenth Amendment; twenty-nine out of forty-eight states had already taken steps in the direction of popular election of senators before the Seventeenth Amendment. The Prohibition Amendment, the 18th, was repealed by the 21st. The 19th Amendment, women's suffrage, was like the 26th, the eighteen-year-old vote, and the Fifteenth, in defining the electorate. All three, however, did not have the concrete results of expanding the actual number of voters as much as had been expected prior to their adoption. These results show that constitutional theory can run ahead of and sometimes behind actual practice.

The 23rd and 24th Amendments, on the enfranchisement of the District of Columbia and the prohibition of a poll tax, respectively, were part of a largely symbolic enfranchisement of ensuring participatory rights for all citizens. They came at the time when the Fifteenth Amendment was finally being fully implemented. Still, with all of the amending efforts to expand the electorate the overall voting rate has continued to decline instead of improve. Ironically the more amendments passed concerning voting the lower the voting rate becomes. The Twenty-seventh Amendment was supposed to be about the equal rights of women when proposed by the Congress in 1972. It failed at ratification after ten years of effort. Subsequently, and very curiously, the twenty-seventh Amendment deals with an entirely different topic, the pay of members of Congress. Strangely the amendment was one of the Bill of Rights proposals from 1789 and never ratified until 1992. This amendment did not have a time limit for ratification, as the Equal Rights amendment had, and so the kindling of some anti-Congress stirrings in the 1980s and early 1990s brought about its ratification.

The defeat of the Equal Rights amendment was not a complete loss since its main legal provisions were already covered in the Fourteenth Amendment's guarantee of equal protection of all "persons" and in other national and state statutes. The proposal was, like many formal amendments, primarily symbolic. The defeat of a symbol is hard to evaluate. Symbols are not unimportant but their effect is slow and uncertain. That uncertainty is precisely the point of interpretative reasoning affecting the formal amendments. The role of interpretation in achieving constitutional significance for particular amendments becomes clear from the foregoing review. And so the formal amending process is not different from the informal process. Only technical matters like the date for sessions of Congress or inauguration of the President are free from interpretation.

The Spirit Of Constitutionalism And The Way Of Life Of A People

Discussion of the difference between formal and informal constitutional growth came about as a result of the effort to draw a contrast between the United States and regimes that have a written constitution while in practice their behavior seems anything but constitutional. The contrast had been made in the understanding that change in public policy and in the constitution itself followed the prescriptions of the constitution in the United States while they were brought about through extra-legal means in the other regimes. The discussion of the informal methods of constitutional growth in the United States shows that extra-legal (informal) means play a large role in the American political system. The American practice does not therefore stand that far removed from those originally viewed as in sharp contrast with the concern for constitutionalism. In fact, and here is a momentarily disturbing statement, in looking carefully at the constitution and practice of many of the other regimes it may be seen that they follow the letter of their constitution better than the United States does theirs.

Other regimes normally considered unconstitutional follow the letter of their constitution better than the United States. This is so in that they follow the letter of the constitution and not the spirit. The old Soviet Union wrote new constitutions in 1924, 1936, and in 1977, so that it conformed to their practical intentions. Other regimes, like the former Iraq regime, change their constitutions in what appears to satisfy the convenience of a political moment. Furthermore, the Soviet constitution and those of others have specific items not found in the American Constitution giving them a literal claim to conformance in constitutionalism. For example, in the Soviet Union the Communist Party was established, which stands in contrast to the political party system in the United States that defies constitutional formulation. Of course, the fundamental contrast was that only one party was legal in the old Soviet system. The new Russian constitution speaks of the power of the people and prohibits state-sponsored or mandatory ideology. What the reality of Russian political life will be is yet unfolding.

A scrutiny of provisions of other constitutions reveals the mention of many rights like those of speech, religion, press, assembly, conscience, education, housing, health care, privacy, and inviolability of the home. The last five are not found in the text of the United States Constitution. Unfortunately the mention of a right or other provisions in many constitutions guarantees little in reality and has the appearance of little more than propaganda statements for internal or external consumption. At best the provisions are goals. Often the reason constitutions may speak of many rights found both within and beyond the scope of the American Constitution and yet not experience them is that the provisions are qualified with statements like "as provided by law," "by the development of," "by providing conditions," "in the manner prescribed by law." The old Soviet constitution did that as does the new Russian, the Philippine constitution, and many others. Each of the alleged rights can be legally intended but realistically inoperative because the necessary development has not yet taken place. A state policy in the Philippines or any similar country to "free the people from poverty" may be praiseworthy but meaningless in the light of domestic and competitive international economic condition. Such constitutional provisions raise serious questions about the meaningfulness of constitutionalism. It may be argued that the constitutional goals are good but that the conditions are bad and they are "not our fault." "Fault" in other words belongs with others outside our community or those within our community who are selfish. Constitutionalism like this takes on the character of rhetoric instead of law.

It is not just the old Soviet system that made a claim to rights of freedom of speech and press based on the assumption that there is only one truth and that truth is already possessed by the government. Censorship practiced in the Greek regime mentioned in the chapter dealing with rights was based on that assumption. One is free to profess the truth proclaimed by the government but not to oppose it since that would be to profess falsehood. It is on the similar grounds that some regimes allow only one political party and only one slate of candidates nominated at elections. To have two parties or two slates of candidates would suggest that the sanctioned one did not possess the truth. No one says it so crudely today yet that is what one-party regimes amount to even as they proclaim their rule according to law. The contrast between the words and the reality of freedom reveals a fundamental point about constitutionalism. A regime can be literally constitutional but not truly constitutional, or a regime can be constitutional while not being literal. If the Constitution of the United States were to be amended according to its legal means ("two-thirds of both houses, . . . etc.") so as to abolish all except one political party that action might be perfectly legal but it would hardly be "constitutional." To formally amend the constitution so as to abolish freedom of speech or religion might maintain the literal form of legally limited government, but constitutional government would no longer exist. This point about literal constitutionalism demonstrates how closely constitutionalism is linked to the discussions in the earlier chapters on the nature and end of the state and the origin and justification of political authority.

The basic philosophy on the purpose of the state and the nature of authority determines in large part what comprises constitutional government. This philosophy is a more critical test of constitutionalism than the usual proposal that "spirit" means conformity of practice to the intentions of the framers. Spirit of constitutionalism has a deeper meaning than that of literal conformity; in the same way limited government is something more than merely following a written document. In these distinctions there emerges a "Spirit of Constitutionalism" which is larger than the literal sense of constitutionalism. It is on the test of this "spirit" that the United States is "actually limited" and that other regimes can be "actually unlimited." The classification scheme discussed at the beginning of this chapter finds a more fruitful dimension under this broader sense of spirit.

Despite its informal constitutional change, which may stand in poor stead by way of literalness, the United States according to the spirit has a soundly constitutional government. It and similar regimes in England, Japan, or wherever exercise authority within a framework of moral force, conducted in a manner consistent with respect for the individual, and guided by principles higher than the determinations of the government. Other regimes may be literally constitutional yet be "actually unlimited" because of one-party rule, a rigid governmental system, and a totalitarian (meaning total or one-truth) perspective. Such regimes are an affront to the spirit of constitutionalism in anything but an organismic-collectivist sense of the nature and end of the state. A strictly mechanistic view of the state could likewise make claims to a literal constitutionalism, which again shows the importance of the earlier discussion.

CONSTITUTIONALISM: POLITICAL STRUCTURE, POLITICAL CULTURE, AND INFRASTRUCTURE

Discussion of constitutionalism basically considers the conduct of government and how the appropriateness of conduct is determined and judged. The discussion has been in terms of conformity to documents and principles where the nature and end of the state are the final determinants of the appropriateness of governmental activity. As just seen the activities of a regime could be deemed constitutionally appropriate *if* it is decided that the organismic-collectivist system or the mechanistic system is the correct one. Earlier discussion of the nature of the state showed the possible dangers in those systems.

There is another way of looking at the conduct of government. Using the political system concepts examined earlier it is possible to gain other insights into constitutional relationships and differences. A deeper understanding of the difficult task of judging regimes can be acquired thereby. The understanding will also show that although the approaches to political science differ they are not antithetical.

The political system model, it is to be recalled, is that abstracted description of the political world involving inputs, outputs, conversion processes, environments, and functions instead of states, powers, authority, and persons. Identifiable institutions, political structures, political cultures, and environments were important to the system, as was the relationship between political culture and political structure. Structures differ by degree, called differentiation, and cultures differ by degree, called secularization in a developmental sense. The relationship of structures and cultures can be descriptively satisfying and show underlying elements that give insights to constitutional character.

Political Structure is not a difficult concept in the context of the political system. It is a pattern of related roles or established relationships among people. Structure is traditionally identified with formal organizations such as courts, the executive, and the legislature. The concept is broadened to include informal as well as formal relationships consisting of party organizations, patterns of voting, or the pattern of power distributions in international politics. All are patterns of related roles or established relationships. Traditional political science has little trouble accepting the broadened concept.

Political structures are usefully related by way of analogy to physical structures such as an Eskimo house or a skyscraper. A simple governmental structure, like that of a small town, can be thought of as analogous to the simple structure of an igloo. A more complex governmental structure can be thought of as similar to a skyscraper with its accompanying support systems. In this manner we speak of degrees of differentiation in physical structures and political entities. Some political structures, or indeed entire systems, are very simple and undifferentiated and others are very complex and differentiated. The acknowledgment of differentiation suggests that political structures and political systems can be compared according to degrees of differentiation just as buildings or other physical, measurable, objects can be. At least political systems can be compared in that manner if it is assumed, a huge assumption, that there exists a "structure micrometer" that can precisely register the exact differences between systems. The existence or nonexistence of a precise micrometer of governmental structures should not disturb the imagined comparison. Even if detailed measurements cannot be made they can be imagined and put to effective uses.

Political Culture can be approached in the same manner as political structures. Culture is understood to be the pattern of attitudes and orientations of a distinct community of people. As Gabriel Almond describes, it is composed of attitudes and orientations toward politics, a subjective realm that underlies and gives meaning to the political system. The concept of culture is somewhat less concrete than that of structure. Nonetheless it involves a set of phenomena that can be identified and measured to some extent or degree. Political cultures are broadly classified into three groups, parochial, subject, and participant, based on a community's awareness of and participation in political events. In a broad sense all the aspects of the life of a particular community comprise its culture. The life surrounding the igloo is simple compared to the life surrounding a complex skyscraper community. Extending the previous analogy, the political culture of the igloo community is parochial in that there is little or no awareness of or participation in separately acknowledged political activity while in the complex skyscraper community there is both awareness and participation. In a subject culture, which has an authoritarian political system, there is awareness but no participation. The increase in the imagined scale from parochial culture to subject culture to participant culture is known as secularization. This classification of cultures does not imply the relative worth of levels of development. It does not imply that participant is "better than" parochial, it merely states that they are "different by degree." (However, those claims of non-normativeness may be justifiably mistrusted due to human inclinations or weaknesses.)

Relating Political Structure and Political Culture

If (again, a very big if) there existed a "culture micrometer," then all the political cultures could be lined up according to their precise degree of difference, from the simplest to the most complex. The political culture scale and the political structure scale that exists in our imagination can be combined for a larger comparison. It can reasonably be expected that the political culture of the igloo community is compatible with the political structure of the igloo community. Technically, the igloo community is understood to be an intermittent political system, in that they have an undifferentiated structure and a primitive political culture. Nonetheless their structure and culture are in continuity, meaning that structure and culture are in step with one another, compatible, or, more technically, that they have an isomorphic relationship. If there were a disparity between structure and culture, that would be referred to as discontinuity.

If perfect continuity existed between all structures and cultures, a perfect world would exist. Comparing the two imagined micrometer-determined scales made up of all present members of the United Nations the country found at position number 47 on the imaginary structure scale would be found at exactly position number 47 on the imaginary culture scale, number 126 in structure at 126 in culture, and so forth through the two scales. If the world were not perfect, if there are discrepancies, discontinuity, between the structure and culture of a particular country, then the scales would reveal how serious that country's problems are. If a country were five steps out of place or forty-five steps out of place, mild or grave discontinuity would be shown.

Examining the two scales, even though purely imaginative, should give another basis for comparing the United States and other regimes. One might expect to find that the United States has a highly differentiated structure and a highly secularized culture. The old Soviet Union had a highly differentiated structure while its political culture, perhaps because of the one-party system, was not highly secularized. On the new Russian regime it is possible to usefully speculate on the degree of structural differentiation, cultural secularization, and continuity between structure and culture. For any regime the degree to which lag or lead of either structure or culture exists can be pondered with respect to the amount of authoritarian rule or freedom that is necessary or possible. A highly authoritarian state will in all likelihood show more than marginal degrees of discrepancy between structure and culture. This suggests a contrast that may reflect underlying elements of a constitutional nature.

If the two scales could be made parallel the United States could be pictured in an advanced position having continuity of structure and culture and the old Soviet Union viewed as discontinuous. While the latter depiction might be regarded as expressing a traditional disparagement, from a strict theoretical-Marxist perspective the Soviet structure would be pleased with being portrayed as a vanguard leading to an eventually advanced classless culture, indeed an eventually classless world. Authoritarian regimes, no matter what their political orientation, commonly make the claim that their actions are designed to advance the country. To correct the discontinuity between structure and culture is the theme of dictators and liberation movements everywhere.

Continuity between the imaginary scales of structure and cultures suggests that the regime or constitution is in accord with the "way of life of the people." This accord is the essential element of constitutional rule for Aristotle. When political structure and political culture are compatible, a constitutional relationship exists. Aristotle acknowledged that it was possible for an evil regime to be in accord with an evil people. In that situation, too, there would be continuity between structure and culture. Though the goodness and badness of a system had to be handled separately, the discontinuity and continuity was at least a starting point for constitutionalism. The earlier chapters on the political system and on methodology showed that the values domain was outside of their consideration but were appropriately found in the nature, origin, and purpose of the state.

A provocative aspect about the old Soviet and American comparison is that the Soviets could not admit of continuity between structure and culture until their dominance was "worldwide." If premature continuity occurred the Soviets would have been obliged to begin the promised "withering away" of their structure. With the danger of competitors taking advantage of the dismantling of the apparatus of the regime the achieved gains would be undone. From the Marxist perspective, basic Western covetousness is the source of all concern and so withering had to be delayed until the revolution was successful worldwide. Once again it is demonstrated that theoretical principles must precede practical constitutional judgments.

Infrastructure: Another aspect in the consideration of the political system, and indeed a close reflection of the continuity and discontinuity of structure and culture, is the character of the infrastructure. The political infrastructure is the internal part of the structure. An igloo, to revert to the earlier analogy, has few internal parts. A skyscraper has many units on many floors and the building includes thousands of miles of electrical wiring, air-conditioning ducts, plumbing, elevator shafts, and much, much more. The infrastructure of a political system consists of political parties, thousands of business and labor organizations, election apparatus, interest groups, streams of lobbyists, the media of mass communication, public opinion networks, and much more. All infrastructure parts process information in the system.

It is possible to compare democratic and totalitarian political systems in terms of the freedom of the infrastructure. The democratic infrastructure is relatively autonomous while the totalitarian one is subordinated to the government. In the democratic countries the infrastructure is "relatively" autonomous since absolute autonomy would be tantamount to anarchy. There is, however, a clear contrast between democratic relative autonomy and close, hierarchic articulation of infrastructure and government in the authoritarian system. In the latter situation the media, interest groups, and individuals cannot act or speak except in a manner consonant with the ruling group. The official position on all public matters is the only one expressed unless one wants to take a chance with being branded or tried as an enemy of the people or a maligner of the state.

Relative autonomy is found in the United States and subordination was found in the old Soviet and other Communist systems. This relative autonomy versus subordination is equivalent to saying that subsidiarity is practiced in the one setting and not in the other. Accordingly, the degrees of relative autonomy or subordination in comparative political systems contains another constitutional measuring device in the sense that the spirit of constitutionalism includes the principle of subsidiarity as well as the other considerations of the nature and end of the state and the origin and justification of political authority. It is with more than passing interest that the evolution in the new Russia and other former Communist systems are closely watched for signs of genuine freedom or the reemergence of authoritarian relations within the infrastructure.

Conclusions About Constitutionalism

Constitutionalism has basically been concerned with the conduct of government, how the conduct is judged, and how that judgment is arrived at. Concrete exemplification of the conduct of government contrasted the United States and other regimes that have similar written constitution to that of the United

States yet have behavior that is very different. Three approaches contrast these regimes: (1) comparison in terms of the fundamental "spirit" of constitutionalism based on the roots of classical and modern constitutionalism and overall political philosophy; (2) comparison of continuity of structure and culture; and (3) the comparison of relative infrastructure autonomy.

The first relates to legal and actual limits on governments and their relationship to fundamental principles of politics. The second, about continuity and discontinuity, was shown to be a way of imagining in a graphic manner the classical notion of constitutionalism as reflective of the way of life of a people. The third, that of infrastructure autonomy, tells of the subsidiarity relationship between the government and the units of society. As the media, political parties, or interest groups would be relatively autonomous, subsidiarity would prevail, and as they would be subordinated, the principle of assumed integrity would be ignored. These contrasts are instructive in understanding constitutionalism.

It was suggested at the beginning of the chapter that constitutionalism in the United States was basically "modern" in the sense of stressing negative limits on government. What was implicit throughout the later discussion, particularly on informal growth in constitutions and on political culture, is that the United States Constitution is and for a long time has been no longer simply a single document. It has come to be that the United States Constitution includes the whole life and scheme of living of its people. In other words, over time the United States Constitution became classical and is not just modern. It is today, like the English Constitution, not just a single document; instead it is the whole body of laws and customs that go to make up the character of the government.

Any attempt to follow the successes of the United States by copying the legal structure outlined in the Constitution fails unless the contrasts between classical and modern constitutions are kept in mind. One country adopting the legal structures of another country must be attentive to the accompanying environments. In the United States the peculiarities of the American culture have been blended over time into the larger American constitution. The similarities and differences between the American culture and the culture of the country that would adopt the American structure must be scrutinized before any changes are recommended. To pay attention to only the strictly legal and structural aspects of constitutional government is to miss a substantial part of constitutionalism.

A Brief Case Study - The Philippines

Imitation is the greatest flattery. By that standard the United States should be pleased since in the nineteenth and twentieth centuries many countries copied its constitution. The Philippines as well as many Latin American nations followed the model closely when drafting their initial constitutions. The specific reasons for the legal and structural practices that were copied varied from country to country. For the Philippines the adopting of American legal forms had historical roots beyond the normal explanation of following a successful model.

The Philippines was occupied by the United States after the Spanish-American War, which had been chiefly a conflict with Spain over Cuba. That war is regarded as not an entirely proud part of United States history because of the greed apparent in some American motives and because of the role of the press at the time in stirring up unfounded troubles. Even though the Philippines was a long way from Cuba the upshot of the war saw Cuba independent from Spain but under American military control for three years and the Philippines, along with Guam and Puerto Rico, coming under complete control of the United States. In light of the world power rivalry at the time, chiefly between many European nations, the American seizure of the Philippines may have spared them from a larger domain of conflict.

A native Philippine resistance to the American takeover sought to establish the independence of the country and even a constitution was written. The independence effort did not succeed at the time but it may have contributed to a quicker than usual promise by a colonial power, the United States, to eventually grant independence. The actual promise of eventual independence came in 1916 and the concrete steps of constitution came in 1934-1935. Independence was scheduled for July 4, 1946. Although a world war with devastating effect in the Philippines intervened, independence was carried out as planned to the delight of both nations.

The Philippine constitution was designed in a somewhat hesitant manner in the period from 1934 to 1940. The process of constitution making lagged for several reasons, including local rivalries and American policy concerns. The interest in this case study is to draw attention to the role that the model of the United States Constitution played in the design of the final product. In the period from occupation to constitution making (1898—1934) the United States poured money, teachers, and an educational system into the Philippines. The education dimension proved far more important than any other monies expended. In that short span of three and a half decades, the education effort produced a nation whose lingua franca was English instead of either Spanish from an earlier 350-year heritage or any indigenous language of the nation.

Philippine identification with the American instruments of government came with the thorough immersion in American educational ways. Philippine children grew up reading "See the apple" in elementary school texts and reciting the Pledge of Allegiance even though their country did not grow apples and the Stars and Stripes was not the native flag. Because of this educational immersion there was a somewhat "natural" affinity for American constitutional ways since they had been indirectly inculcated. This is a concrete example of what is called the socialization process described in an earlier chapter. Through informal learning as well as through deliberate efforts, Filipinos came to accept American ways. In addition to learning about American products and American habits and customs, the positive values of the American political system were stressed and Philippine leaders came genuinely to embrace them.

It should come as no surprise to learn that the records of the debates related to the drafting of the 1935 Philippine constitution reveal arguments as if from American textbooks over the relative merits of various governmental structures. The drafters of the constitution were all Filipinos. There were no formal ties to any American advisors. One can well imagine, however, the careful attention to American practice as the resulting document came to parallel the American constitution. The records of the debates at the Philippine constitutional convention clearly indicate that the copying was not from paper but from what had been inculcated in the process of socialization. The copying was close except for avoiding what were perceived even then as "mistakes" in the American design.

The main features of the Philippine constitution were a separation of powers among three branches, including an independent judiciary, and a bicameral legislature. There was also a bill of rights and, as in all constitutions, a preamble and provisions for amendments. The new ingredients in the Philippine constitution were all items that had been omitted from the American constitution. Over many decades many of these omissions in the American constitution had been added to it or had come to be regarded as important parts of the constitutional posterity. These missing ingredients included the definition of citizen, specifications on suffrage, establishment of a general auditing office and a civil service procedure, and provisions for the protection of natural resources. All these items had become part of the larger American constitutional system but only the first two had come to be formal amendments to the constitution. One structural change of particular note in the new Philippine constitution was the procedure for electing their President. American academicians and others had come to regard their own indirect system of election through the Electoral College as anachronistic and would not advise its use in any other system, let alone their own. Heeding this conventional wisdom of the time, the Filipinos opted for the direct popular election of the president.

Another change in the Philippine constitution from that found in the original American Constitution but which had also undergone mutation was the system of electing Senators. One hesitation in the design of the new governmental structure was over a unicameral versus a bicameral legislature. Initially unicameralism was embraced though shortly in 1940 amendments the bicameral form was chosen with a Senate and a House of Representatives, using the identical names as in the American legislature and which had been in use in the Philippines National Assembly from 1916 to 1935. The arguments in favor of bicameralism were familiar to Americans: "Two heads are better than one," "Avoid hasty and ill-considered legislation," "Less susceptible to bribery," "It would attract more mature, experienced, and able office holders." The criticisms of bicameralism, like the arguments in favor, were echoed in the dreaded "D's" of textbooks at the time: "Deadlock, delay, duplication, and diffusion of responsibility."

In establishing the two-house legislature there was little difficulty in determining the representational base for the lower house. It was to be, as in the United States, on equal population districts. The Senate was not as easy. Senators were to be popularly elected, as had recently come to pass in America, but the representational base was problematic. Established territorial districts comparable to American states were not readily available in the Philippines. Islands could not be used as a representational base because there is a tremendous variation in island size and there were too many, more than 7000. Provinces and language or dialect areas likewise could not be used since they also varied in the population size of the language groups and they were not fully developed in political identity. The stratagem chosen was to have all senators elected from the nation at large with one third elected every two years for a six-year term. Clearly this final design closely followed the American model with only the representational base being different.

The new constitution was fully implemented in 1946 and the Philippine structure worked according to design for twenty-five years except for one problem – no president was ever reelected to office. Other national leaders, particularly senators, continually challenged the chief executive. The rivalry between President and Senators encouraged a rivalry between the executive branch and the legislative branch resulting in policy stalemate and confusion. A complete picture of the Philippines and its government cannot be taken from this brief case description and the reader should not get the impression that everything went poorly. There were, however, definite governmental problems and accompanying social and political frustration.

An attempt to overcome the defects in the Philippine constitution was undertaken in a constitutional convention of 1971-1972. The convention had been mandated earlier but the particular circumstances of its occurrence may have brought as many problems as it sought to eradicate. The convention was held during the second administration of President Ferdinand Marcos, the first president to be reelected. That reelection in 1969 was perceived to have more irregularities than usual. At the same time there was growing restlessness in the country about economic hardships, corruption, and subversion. With the strong encouragement of President Marcos the convention moved in the direction of proposing a shift to a parliamentary form of government, meaning one house electing a prime minister. As the convention was coming to a close other events seemed to move the president to declare martial law and to rule by edict. The convention finished its work in the months following the declaration of martial law, and the parliamentary proposal that came forth from the convention was looked upon as a vehicle for Marcos to continue in office for an unlimited number of years since the outgoing constitution prohibited the President from serving for more than eight continuous years.

Marcos continued in office and the new constitution of 1973 with its new governmental structure stood below Marcos in power and importance. The President was to be "head of state and chief executive" though the Prime Minister, elected from the unicameral National Assembly, as was the President, was to hold "the executive power" and be "commander-in-chief." That there was confusion in this arrangement is confirmed by the 1976 amendment in which, in a new national assembly with a native name, the President was also to be the Prime Minister. It is clear from a purely structural consideration that the conversion of the established Philippine constitution from a system with three branches and a bicameral legislature to a parliamentary unicameral legislature would receive tremendous opposition, whatever its objective merits or intentions. A period of authoritarian rule was perhaps intended to temporarily provide a forced calm during which the dramatic structural changes were introduced. Senators in particular opposed the new parliamentary form since their special legislative and societal position was abolished. Prominent among those arrested during the early days of the martial law era were some former senators and other legislators. Logically it is reasonable to expect that political leaders would "take the lead" whether in opposition or support, so no definite conclusions can be drawn from the role of the former senators.

It is difficult to sort out the constitutional and structural aspects of the changes and their partisan and personal dimensions. As a case of structural constitutional change the parliamentary move eliminated both the personal rivalry of the president with each of the senators and the rivalry of the president with the Congress. By the change also, the problems of representational base and multiple representation were settled once and for all since the offices of separate President, vice-president, and twenty-four senators would no longer exist. If martial law was in any way coordinated with the needed transition period from the earlier constitutional form it could be viewed, in that respect at least, as salutary. Nonetheless, the institution of the senate and the whole governmental form modeled after the American form was well ingrained not just since independence in 1946 but after seventy years of immersion in American ways. Change to a new form, even if a highly desirable structural change, would be difficult under the best of conditions.

Marcos did not last. After the assassination of former Senator Aquino upon his return from exile in the United States in 1983 and another highly flawed presidential election in 1986 Marcos himself fled into exile and was replaced by the wife of the assassinated senator. A provisional "freedom" constitution was established in 1986 that was replaced by the constitution of 1987. The new constitution restored the major structural provisions of the pre-Marcos order, notably the Senate of twenty-four members elected at-large. Another feature, actually a revival of a provision of the pre-1940 amended 1935 constitution, was the one-term presidency limited to six years. The new design of the presidency eliminated part of the rivalry with senators since once elected the incumbent had no concern about a would-be opponent in the next election. The design did not obviate the other structural problems of all twenty-four senators coming from the same base as the president or the competition between the two quite distinct legislative chambers and of the senators amongst themselves.

It seems inappropriate to say that the structural design of the Philippine government with its separation of powers, a bicameral legislature, and the unusual electoral base of the Senate is not well attuned to the indigenous circumstances since there have been at least four occasions for the people to express their sentiments on it. In almost three generations there has been debate on governmental design: in the original constitutional drafting in 1935, the amendment to it is 1940, the debate and resistance to the Marcos redesigns of 1973-1976, and the new constitution of 1987. The Senate appears to be an integral part of Philippine life whether or not it satisfies the design symmetry of political scientists. While the merits of abstract competing structural designs of governments will be examined in a later chapter, concrete constitutions and governments must be judged in the light of accomplishment rather than theory.

The new 1987 Constitution has extensive passages setting forth goals and policies. As mentioned the 1935 constitution closely followed the United States constitution but went beyond it in areas not yet accomplished in the model. For example, the Philippine constitution set a two term limit on the president, a provision not included in the United States at the time, it defined citizenship, something missing in the U.S. Constitution, and it gave the president the line-item veto, which has never been incorporated in the U.S. In addition, the Philippine constitution had provisions for a Commission of Elections, a Commission on Appointment made up of twelve senators and twelve members of the House that confirmed or denied presidential administrative and judicial appointments instead of using the majority of the Senate as in the U.S. The Philippine constitution established a General Auditing Office with an Auditor General and it provided for the Civil Service, both of these items had to be established by law in the U.S. and not in the constitution. Another item was a constitutional provision on "conservation and utilization of natural resources" which again was sought and not included in the U.S. Each of these different commission, office, and provisions were in separate articles in the constitution. With all of these additional provisions the 1935 Philippine constitution with about 7800 words was only about 600 words longer than that of the U.S.

Length of the constitution is mentioned because the Marcos constitution of 1973-1976 had much more detail at around 12,000 words. An intriguing addition to this later constitution in the authoritarian regime of Marcos was an article, following the bill of rights, on the "duties and obligations of citizens." It seems the dictator wanted to tell the citizens how to behave. He himself was cast out for his own behavior in 1986 and his constitution was replaced by one of almost 22,000 words. It is as if the response to years of abuse and perceived abuse was a constitution stipulating greater safeguards from government. Among other provisions the new constitution prohibited "political dynasties as may be defined by law." A related clause stated that the spouse and relative by consanguinity or affinity within the fourth civil degree of the President shall not, during his tenure, be appointed to high governmental office or that of government-owned or controlled corporations and their subsidiaries. It was a case of locking the doors after the house has been pilfered. Unfortunately such worthy ideals do not guarantee, for the Philippines or for any country, that the next would-be dictator will not find other stratagems for accomplishing evil.

The limitations of constitutional restraint was manifest less than a decade and a half later when the popularly elected former movie actor President Joseph Estrada was forced from office and eventually impeached. The limitation of constitutional provisions is further pointed out in the ironic fact that while the new document is very specific in ensuring "the fundamental equality before the law of women and men" in its other gender references always uses the masculine pronoun, him or his or himself, especially when referring to the president. Yet, two of the first four post-Marcos presidents were women.

That the new constitution went further than previous ones in seeking to advance the interests of the Filipino may be seen in its provisions to "free the people from poverty," "promote social justice," "recognize the sanctity of family life," "protect the life of the mother and the life of the unborn from conception," "give priority to education, science and technology, arts, culture, and sports," "promote total human liberation and development," "protect the right of workers and promote their welfare," and "promote comprehensive rural development and agrarian reform." The bill of rights provides the "right of the people, including those employed in the public and private sectors, to form unions." All of these provisions stand against a reality of an economy which precludes all but the minimum, if that, for the vast majority of the people. Labor unions may be legal and a basic right but both the domestic and competitive international labor markets give them scarce chance of advancing the workers. Once again, such goals in a condition in which they cannot be realized raise serious questions about constitutionalism as to whether it is a statement of aspirations, political rhetoric, or legal phantasm.

Less literally problematic are provisions that declare "freedom from nuclear weapons in its territory" or that "foreign military bases, troops or facilities . . . [are] . . . not allowed . . . except under treaty concurred in by the Senate and, when the Congress so requires, ratified by a majority of the votes cast by the people in a national referendum." (The constitution also stated "Congress shall provide for a system of initiative and referendum.") This foreign policy making by way of a written constitution appears reasonable by the standards of the time of drafting but the realities of domestic and international affairs as in the case of international terrorism and the Muslim insurgency in the southern islands within fifteen years shows its weakness. The Japanese constitution written after World War II at the urging of the United States likewise restricted their foreign policy by renouncing the right to wage war and yet less than sixty years later it is the United States that wanted them to take more military responsibility on the international scene as they have done to a small degree in Iraq.

That no "death penalty" shall be imposed sounds great until followed by the qualifier that states "unless, for compelling reasons . . . the Congress hereafter provides for it." Unfortunately the constitution has many places where the qualifier "except" appears and is usually followed by "as provided by law." The qualifier is perfectly reasonable in a constitution of such length. It is found in many of the state constitutions within the United States or the provisions are supplemented, for example, in California or Alabama, by hundreds of constitutional amendments. The reasonableness of the qualifier furthers the questioning about constitutionalism as such.

There is no established set of criteria for judging the effectiveness of a constitution or its regime. Change in volatile situations brings about resistance and turmoil from those adversely affected just as the old order would bring about its own form of turmoil. Yet, it is the nature of political world that no situation will stand still to allow time for historical judgment. It is impossible to judge whether the 1987 constitution will be better suited than the previous attempts to the needs of Philippine political life. The changes undoubtedly at the time reflect the broad consensus of the country's leadership for the separation of powers model. Time and experience will be the measure of that judgment. Yet, there is once again talk in the Philippines about change. In 2003 that continues in 2006 a movement started for change to a parliamentary system. Again the theoretical arguments about structure are sound. Thus writing about a fluid constitution that may change at any time is difficult. Nonetheless structuring principles give insight no matter what the eventual outcome. It is current President Arroyo who is urging the adoption of the parliamentary system and it may be wondered whether Marcos's need for martial law to establish the new form will be needed (although there is at the moment no sign of such a move).

Twenty-four centuries ago Aristotle commented that the chief lawgiver is the principal benefactor of a people if that law reflects the country's internal natural liberty. The merit of the Philippines situation is that so far at least their troubles have been set in constitutional and legal terms without the reoccurring practice, as in other countries, of military take over of the government for long periods of time. To have examined and temporarily experimented with alternative governmental structure gives the Philippines a maturity lacking in regimes whose troubles are resolved in a tradition of military rule. Perhaps the blessing for the Philippines is that they are a nation of islands with no imminently threatening neighbors and so they can afford to engage a legal and academic debate about their governmental structure and constitution. Whether that blessing, if indeed it is a blessing, is sufficient to withstand the pressures of the internal social and economic situation must give them reason not to rest.

CONCLUSION

The Philippines' experience is an example of visualizing constitutional crisis in terms of the discontinuity between political structure and political culture. The aspects of political culture were reflected in the indigenous situation, which was not amenable to the American constitutional structure. The Americans who sincerely encouraged the Filipinos to draft an original constitution similar to that of the United States seem to have done so with insufficient or no attention to subtle changes in their own constitution. The American constitution had become "more than a single document" or few closely related documents. Through formal and mostly informal growth the American constitution had become an adaptation of structure and culture. The parliamentary reforms introduced into the Philippines in the 1972 constitution could be justified as an attempt to adapt their structure more to their particular culture. Perhaps that is why it is again proposed.

The Philippine situation, as representative of most countries, demonstrates that constitution making, structure making, is not easy. Constitutions cannot be made in the abstract, although many conceive of them in this way and academic analyses encourage such conceptions. That those countries that have continuity between structure and culture do not themselves have a perfect textbook grasp of what their success is made from, that they do not know what formula goes into making "continuity" of structure and culture, is demonstrated by their inability to export constitutional stability to the many other countries desiring it.

Constitutional government remains an inexact art. It is not much of a science at all as a momentary mental review of the nations of the world will show. Various attempts at scientific proposals for "national building" have been put forward. Those programs often turn out to be merely new versions of the old art of tyranny now pushed with the aid of a plethora of allegedly scholarly consultants. The precise nature of constitutional government remains elusive even for those who have had the good fortune of enjoying it.

Chapter 13

Forms Of Government: Geographic Distribution Of Power

A question with any large or small organization is how to combine effectiveness and efficiency. Frequently that purpose is achieved by the way power is organized, whether it is geographically dispersed or concentrated. The names of geographic organization of governments are unitary, federal, and confederate. These are real or imagined ways in which authority is distributed between national and local levels and are referred to as the forms of government. There is another set of categories referred to as forms of government, namely, the parliamentary form on the one hand and presidential or separation of powers form on the other hand. In other words, "forms of government" is used in two different contexts. The geographical forms and the functional forms can theoretically be mixed in many combinations of ways. For clarity the two sets must be described separately. The geographic forms will be discussed in this chapter, the functional forms in the next.

Definitions Of Forms

A distribution of governmental duties between central and local levels is found in all countries. The distribution is not always according to the names assigned by political scientists. Still, all states have some centralization as well as some dispersion of power. The degree of national versus local jurisdiction and the locus of who decides is the essence of "geographic distribution." Descriptions will show the real and imagined legal and actual characteristics of the forms. This extends the earlier discussion of sovereignty in giving concrete consideration to who exercises political authority.

Confederacy: A confederacy is a loose union of states where each state retains its sovereignty, freedom, and independence, and is free to withdraw at will. For present purposes the best examples that can be given are the United Nations, the old League of Nations, and various alliances such as the British Commonwealth, the North Atlantic Treaty Organization (NATO), and the Organization of American States (OAS). They all fit the definition. The European Common Market, on the other hand, has been another example but with the advent of the European Union (EU) its character may be undergoing a change. The point of the typical confederacy is that the members freely associate with one another and can just as freely choose to break their association.

The Constitution of the Confederate States of America of 1861 is so similar to the original United States Constitution from which the southern states were claiming secession that it cannot serve as a workable example of a confederacy. The "Articles of Confederation," the first American national constitution, has special considerations that complicate and ultimately obviate its use as an example. The critical point about a confederacy is that each member retains autonomous decision-making authority. If a member decides to withdraw from the organization, it can do so. If it remains it does so on its own terms.

Unitary Form: In a unitary state final decision-making authority is vested in the central government. The central or national government decides the distribution of powers for the country. It decides what powers will be distributed and how much power will be dispersed. England and France are both examples of unitary systems, even though they differ widely on centralization and local autonomy. In England local units have a greater share of political power than in France. In contrast in France the central government sees fit to retain more control. It is not the case that all power is centralized, it is just that in comparison to England there is less local autonomy. In both countries any decision about distribution is made by the central government, whether the decision means less local rule or more.

It is the central government's ability to decide that makes both France and England unitary systems. Recent governments in France, which were expected to further centralize power, took steps to disperse powers and the "image" of extreme centralization. Succeeding governments in France again switched direction. The outcomes of such alterations do not normally become clear for many years so a judgment on how "real" the changes are cannot be made now. Whatever the final results, the essential point is that the change comes about by direction of the central government.

Within the United States each of the respective states has the relationship to its local governments that the central government in the unitary form has to its local jurisdictions. For example, within the state of Pennsylvania, as in England, the local cities and towns are granted or not granted decision-making authority by the state government in Harrisburg. According to the state constitution, the state legislature can grant to local cities, counties, or towns "home rule" charters whereby the local units receive varying amounts of autonomy. Discussions of a similar nature have occurred in England resulting in the granting of home rule to Wales and Scotland. Whatever the "degree" of autonomy granted in plans of devolution, unless complete autonomy is granted, the local unit still remains subject to the final jurisdiction of the central government. Complete autonomy is something utterly unthinkable in American states and only true in England to the extent allowed (normally to set "colonies" free).

In states within the United States, and in governments elsewhere, home rule requires central government approval and any granted home rule can be taken away in whole or in part without local approval. Local control over education likewise is subject to state rules that ebb and flow over many years. Usually home rule is taken away in piecemeal fashion by the passage of new central government legislation with no exceptions mentioned for "home rule" entities. Education policy seems more unidirectional in "favor" of state dicta. Home rule is in large part a rhetorical device even though it is a legitimate and genuine administrative device. As a tool it satisfies temporary concerns while the process of time and experience works out long-term solutions. To use states within the United States as examples of the unitary form is unusual because most people do not know about these relationships. People know they elect state officials, like governors and legislators, but they do not know the legal character of the state or what its relationships are to individuals or to their local government. Local governments are known and the national government is known; the intermediate of states are little known or if known are regarded as bothersome.

By this definition of the unitary form it should be understood that a confederacy is a loose union of unitary states. Each state that retains its "sovereignty, freedom, and independence" is unitary in relation to the larger confederacy. Each unit in a confederacy independently decides whether it will go along with the other states on any matter whatsoever. Stressing this fundamental aspect of confederacy points out that so far as unitary and confederate go there is only one form of government, the unitary. Confederacy pretends to be a government while in essence it is not, since it does not have separate decision-making authority except by consent of each member. To call a confederacy a form of government is for the most part a rhetorical device applied to temporary national unions that are on their way to either falling apart or to creating a real unified rule. The United Nations and other international associations are therefore, as mentioned earlier, the better examples of this "form of government," because it is known in advance that the separate states do not concede to the UN independent "governing" authority. A review of the constitution of the (Southern) Confederate States of American and a comparison with the constitution of the United States shows that it pretended to be a confederacy. The government of the Confederacy was stated to be "permanent," a word not even used in the original United States Constitution.

Federal Form: The United States, Canada, and Russia are prominent examples of the federal form of government where authority is said to be divided between a central national government and local units. It is expected that any distribution of governmental power is done by the basic constitution, and it is expected that the distribution cannot be altered by the unilateral action of the central government or the local governments. In federal systems the distribution of powers to local units of government may be broad or minuscule. Often the breadth of distribution reflects a blending of the geographic and population size of the country, although the correlation is not uniform.

The Soviet Union was a difficult state to classify since its constitution identified it as "a unitary, federal and multinational state, formed on the basis of the principle of socialist federalism and as a result of the free self-determination of nations and the voluntary union of equal Soviet Socialist Republics." They were making the unusual claim to be simultaneously unitary, federal, and confederate. The confederacy part was based upon the membership of the nominally autonomous republics, two of which had membership in the United Nations as independent states. In reality the Communist Party so dominated all the republics in the Soviet Union, because of the "solidarity of the workers of all nations," that it was usually and accurately thought of as one unitary state. It is because of the combination of unitary and confederate factors that the Soviet Union was loosely referred to as federal. The new Russian Federation does not claim the combination of forms and the constitution makes clear provisions for the separate government of the local republics, administrative regions, and autonomous territories. The freedom that exists in theory though for the local areas may not stand in practice, especially if their action is seen as being harmful to the federation. That later consideration is not unique to Russia.

THE PROBLEM WITH FEDERALISM

The problem with the federal form goes beyond the discrepancy between theory and practice in the old Soviet Union or the new Russian Federation. The problem is intrinsic to the concept of federalism itself. The earlier discussion of the "indivisibility" attribute of legal authority in the chapter on sovereignty pinpoints the theoretical problem for federalism. That attribute means that authority, or sovereignty, cannot be divided. Just as one cannot be "half pregnant," authority cannot be divided in half. The federal form, federalism, suggests that the authority of the state is divided with the national government having authority over some matters and the local governments have authority over other matters. The division is supposedly made by the constitution, which is what identifies the federal form. The major question for federalism is who decides the distribution and redistribution. If the authority to decide is vested practically in one particular level of government, then that locus ought to be examined carefully to see if it reveals the form as different from what is assumed. A small classification scheme can help make clear the primary aspects of the forms. Using the theoretical forms of unitary and federal it is possible to classify forms in the following manner: 1. Legally federal and actually federal, the United States; 2. Legally federal and actually unitary, the old Soviet Union; 3. Legally unitary and actually federal, England; 4. Legally unitary and actually unitary, France.

The United States is listed as legally and actually federal because the division of powers is said to be constitutionally guaranteed and because relative decentralization does exist. The Soviet Union, on the other hand, despite its proclaimed federal form, is classified as actually unitary because of its highly centralized reality. (The old Soviet Union is used because it is a convenient scapegoat or foil and avoids identifying some current state that would cloud the legitimate point about theoretical federalism that is under discussion.) England is classified as legally unitary and actually federal due to its centralized authority combined with a fair amount of local self-rule. France, at least as compared to England, is legally and actually unitary because it is more centralized in theory and practice. Whether the practice in England and France are actually as just described is indifferent to the understanding that they can change at the behest of the central government.

Certain theoretical advantages are said to hold for the competing forms. The unitary form provides unity, simplicity, uniformity, efficiency, and flexibility. This means that there is very little discrepancy in practice between various parts of the particular nation when uniformity is desired. Governmental and legal procedures in one part of the country are the same in other parts thereby simplifying rule and producing efficiency. Furthermore, change can occur without awaiting local approval thus giving enhanced flexibility. Nonetheless, the unitary has certain liabilities that turn out to be the advantages of the federal form.

These liabilities of the unitary form are the absence of local autonomy and local incentive for handling responsibilities, the inadaptability to a large state with a heterogeneous culture, the lack of experimentation for innovation in government policy or practice, the lack of opportunity for greater levels of citizen participation in government, and the tendency toward the development of a centralized bureaucracy which runs contrary to the claimed simplicity and efficiency. Corresponding advantages of the federal form are then the presence of local autonomy and local incentive for handling responsibilities, the adaptability to a large state with heterogeneous culture, the presence of experimentation for innovation in government policy or practices, the opportunity for greater levels of citizen participation in government, and the lack of a centralized bureaucracy thus giving simplicity and efficiency in governmental operations.

While these disadvantages and advantages work out nicely in any theoretical consideration they do not hold up practically. The political scientist William Riker, a past president of the American Political Science Association, made an instructive comment many years ago in calling attention to the discrepancy between the theory and practice of federalism. Though the situation in many of the countries mentioned has changed many times since he made his comments, the basic point he made about imagined federalism in contrast to the reality goes to the heart of its theoretical underpinnings. In citing what are matched pairs of unitary and federal regimes, Riker points out the misunderstanding that usually occurs. He cited Australia and New Zealand with common political culture and lower class England origins. Australia is very much a federalism while New Zealand tried it and then rejected it. Yet, he says, the citizens of one country moving to the other would experience little difference. At the time of his observations Riker noted that unitary Ghana and federal Nigeria along with unitary Chile and federal Argentina also showed the inconsistent patterns and unexpected performances from the theoretical definitions of their forms. He also cited all too obvious inconsistencies of so-called federal and unitary governments in eastern Europe at the time.

Again, though the particular circumstances have changed the essential lack of practical differences remains critical for the theoretical forms. In practice the similarity of regimes thought to be legally different can be expanded from the above matched pairs. Yet, the list is limited since the total number of regimes said to be federal is only about twenty-four out of one hundred ninety-two or so nations. Federalism is somewhat loosely correlated with large geographic size. Notable exceptions of China, Algeria, and Zaire, all large but not federal, prove that correlation specious. A reflection on the world scene of many different regimes, with various bureaucracies, different levels of citizen participation, and greater and less complexity and efficiency, reveals no pattern of preferred form. Still, some experts, especially in academe and the media, like to maintain the reality and the preferred character of the federal form.

RESERVE POWERS

The classification of the legal forms looks tidy and accurate. Analyses show that practical distinctions are difficult to make and that the federal form in particular is quite ambiguous. The problem in federalism arises from the discrepancy between the legal expectations and the practical operations. A constitution may spell out an initial distribution, but what is important is how the powers come to be exercised and how adjustments are made in the functioning regime. Since no constitution can spell out how all contingencies are to be handled, it is necessary to have some provisions or procedures for redistribution. Redistribution has a profound bearing on the exact legal and practical nature of the form.

In a unitary state decisions about redistribution are legally and actually the responsibility of the central government. Local units may take some initiative in introducing new practices or policies, however if the central government wishes to prohibit the moves or to assume them for itself there is no question about their authority to do so. In the federal system, on the other hand, there are elaborate and diverse provisions on how to handle redistribution. The essential nature of federalism suggests that redistribution is reflected in the constitution. Supposedly change would come about by a constitutional amendment specifying more powers for the central government and less for the local governments, or the other way around. Since amendments are not always possible or practical, some other provisions are made in the constitution for allocating the "reserve powers."

Reserve powers or "residuals" are powers that are not mentioned in the original constitution. They are "leftovers" that accrue to one level of government or another according to the provisions of the constitution. Which level actually receives these reserve powers is not the final determinant of the form since a unitary form can allow for local autonomy, as occurs in England and within the American states. The actual form of government is determined by who decides whether a questioned power is national or local. Some person or agency must settle the issue since a constitutional document has no voice without an agent.

In the United States the reserved powers and the basic statement of federalism is found in the Tenth Amendment. It states:

> The powers not delegated to the United States by the Constitution, nor prohibited by it to the states, are reserved to the States respectively, or

to the people.

By reason of this statement the amendment is commonly known as the "federal amendment" or the "federal principle" and is taken as saying that powers not mentioned in the original Constitution belong to the states. Notwithstanding this impression, the actual growth in over two hundred years has been national. New powers have accrued to the national government, and even powers thought originally to belong to the states have, through a steady stream of legislative and executive actions as well as court cases, been assigned to national jurisdiction.

In Canada: Besides the United States about twenty-four other countries are thought to be federal, although the number shifts as countries make changes in the expectation of improved operating conditions. Changes go from unitary to federal and from federal to unitary. Large states in Africa, like Sudan, have adopted the federal form although incompletely. Unfamiliarity and remoteness make it difficult to study most of the other countries. One that is not remote, although not particularly well known, is the United States' neighbor, Canada. It provides a surprising "federal" growth pattern in comparison to the United States. The growth is also in contrast to what appears to have been legally intended.

The Canadian constitution, earlier known as the British North America Act, provided that the national parliament, after certain specified powers were granted to the provinces, would have the authority "to make laws for the peace, order, and good government of Canada in relation to matters not coming within the classes of subjects by the Act assigned exclusively to the provinces." According to this statement residuals belonged to the national or Dominion government and not the local government or provinces. In many respects the growth for a long time was actually local. Even with that local growth there was restlessness in some provinces with what they saw as national domination. This kindled separatist feelings in Quebec and in some western provinces that sought further local growth. All this occurred despite the formal placement of reserve powers at the national level. Separatist efforts stirrings are currently at rest.

The Canadian constitution was rewritten when the British North America Act became the Constitution Act of 1982. Both the dominion (national) government and the provinces sought to consolidate their position in the new act and both claimed that they succeeded, although not completely. Because of this change and because of the absence of any imminent separatist crisis, the new constitution's character has not been fully tested. Although some of the provisions of the new constitution do grant exclusive jurisdiction over some responsibilities to the provinces, the real test of the ostensibly federal ingredient can only come when there is a dispute. If the provinces and the dominion government disagree on an area of exclusive jurisdiction, that dispute, like Quebec's challenge to the constitution itself, will be settled in the courts. As will be discussed in a moment, the manner of settlement answers the question of legal form.

FEDERALISM: CENTRIPETAL OR CENTRIFUGAL?

Centripetal force is center directed. A centrifugal force moves outward. The discrepancy seen in the operation of federalism in the United States and the general discrepancy seen between expectation and practice is a manifestation of federalism's centripetal nature as a concept. In any federal form there must be either a centrifugal or a centripetal movement. Either a national or a local agent must make authoritative decision about residuals and redistribution. The constitution, the document of the original distribution, does not act alone. In the United States, and in Canada too, final decisions about reassignment of powers have always been made by one of the branches of the national government, dramatically the Supreme Court in the United States. About half the federal systems provide for the adjudication of federal-state conflicts in a designated high court.

In the United States the Court is not the sole arbiter of national-state relations although it usually receives the greatest amount of attention (or blame). In reality the landmark decisions of the Court are often an upholding of an earlier action by the Congress or the President. In the *Gibbons v. Ogden* case (1824), when the Court is said to have established the national commerce jurisdiction by its interpretation of the Constitution, the Court was ruling in favor of earlier action by the Congress. In *McCulloch v. Maryland* (1819), concerning an attempted state tax of a national entity, the Court ruled in favor of earlier presidential and congressional actions. The same was true when the Court helped the Congress and the President get around restrictive treaty procedures in order to establish wildlife policy, which is usually reserved to the states (*Missouri v. Holland*, 1920). Even in the instances when the Court rules "in favor of" the states, the centripetal force still prevails since it is a national agent, subject to other national branches, which makes the decision. The newspapers, major ones at least, tend to keep score of Supreme Court decisions showing an alleged pattern toward state's rights or away from it. The score keeping is not consistent and often only satisfies the parameters of the immediate account. And always the report fails to take note of the essential fact that it is the Court as a national entity that makes the decision and can later reverse it.

Federalism in Theory and Practice

The theoretical claim about federalism is that the distribution of powers is made by a constitution that cannot be unilaterally altered by the central government. Yet, in the United States the Constitution has been, can be, and is changed most significantly by the unilateral interpretative actions of the national government. As seen in the previous chapter, when judicial, congressional, or presidential actions alter the Constitution it is done without the formal amending process coming into play at all. The process of informal constitutional growth has played the dominant role in defining and redefining the jurisdiction of the national government and the states. The interpretations that result in national growth are not usurpations by a voracious government. The growth that occurs is usually a necessary response to a particular set of circumstances.

National growth is most often the response to a demand for uniformity needed to overcome the confusion and dysfunction of disparate state rules. National highway legislation financed construction of a network of major roads throughout the country, provided for uniform construction materials, widths, shoulders, etc. National business regulations, for example, the too much maligned Occupational Safety and Health Administration, support uniform safety standards and prevent certain businesses from hiding behind state law to take advantage of workers and consumers. There is a geopolitical logic to the growth of national powers in the United States. The land area of the United States combined with its population and resource distribution necessitates national rules and national rule makers. National rules are necessary for interdependence in the country and to avoid unwanted disorder.

Interdependence produces both problems and solutions. In the United States a labor strike, a disaster, or an agricultural problem in one part of the country quickly affects most all parts of the country. When such situations occur there is no concern that the Northeast should not be helping the Southwest. There is fair recognition that the sections of the country have interchangeable roles of producers, consumers, developers, marketers, borrowers, lenders, friends, and neighbors. All parts of the country profit together so they help out and suffer together. In Canada, to refer again to their counter-dynamic practice, the combination of area, population, and resources is different from the United States. With a population one tenth that of the United States in slightly larger territory, there is less interdependence, and accordingly more localizing developments. The instrument to oversee this national dynamic in the United States is bound to be the Congress, President, or the Courts, or a combination of them. Even under the new Canadian constitution, though there have been signs of concessions to the provinces, there is a necessity for a national overseer and so it also is not an exception to this centripetal force. In fact there has been national growth in the area of social policy and the provincial resistance is not yet fully resolved. According to the constitution the provincial legislatures can in effect veto the derogation of their power, however such a proclamation never occurs simply and so power erodes rather than is taken away.

*UN*FEDERALISM

In the United States, the "federal" prototype, the inevitable national growth has its foundation, most surprisingly, in the "federal amendment" itself. The Tenth Amendment is thought to proclaim local growth. It speaks of powers that are "delegated" to the national government and powers that are "reserved" to the states. The delegated powers, however, are expanded chiefly through the implied powers doctrine of the "necessary and proper" clause and other clauses of the Constitution. The implied powers doctrine holds that certain additional powers are implied in the powers specifically delegated to the branches of the national government, although it should be noted that the Constitution itself does not use the word "specific." As shown in the earlier discussion of constitutionalism there is no longer any important dispute over the concept of implied powers.

What makes the "federal amendment" the source of the national growth is that there is nothing in the Constitution that is specifically "reserved" to the states. There is no substantive power of government that the Constitution mentions as belonging to any agency other than the national branches. Originally, for example, specification of qualifications of voters belonged to the states. Out of necessity this power was over time mostly taken away from the states. And, in truth, the power is a procedural and not a substantive responsibility. It might be thought that the switch from state to national jurisdiction in the matter of voter specification had to be accomplished by formal constitutional amendment, which therefore proves the true federal character of the system. That contention is reasonable except for the consideration that the history of the various voting amendments shows that they were only effectively implemented with the interpretative efforts of the national government. Ratification of the voting amendments did not occur one day and they became effective the next day. It took ninety years and the passage of the 24th Amendment for the 15th Amendment to be implemented. Women's suffrage and the eighteen year-old vote each needed much assistance to realize their potential.

There is a single provision of the Constitution that grants a specific substantive jurisdiction to the states. That single provision is in the Twenty-first Amendment granting the states the power to establish local prohibition if they so desire. Few people want to expand upon this substantive state power of prohibition. It is by way of this amendment that each state has its own rules for sale and distribution of alcohol beverages. Some, like Pennsylvania, have a state monopoly liquor and wine sales system; others have the sale of beer in supermarkets, and others at pharmacies. Yet even here the states' control has been eroded. Congress, with the threat of withholding "federal" highway funds, forced all states to raise the drinking age to twenty-one because of youthful drunk driving. The twenty-one-year-old drinking laws, like the automobile air-bag law, are recent examples of reasonable national action. Congress has also forced the states to accept a national standard of blood-alcohol content for all cases of drunk driving. The states might like to regulate on their own in these areas but local political pressure and interest group pressures often preclude effective action and so the national government acts.

The recognized "police powers" of the states, the inherent authority to promote and safeguard the health, morals, safety, and welfare of the people, is itself not based on a specific substantive provision of the Constitution. The police powers are based on the interpretation of the reserve clause itself. Since what can be interpreted into the reserve clause can also be interpreted out and since nothing is specifically reserved to the states except for the anomaly of prohibition, the "federal amendment" turns out to be not so much federal as "*un*federal." In other words, because of the reasonableness of implied powers and the lack of substance to the powers said to be reserved to the states, the Tenth Amendment turns out to be the *un*doing of federalism. The United States is therefore *un*federal or unitary rather than federal.

Support for *un*federalism

Writers like words. Sometimes they use words to excess. At other times they do not use them effectively. Sometimes they coin new words. *Un*federalism is a new word. The prefix "un" negates the word that follows, as *un*like takes away likeness. The word "*un*federalism" may be unsettling for the reason that it strikes at the notion of states' rights. Advocates of states' rights maintain that the states had a core of sovereign power that could never be taken away. *Un*federalism shows that the states legally never had that core of authority. Justification for *un*federalism comes from the many considerations of the logic of the 10th

Amendment and the necessity, interdependence, and the national desire for uniformity already mentioned. "Support," however, is a matter of citing past or present factors that contribute to the general condition of *un*federalism without overtly or formally intending to do so. There are many such supports.

1. The Articles of Confederation.

An unexpected support for *un*federalism is the Articles of Confederation. This document, the first constitution of the United States, is said to have established the "confederacy" that preceded the "federal" Constitution of 1787. In the process of showing that the "federal" Constitution is not so federal, it becomes important to see that the Articles of Confederation were not so confederate. This venture may seem preposterous when it is acknowledged that Article I of that first Constitution states, in its original spelling, "The Stile of this confederacy shall be, 'The United States of America.'" That should make the situation fairly unequivocal: the Articles of Confederation established a "confederacy." The Second Article should establish conclusively that the intended form of government was a confederacy. As it is usually quoted, the Second Article reads, "Each state retains its sovereignty, freedom and independence." The essence of a confederacy, as indicated earlier, is that the member units retain their sovereignty, freedom, and independence; they are free to withdraw at will. Nonetheless, there is a problem. The usual quote from the Second Article leaves some material out; quoting out of context makes a big difference. The article actually reads,

> Each state retains its sovereignty, freedom and independence, and every Power, Jurisdiction and right, which is not by this confederation expressly delegated to the United States in Congress assembled.

Rereading the full article may not seem to make much of a difference. Attention should be directed, however, to the distinction within it between delegated and reserved or "retained" powers. Though the article speaks of "expressly" delegated powers, that word does not take away the division. A look at the expressly delegated powers shows that they are the same powers stated in the same manner in the subsequent Constitution of 1787. A close reading of the Articles and the Constitution shows a great similarity of powers of the national government, restrictions on the states, and obligations of the states to one another, such as full faith and credit, privileges and immunities, and rendition. In these respects then, the Articles are similar to the later Constitution.

The Articles of Confederation, it is clear, did not provide for a well-designed government. Its mechanism for interpretation, its decision process, and its means of implementing policy were clumsy. The reasons for the Articles' faulty procedures may be that a genuine spirit of confederacy motivated the drafters, or it may be the result of overly optimistic assumptions based on existing unity. Optimistic assumptions of unity might have been based on the Americans successfully waged war against England. That the euphoric unity of victory was broken by the rivalry of peace can be extracted from Robert E. Brown's thorough critique of Charles Beard's conventional conspiracy thesis of the American origins. No matter what explanation is given for the defects in the Articles, it is clear that the political leaders at the time saw and acted upon the need for change without delay. In a series of meetings at Alexandria (1785), Annapolis (1786), and then Philadelphia (1787), the leaders brought about the drafting of the "more perfect union" of the present Constitution, replaceing the Articles within six years of its ratification in 1781.

The argument that the Articles are not convincingly confederate relies on more than the reserve clause within the Second Article and the similarities with the later Constitution. Striking contrasts to a truly confederate intention are the many passages that speak of the confederation as a "perpetual union." Six times the union is referred to as "perpetual." Furthermore, it is stated twice that the Articles shall be "inviolably observed," which is then followed by the phrase that "the union shall be perpetual." These statements hardly suggest a primary focus on the sovereignty, freedom, and independence of the states. The sovereignty word appears only once and that is in the above quoted Article Two. The right to withdraw at will is never mentioned. The more perfect union, of which the later Constitution's preamble speaks, may indeed reflect a perfecting of a union that already existed. No final determination has to be made here about the precise character of the Articles of Confederation. The point of interest in this discussion is to show that there is a basis even in the earlier document for the contention that true union was the intention in the design of the Constitution of 1787 despite the convincing rhetoric of "federalism" that surrounds it.

2. "New" Federalism

A more contemporary source that supports the contention that the United States is unitary, or to use the coinage *un*federal, is the "new federalism" which presidents, particularly Republican presidents, regularly espouse. By new federalism they maintain that the fiscal resources and responsibilities of the national government should be returned to the states usually in the form or revenue sharing or block grants. Such proposals are usually winners with Congress because the members, even Democrats, want to be able to tell their constituents of their efforts in behalf of returning money to the district. Former President Nixon in 1969 in a major speech announced a plan of responsibility and revenue sharing. President Reagan also gave much attention to new federalism. Both Presidents George H. W. and George W. Bush intoned the rhetoric of new federalism. President Clinton and to a lesser extent President Carter were too smart to employ the language of the Republicans, but they also espoused programs that would turn responsibility away from Washington. The rhetoric of the return of revenue and responsibility to the states is consistent with the tactic of presidential campaigns of "running against the government the candidate seeks to lead."

Much fanfare always accompanies the idea of sharing the largess of national revenues with the states. What might dampen the federalism euphoria is to understand that: 1. the President is making the proposal, 2. the proposal is going to Congress, 3. the "federal" restrictions that are always a part of any change are not so minimal, and, 4. the manner of channeling the funds is the first restriction on the states. In other words, though the presidents use the term "federal" effectively, it is one national agent, the President, making the proposal to another national agent, the Congress. No program is passed without national rules about how the program is to operate. Every revenue sharing measure has an element in it to ensure that the funds are spent by the states for the national purpose intended. New federalism, like the old one, is *un*federal from the very beginning.

3. Statistics on Unfederalism

Statistics on governmental spending support unfederalism. Over the years there has been a massive shift from local to national power. In 1902 local governments spent 59 percent of all governmental budgets in the United States, the states spent 6 percent, and the national government had 35 percent of the expenditures. By the 1970s the local figures hovered around 24 percent, the state figure had increased to around 16 percent, and the national percentage had increased to about 60 percent or higher for a number of years. By the year 2000 the national government's percentage is at about 62 percent with combined state and local spending at about 38 percent of total government figures. Even these figures are misleading because about 19 percent of state and local general revenue comes from the national government. Revenues derived from national sources translate into a higher national percentage of total expenditures and a lower state and local percentage. Clearly the national government has grown vis-à-vis the states and local governments. (Related, but not explored here, is the dimension of a large increase in overall government spending in relation to the total economy.)

It is often argued that the growth is primarily a result of the better national revenue source as a result of the Income Tax (Sixteenth) Amendment. Aside from the questionable post hoc, ergo proper hoc reasoning, the contention does not consider the particular situations that compelled national action in order to provide necessary uniform practices. The grant-in-aid programs that provided national monies for the building of highways, airport terminals and runways, hospitals, educational facilities, and many other undertakings were the result of the need for certain minimum national standards. The cynic would say that these programs are the result of a reasoning that says, "We've got the money, let's find a way to spend it." An objective analysis would consider whether driving from the east coast to the west coast or flying the same distance with many stops in between would be more commodious with different road and airport standards along the way or with national standards. One can imagine what it would be like to undertake an automobile trip from Florida to Oregon and find in each state along the way different rules and road specifications. It would be like traveling through fifteen Englands where there are alternate rules of "driving on the 'wrong' side of the road."

The same type of observation about minimum national standards holds true for water and air safety standards, fair housing practices, and a host of other commercial, social, economic practices. To name a few more there are additional programs in labor practices, banking procedures, handicap access requirements, food and drug handling, and building and safety standards. The national standards in all these areas make certain that unscrupulous individuals do not hide behind state laws to take advantage of consumers or the unsuspecting public. There is also a convenience in national requirements that outweighs the inconvenience of the remote bureaucracy administering them. The convenience is the certainty, when conducting business or traveling, of knowing that standards and practices will be the same.

4. Statutory Supports for Unfederalism

Additional evidence of the growth of the national government can be seen in other areas. For example, chief justices have complained that beyond the traditional upward movement of litigation from the state courts, Congress has contributed to the expansion of national courts' duties by enacting statutes that expand the jurisdiction of the national courts at the expense of the state courts. Twenty-five years ago Chief Justice Warren Burger lamented the "piecemeal shifts of jurisdiction away from state courts and into Federal courts." He asked state judges to thoughtfully and effectively inform Congress that the state courts could do a better job. National growth continued and the Court contributes to it as it did in Maine v. Thiboutot, (1980) by enlarging the justification for citizens to sue their states. Burger dissented. Congress did not reverse the trend as it saw the need to overcome the disparateness of different state rulings.

The complaint about minor cases clogging the court docket may be well taken in the case of the man who brought suit on the grounds that his constitutional rights were violated when he was not permitted to drive his Sherman tank on the streets of Cincinnati. Any casual observer of the news is aware that there is no end to the seemingly frivolous cases and everyone might desire that other procedures could resolve disputes without involving the national courts. Nonetheless these minor matters may well be the price that must be paid to maintain a system that protects uniform treatment in more substantial cases. The savings gained in caseload efficiency must be weighed against the social cost and the Court itself accepts this logic when it accepts appeals from lower court and state court decisions. Expanding the responsibility of the national courts is a way for Congress to ensure the intent of legislation it passes. In 1999 some members of Congress proposed legislation known as the "Federalism Accountability Act." The purpose was to make it harder for Congress and the executive branch to adopt laws and rules that preempt the states on a wide range of issues dealing with drugs, the environment, health, and worker safety. Hearings were held. The opportunity existed to defend the states. The proposal did not pass.

5. The Rhetoric of Federalism

Several times in the preceding comments federalism has been referred to as rhetorical. Strictly speaking it is nothing more than a rhetorical term used for political purposes. At the beginning of this chapter William Riker was mentioned for drawing attention to matched pairs of unitary and federal systems and his finding of no discernible difference in the effective functioning of the forms. Putting the issue as a question, "Does federalism exist and does it matter?" a scholarly qualified "No!" was his answer. He called federalism a "fiction" and commented that scholars accept federalism as real while ordinary citizens treat federalism as a fiction. He is on target in the view that ordinary citizens do not concern themselves often or seriously about federalism while scholars treat it as a real thing. Scholars seem overly taken with the fiction persuading regional politicians to accept the formation of a central government. Riker's main point was that no matter how useful the fiction, one should not overlook the fact that it is a fiction. Political scientists seldom speak so directly.

FEDERALISM UNDONE

In this chapter federalism has been undone. Examination of the usual forms of government in concrete setting shows that governments can either bring about change by making decisions or they can bring about change by not making decisions. There is no option that half the decision belongs to someone else. In this way the original three forms of unitary, federal, and confederate are reduced to one, unitary. The confederate form is a loose union of unitary states. The federal has been shown to be *un*federal. The earlier classification of forms between unitary and federal breaks down because they are established on a fiction. Nonetheless, the conventional distinction of actually federal or actually unitary remains important since it suggests degrees of centralization or relative decentralization that prevail in particular countries. Unbeknownst to most arch defenders of federalism it stands as a substitute for the more accurate concept of subsidiarity.

The term federalism still has some utility even though it does not have the legal content previously assumed. A consolation of some value for the friendly old term will be shown in a moment. First, however, it might be said that having exposed the fiction of federalism and the reality of *un*federalism, it may be useful to place the discussion in the context of "world federalism" discussed earlier. World federalism is presented as an alternative to world government. That proposal can be looked at now in a new light and it can be asked if its advocates truly know what they are saying. In the discussion in the chapter on the "state and groups" the responsibility of the state as the highest authority was pointed to as the only viable option even though advocates of change want to blame the state system for the world's problems. Politics is full of rhetoric that tries to achieve lofty goals while claiming to be something less or claiming something less and hiding loftier ambitions. If the World Federalists can help mitigate problems and improve the relations of states it is difficult to oppose since it is hard to contest the elimination of evil. The challenge is to be clear on principles and not to allow the rhetoric of indirection take over.

FEDERAL CONSOLATION AND THE FUTURE

Discovering the fiction of federalism and the reality of unfederalism may be unsettling. Showing the fictional character of a familiar description of reality does not change the reality. B. F. Skinner makes the consoling and wise observation, perhaps to calm those who get ruffled by some of the things he says, that "a theory does not change what it is a theory about." While that is not absolutely true since in the short term a theory can cause damage or harm, Skinner's comment is sufficiently true to merit consideration. His statement amounts to saying that one should not get terribly upset when first coming across something that deviates from previous assumptions. Learning something new can lead to a synthesis of understanding.

Federalism is not what it is usually described to be. Because a major element in the conventional stock of political science and American government is challenged in the comments on unfederalism a further word may help. To reveal its fictional use does not eliminate the Tenth Amendment. It only changes the perception or understanding of that amendment. The *un*federal understanding eliminates the basis for the old doctrine of states' rights according to which the states were thought to have, but never practiced, legal autonomy. From the new perception a more useful understanding can develop.

Federalism as Subsidiarity

In place of the old reading, the new insight on the Tenth Amendment places it in the context of subsidiarity. To maintain that "all powers not delegated . . . are reserved" says that a function or power ought to be assumed as best performed at a lower level before it is taken over by the national government. If the states can perform a function rather than the national government, they ought to do so; if the people can perform a function rather than the states, they likewise ought to do so. A subsidiarity reading of the Tenth Amendment is perfectly reasonable. It is far superior to the states' rights view of an unspecified area of jurisdiction absolutely off-limits to the national government. Subsidiarity addresses distribution of responsibilities and powers on the grounds of principles. Subsidiarity has a rational character about it instead of an emotional one. The study of politics should be a rational undertaking.

In the past when states' rights was proclaimed it was not practiced except in temporary obstreperous delaying fashion. Consequently, the only significant change in the new doctrine of *un*federalism is to admit the authority of national jurisdiction and to deny the doctrine of states' rights. When "federalism" is understood as no more than a statement of subsidiarity, there is no problem with its use. Indeed, understood as subsidiarity federalism should be a forceful reminder that decisions are to be rationally and not emotionally based.

States Continue to Exist - Make Use of Them!

It is important, if the national government has the right, as in any unitary system, to decide what powers shall be exercised nationally and what should in reason be left to local governments, that there be some mechanism whereby the national and local interests can be effectively debated before decisions are made. In the United States that mechanism is in the whole structure of the government ranging from the two houses of Congress, to the separation of powers, to the courts, to the electoral system, to the guaranteed existence of the states and their guarantee of a republican form of government. According to the latter guarantees (see Article IV of the Constitution), (1) states may not be divided up nor joined to another state without the state's consent, (2) the national government must come to the defense of the states, (3) the states may not be denied their equal representation in the Senate, and (4) their representational form of government shall be assured. The last point, the guarantee of a representational or "republican form of government," means at its essence that internally the states can continue to elect their governors and other state officials. In other words, the assurance of "a republican form of government" means that the Constitution guarantees the existence of the states and the continued election of governors even though it does not guarantee, according to unfederalism, that the states and governors will have anything to do. The better part of wisdom suggests, therefore, that since the existence of the states is fixed they ought to be utilized in the best way possible. That is subsidiarity.

Political Party Structure and Federalism

The whole governmental structure, the guarantees of states' existence, and the republic form of government have another mechanism whereby the national and local interests are aired effectively, namely, the political party system and the electoral process that accompanies it. American political parties, despite the appearance of being national in name and character, are in reality loose coalitions of state parties. The national parties are confederacies of state parties. The state parties are confederacies of local units of the party. This inverted pyramid of party organizational authority is a result of voter turnout as the ultimate electoral authority.

At the national level the parties come together only once every four years to nominate candidates for president and vice president. At those national conventions and afterwards the parties often openly demonstrate their confederate character by failing to unite behind the nominee, except perhaps nominally. When the state units or lower units of the party fail to back the "party" nominee extraordinary effort must be mounted to overcome the handicap. The recalcitrant lower units cannot normally be disciplined because that would only drive a larger wedge, adversely affecting future elections. The same lack of unity and lack of disciplined voting enforcement even applies within the Congress and state legislatures.

Party loyalty is not legally binding within legislative bodies and frequently legislators are found voting according to local wishes instead of according to the wishes of the party leadership. Sometimes elected representatives change party affiliation while still holding their office and look to be sustained, as they usually are, by their constituents at the next election. This reinforces the confederacy of the party system. The 2004 election witnessed, as in most presidential elections, numerous local parties "sitting out" the election by not working on behalf of the party candidate for the presidency. Prediction of elections is difficult for this reason. Subsequent to the election the lack of cohesiveness during the campaign makes governing more difficult in the relationship of the President with the Congress as well as the relationships within the legislative bodies.

Uniformity and Reality

The party system combines with the unitary (*un*federal) legal system to result in "federalism" in the overall political system. This system federalism is not a legal one; it is the product of the dynamic interaction of the unitary and confederate parts of the political system. This interactively realized federalism might not be a fully satisfactory substitute or a complete consolation for the familiar fiction. It does, however, identify more accurately a major means of local input on the decision process concerning national and local interests. That identification helps in insuring that decisions are as biased for local preference as is reasonable, a bias consistent with subsidiarity's assumption of the competence and integrity of the lower unit until demonstrated to be lacking. That competitive political parties contribute to the dynamic of "federalism in society" is demonstrated by what happens in one-party systems where centralization of responsibility often stifles genuine growth at any level.

The need for national uniformity was evident some years ago. Birth certificates, death certificates, and drivers' licenses seem the quintessence of local jurisdiction. Yet a Justice Department study in 1976 pointed out the need for uniform standards and procedures in these and other identification card areas. The need for uniformity flows from a growing criminal use of false identification in illegal immigration, check, credit card, other business frauds, welfare fraud, and drug abuse through false identification. The matter has only gotten worse. Billions of dollars a year are lost in identification theft, with welfare and related fraud being the least costly although the ones most likely to receive attention. National legislation is required because state action is piecemeal, producing gaps and loopholes that perpetuate the problem. Greater efforts and vigilance are needed following the 9/11 terrorist attack. Of course, as discussed earlier a complicated balance must be struck between freedom and security. Local governments, the national government, and the courts are still sorting out the appropriate response.

Uniformity is looked upon as being the first step in establishing a national identity card, feared as a type of internal passport and a threat to civil liberties, a mark of the national government in the pocket or purse of every individual in the United States. Perspective might remind us that the social security card and earlier even the dollar bill were regarded in the same way. The challenge over "national" currency was settled long ago while the social security card as a common identity number is in one respect the source of the need for a more sophisticated card. The social security number is used in banking, business, tax, and health matters to insure that unscrupulous persons do not cheat. It has been used for numerous other identification matters, even, though declining in practice, as faculty and student identification numbers at universities. The telephone company and the cable television company use it when the homeowner subscribes for service. Because of its wide use it has the same problems of counterfeiting and fraud as currency. These problems prompt the call for a better-designed card. National standards or a national card will be the result of necessity and not usurpation. Hopefully its introduction will be explained in a levelheaded manner instead of having a great national debate based on emotion.

Chapter 14

Forms Of Government: Functional Distribution Of Power

Functional distribution concerns governmental organization at a particular level rather than, as in the previous discussion, what organizational relationship exists between national and local government. All governments have certain common functional activities in making law, enforcing law, and judging violations of the law. Plato and Aristotle spoke of these separate activities. Another ancient, Polybius, the author of the earliest history of Rome, wrote of a separation of powers and a system of checks and balances, which, he explained, contributed to Rome's greatness. Locke and Montesquieu in modern times gave attention to the same topics. It is often claimed that separation of powers and checks and balances found their way into the United States Constitution through the later two authors, although historical experience played a substantial role.

Functional distribution is about how to handle the making, enforcing, and judging law. There are two principal ways of organizing the three functions. Separation of powers is one way. Fusion of powers is the second. French governmental reforms developed a third way, referred to as a "mixed" form. The mixed form also will be described, but primary attention will be focused on separation and fusion.

Separation Of Powers

Separation of powers means separate branches perform the different functions of government. The title usually associated with this system is "Presidential" taking that name from the separately elected, fixed-term president or executive with real, not just ceremonial, powers. Having such a president necessarily implies that there is also a separately elected, fixed-term legislature that has activities and responsibilities independent of the president. In addition to the legislative and executive branches, the system has an independent judiciary. That describes the United States national government and also its states.

In the United States, in nursery rhyme fashion, "Congress makes the law, the President enforces the law, and the Courts judge the law." The rhyme (Cf., poetry discussion: *supra* p. ix and *infra* p. 242) is based on the constitutional prescription that vests legislative power in the Congress, executive power in the President, and judicial power in the Courts as found in the opening passages of Articles I, II, and III, respectively, of the Constitution. A sharing and overlapping of powers is also prescribed in the Constitution, which produces the checks and balances that prevent undue concentration of power. As Aristotle, Polybius, and Cicero saw, the functional value of avoiding concentration is that law and policy reflect the wishes of the diversity of the community and not just the preferences of a few.

In the Constitution the President becomes involved in the making of law by signing or vetoing legislation. Also, the President is entitled to propose legislation to the Congress. The legislative body becomes involved in executive responsibilities by approving the establishment of executive departments and by the requirement that the Senate approve appointments of executive officers and that it ratify treaties. The courts are part of the checks and balances function by reason of their separate hearing of cases brought under the laws. The members of the courts are not separately elected and instead are nominated by the President and confirmed by the Senate. Once the appointment is completed, the Justices normally serve for life and thereby are independent from the other two branches. The same pattern is followed in other presidential systems. The pattern of separation of powers with checks and balances is also followed in the states within the United States except for variation on selection of the judiciary.

The constitutional prescriptions are all followed: Congress legislates, the Courts judge, and the President enforces. The system appears to work as prescribed. There are some impediments, however, when the Court exercises judicial review of laws passed by Congress, when the President in practice determines war more than the legally designated Congress, and when Congress intrudes on areas of executive prerogative. Thus questions arise about the precise designation of the relationship between the branches and the exact distribution of powers. The questions about who performs what role in the Presidential system will be addressed after first introducing the fusion system.

FUSION OF POWER

The fusion of powers, usually entitled the "Cabinet" or the "Parliamentary" system, means that the legislative, executive, and judicial powers are fused into one body, understood to be the cabinet or the parliament as a whole. England is the primary example of this form, but Canada, Japan, Germany, and many others could just as easily serve. A parliamentary body is normally composed of two houses, an upper house with generally ceremonial roles, and a lower house or "commons" where the fusion of powers is found in more specific form. The members of the commons are elected from separate districts and these members in turn elect a prime minister who exercises executive power. In the parliamentary form there is no independent supreme court that can veto acts of the prime minister or the commons. There is a separately operating court system but it lacks the judicial review function. This lack only reinforces the fusion of powers in the parliamentary body. There are some anomalies to this generalization about judicial review. Canada, for example, as mentioned in the previous chapter, lets its Supreme Court decide disputes between the provinces and the dominion government. The word "lets," however, maintains the fusion identity.

In the parliamentary system the prime minister has the power to call elections at will. While there are some limitations on this power it does constitute a major contrast to the regular fixed date of elections in the presidential form. The ability of the prime ministers to schedule the date of elections gives an advantage of selecting the most opportune time to take on opponents. This power, combined with a discipline on party members, gives the prime minister a leadership edge that presidents lack. This edge does not always work advantageously. Other factors make some parliamentary governments strong and some weak.

Strong and Weak Parliamentary Systems

In England, Canada, Japan, Germany, and other "strong" parliamentary systems, the fusion of powers is in actuality found in the prime minister and in the cabinet, which is appointed by the prime minister. The locus of power in the cabinet explains the alternate title sometimes given to this form. In contrast to the strong parliamentary system, there is a "weak" counterpart, as was the case in Italy, Portugal, and Spain until recent decades. The contrasting terms, weak and strong, do not refer to the degree of fusion or even whether fusion occurs. It refers to the location of the fusion. In the strong system the prime minister or the cabinet are the ones who really exercise power. In the weak system the locus of the fusion is more accurately found in the parliament or assembly. This parliamentary locus often means that power is diffusive or dormant. In the strong cabinet system, there is usually a two-party system so that one party has a true majority at any particular time. Third parties and coalitions do exist in the strong systems, but their existence does not disturb the major parties that continue to dominate the political scene.

In the weak systems it is precisely the existence of many parties that undermines any potential strength of the government. ("Strength" is understood to mean the ability to make and implement durable decisions.) In the weak systems it is not unusual to have three- or four-party coalitions forming a parliamentary majority to select a prime minister and cabinet. An inherent instability exists in such coalitions since at any time a party can withdraw support, causing the government to lose its majority, and the process of selecting a prime minister or cabinet must begin again or a new coalition must be formed by the incumbent prime minister. Changes in prime ministers frequently result in new elections. Surprisingly, perhaps, the results of new elections usually differ little from the previous distribution of members in the assembly, since the voters have no clearer focus of issues or candidates than earlier.

The wide variety of choices available to the voters in a multiparty system may be more representative in democratic terms. However, the lack of concentrated responsibility that comes from such a multiparty practice makes it less likely that public preferences will be translated into specific policy. As a result the system is in this manner less representative. In a two-party system where there is a choice between somewhat contrasting policies or, consistent with what was said in Chapter One, contrasting personalities, the voter preferences will ultimately be registered in the composition of the government as competing candidates play to what they perceive as public preferences. (A diagrammed sketch of the presidential and parliamentary systems and the strong and weak versions of the latter are provided in *Appendix I.*)

Presidential Versus Parliamentary Systems

When comparing the parliamentary system with the presidential system for respective advantages and disadvantages, it is only fair to use the strong form as the point of reference. Accordingly, the parliamentary system's advantages are unity, efficiency, and flexibility. At least these are purported advantages in comparison with the presidential system. In many descriptions the presidential system is noted for deadlock, delay, and buck-passing whereas in the parliamentary system there is by definition a unity between prime minister, cabinet, and commons. In this unity the prime minister and the cabinet set policy, which is ratified by the commons, since the prime minister's party dominates it. If the parliamentary body did not support the policy of the prime minister, there are two likely outcomes, either the prime minister resigns and is replaced by a new leader of the same majority, or the parliament is dissolved and new nationwide elections are held with the prime minister seeking to mount new majority support. The result is the quick restoration of unity.

In the presidential system, by contrast, the president at any given time may be of one political party and the legislature of the other party; the two houses may even be of opposite parties. The courts are independent of the other two branches, though the judges are always a mixture of individuals from both parties. In this system the policy objectives of the three branches may differ widely and the situation cannot be changed until possibly the next election. When the president and the congress are of two different parties, neither will voluntarily resign and seek to be replaced by someone from the other party to achieve unity within the government. Historical experience shows, however, that having the legislative and executive branches controlled by the same party is no guarantee of unity.

The unity in the parliamentary form produces the qualities mentioned earlier of efficiency, flexibility, and effectiveness. Unity means there is no delay in awaiting the approval of another branch. Once a policy is decided upon, it becomes policy. If the prime minister and cabinet are convinced of the merits and importance of a policy, it can be enacted without concern that some legislative chairperson can obstruct. The policy is implemented when it is needed in the judgment of the executive. Therefore the only limitation on the efficiency and effectiveness of policy is the timing and judgment of the prime minister.

In the parliamentary system responsibility is clear. Elections are contested on the basis of the performance or the potential performance of the candidate for prime minister. There is no confusion in this system of the candidate for the executive holding the legislature or the courts responsible for policy initiative or its failure. There is no exploiting of partisan differences for electoral advantage in one branch or the other. Individual members of the parliamentary body assume less importance than the party and its leadership. Consequently, the public is not distracted by colorful but impractical proposals by all sorts of candidates for legislative or executive offices who could never be held responsible even if elected. The same "irresponsible" posturing from the presidential system is in evidence in the multi-party parliamentary system also. When and if elected, the party or candidate in the separation of powers system who makes unreasonable promises can always blame everyone else for the inability to get the policy enacted. In the two-party parliamentary system, attention is focused sharply and clearly, which stands in contrast to the diffusion in the presidential system.

However, although there are grounds for the advantages just cited for the parliamentary system, they do not lead to an unqualified endorsement of the form. The advantages and disadvantages just discussed of the two systems may be classified as "theoretical." Theory is not to be taken lightly but theories differ in quality, especially weak empirical theory that is neither universal nor necessary. The problem with the theoretical advantages of the parliamentary over the presidential system is that, although the observations about the different partisan and structural configurations may be mostly accurate, the actual performance, the actual policy outcome, of the two systems is not noticeably different. The governments of England, Japan, Canada, Germany, or any other parliamentary example are not clearly superior in the governing function to that of the United States. In managing their economies, in handling foreign affairs, in establishing successful domestic policy, and in undertaking all that government does, one system does not have better results. One country may appear to handle one area of responsibility better than another country for a period of time. It may appear that a temporary better policy is a result of better governmental organization. Then the performance record shifts and there is no correlation between organization and policy. West Germany and Japan's "management" of their economies were for decades given as examples for the superiority of their governing systems and policies. A few years later that boast no longer held.

The political world remains serenely independent of the efforts of generations of politicians and scholarly experts claiming discovery of the formula for government problem solving. Political, social, economic, cultural, religious, and other variables no more conform to expert plans than the weather. That does not mean that organized and scientific efforts are useless. That conclusion is nonsensical. The science of politics may never be any more exact than the science of meteorology, but few of us would fly in the face of a hurricane warning any more than we would freely vote for a committed tyrant. Exact cause and effect relationships have not been established in the world of politics. Accordingly, there is no scientific basis for saying that one organization scheme is superior to another. There is no proven reason to abandon presidential for parliamentary government or vice versa. (That countries flirt with change from time to time, as the Philippines has, is understandable in light of the desire to improve performance. Changing from presidential to parliamentary forms, however, is no guarantee that a stronger government will be achieved. It may well end up, at least temporarily, with a far worse situation like a weak parliamentary system.)

Exaggerated notions of "separate but equal" branches often handicap descriptions of the presidential system. Attention is usually given to the rivalry of the branches over power and prominence, and to the ever-expected threat of erosion of the constitutionally intended equality. Much is written about "the era of Congress," or about the "imperial Presidency," or the "usurpation" of power by the courts. Scholars, news stories, radio and television, candidates, and officeholders all speak of the separate but equal branches and how one branch is intruding on or falling victim to another. These accounts of the rivalry overlook a simple point, namely, that the phrase "separate but equal" does not appear in the constitution. It is a derivative principle from the Constitution.

An equally acceptable deduction from the Constitution may be that the branches are "merged and co-dependent" because the checks and balances bring them together as much as separate them. Taking a step back from the tussling of the political world it is easy to observe that the United States does in fact have a government, it does have a foreign policy, it does have an economic policy, and it does have important domestic policies. The policy that the United States government has is not the policy of the President or the policy of the Congress, though it is most often described that way. It is the policy of the United States. No matter its genesis, through the initiative of the President or the insistence of the legislature, the policy in place is that of the United States.

An American looking at the policy of England, or France, or Germany does not ask about the policy of the Bundestag, or the Chancellor, or the Prime Minister, or the National Assembly, or the President, or the Commons, or the Queen. The interest is in the policy of France, or England, or Germany, or whatever country. That is how those whom it affects receive the policy. The recipients of foreign aid or Air Force bombs view the United States as responsible. In the same way, the American coal miner, the malnourished child, the criminal, the librarian, or the farmer is the recipient of policy even though there is an inclination to point to or credit one branch or another with dominant influence in the making of that policy. Because of this simple but often overlooked truth, the reality of governmental policy is missed and attention is focused on the theater of institutional and partisan competition.

Partisan competitors within the Congress and between the branches of the government often receive attention because of a symbiotic relationship with the media. Partisans exploit the media's desire for colorful stories of competition and the media casts partisans in a competitive role for the same purpose of attracting attention. The news is presented as a never-ending civics lecture about what Congress, the President, or the Court did to each other. Little excitement would be generated by the norm, that is, in saying, "Government works," or "the branches of the government continue to cooperate." Hearing about the contrast of colorful trees stirs more attention than pointing to the beautiful forest of cooperation. Thus most news about the American political system is both widely listened to and very misleading.

A Shift Within The Presidential System

Because of the attention to rivalry over the assumed constitutional roles even the slightest change is presented as alarming. A seeming shift in the decisions of the courts or an alteration in the management of the war powers or in foreign policy management or changed responsibility for direction of the economy are reported as threats to the constitutional structure. If the classic separation of powers is referred to as a "nursery rhyme" or if it is said that a quite different division of labor exists, the suggestion is regarded as heretical.

Nonetheless, a shift in the original division of labor has occurred. If a proper comparison between the parliamentary and presidential systems is to be made the shift must be understood. And, it must be understood as not endangering the system. Instead, it is strengthened. Forty years ago is was becoming obvious, as Gabriel Almond commented (*Comparative Politics,* 129), that the courts, Congress, and the executive had established a division of labor quite different from the classic separation of power-checks and balances doctrine. The courts had become lawmaker because of judicial review, the executive had become the principal source of the rules through initiating most new proposals, and the Congress was not so much lawmaker as the ratifier of the rules and spokesperson for interests. Those role descriptions are commonplace except that the standard nursery rhyme depiction remains.

The role changes have been under way for more than a century, going back to the policy initiatives of William McKinley, Theodore Roosevelt, and Woodrow Wilson, if not earlier by Lincoln. In a formal way Congress insisted on presidential initiative in the Budget and Accounting Act of 1921 by shifting responsibility for organizing and managing the budget to the President. Congress had struggled with compiling the budget, with all its policy implications, for many years and directed in 1921 that henceforth the responsibility and the accompanying opportunities were to be the President's. Subsequent changes have not altered this relationship except that in 1974 Congress set up the Congressional Budget Office as a means for it to better respond to the full implications of the executive budget. Although adjustments continue, the basic relationship enacted in 1921 is fully entrenched.

The President's role as chief policy initiator in foreign affairs started even before the nineteenth century, so there should be little surprise that twentieth-century Presidents request a "declaration" of war only after a state of war already exists. By one count the United States has been engaged in more than 100 overseas military actions since 1789, and Congress has declared war only five times. Since the Second World War there has been no formal declaration of war. Often it is best to have no formal declarations to avoid undue escalation. Congress has a sizeable role in appropriating the funds to finance foreign and defense policy and in questioning those policies, although admittedly its role is one of response, not initiative. The two wars with Iraq showed presidential initiative and the seeming manipulation of Congress and the public to support the effort. In subsequent formal and public questioning of what is said to have been misleading commencement of war it is difficult to sort out the partisan from the truly legitimate congressional reexamination. The Executive and Congress are acutely aware that false steps can result in the diminution of important future initiatives.

In addition to foreign policy and defense initiatives and to general policy initiatives, the President is looked upon as chief director of the economy because of the general economic tone set by the budget and other economic policies. It is most fitting that the President be the principal source of policy because, as discussed in Chapter Three, policy or legislative initiative is an effort at "predicting the future." New policy can change or affect only the future. No policy can change the past or the present. Predicting future policy requirements is a task better suited for one person than by many. One person, the President, can be responsible for coordinating and giving priorities to all sorts of studies, analyses, forecasts, trends, and speculations. If such a task were given to two legislative bodies composed of 435 and 100 members, respectively, broken down into endless committees and subcommittees, the ability to reach unity through majority agreements would be handicapped to the point of inaction.

Presidents may not always be successful in having coherent programs of integrated priorities explained adequately to the public and to the Congress as seems to have been the case with the Social Security reforms proposed in 2005. Presidents by form begin with unity and it is this initial unity that the Congress seemed to recognize in mandating the executive preparation of the budget and in allowing the President the policy initiative in over a century of development in more and more areas. The Congress itself could only approach this necessary unity if it organized itself more strictly along parliamentary lines, something that would be especially difficult to do with two separately empowered and independent legislative houses. The president must convince the Congress of the wisdom of the program and budgets and Congress can demur. If Congress alters the president's program the resulting disagreement can be the subject of the next election as the competing candidates establish their rhetorical contrasts.

The shift in policy responsibilities from those in the original constitution does not leave Congress bereft of power. It is, or can be at least, more powerful. The size and composition of the modern Congress makes it better suited for some tasks than others. The design of the division of labor between three branches as it has evolved intends that each be effective and efficient and that they not duplicate one another. Furthermore, good design intends that effort not be wasted in endless disputes over jurisdiction. On the congressional side, this design is fulfilled by the organizational scheme, whereby the hundreds of members of both houses are divided into many committees and subcommittees. Each committee and subcommittee is specialized in its tasks. To have policy initiated in the Congress would be slow and frustrating. There is no one individual within the structure of Congress who can compel the hundreds of others to support a proposal. Each member within his or her respective chambers, as each chamber itself, is equal. The congressional structure, which cannot be used effectively for policy initiatives, is used more effectively to respond or react to the policy proposal made from outside the structure. To review the initiatives from the executive, to give oversight to the implementation of already agreed upon policies, is an effective use of the congressional structure. Acting in this manner Congress serves as the legitimizer of the initiatives taken by the President. With Congress exercising this review or oversight function, the presidential system maintains both the policy leadership and responsiveness.

The review function of Congress is not a rhetorical construct designed to salvage the separations of powers-checks and balances doctrine. Vietnam, Watergate, Iran-Contra, 9/11 Intelligence failure, Challenger explosion, August 2003 Power Grid blackout, the second Iraq war and occupation, the extent of domestic surveillance by the National Security Agency under authority of the Patriot Act or by discretion of the President are areas where congressional investigations assume a legitimate prominence. Frequently congressional hearings are of a mundane nature, looking at presidential proposals, budget or otherwise, and judging them on past performance. Celebrated high-profile hearings are for the larger purpose of establishing a public record as a basis for possible significant change.

In their role as the closest link to the public, members of Congress regularly receive reports from their constituents, whether large business or single individuals, on the effectiveness of rules and regulations to which the public is subject. The member's response ranges from polite letters and no action to inquiries that produce results. In this process Congress is attuned to what has or has not worked. Congress may follow public input with inquiries to appropriate administrative agencies, depending on the response hearings may be held, and official testimony may be sought if the preliminary inquiries do not produce satisfactory results. Occasionally Congress suggests improvements. If the problems are not abated there are a number of options: to hold further hearings, withhold funds, require changes, or drop the program. The last option based on substantial evidence gives leverage when a committee seeks information from agencies. The 2006 congressional elections appear to point in the direction of closer oversight and mandated changes in several presidential policies, in foreign, military, and domestic policies.

Members of the House and of the Senate tell their constituents that they have "introduced" certain important legislative proposals of obvious local benefit. This gives the impression that they and their chamber are taking the lead in making policy. Of course what they say is technically true, except that the substance of the proposal came from elsewhere. Today there is no such thing as a congressional policy initiative being imposed on the President. Various members of the Congress might propose health programs, tax programs, weapons programs, farm programs, or banking programs. If they do not receive the approbation of the President and sizeable input from the affected department the proposals go nowhere.

The changed basic function of Congress means that in performing the review function, Congress "sees to it that the law is faithfully executed." Though the latter is a phrase from the presidential article of the Constitution, today it describes Congress's basic role. The reversal of the original division of labor is completed. No constitutional amendment was passed to bring about this new division of labor. Almost two centuries of evolution produced it. For years political science and history books have reported on the evolution of the powers: the growth of the presidency, the early emergence of the Court, and changed responsibility of the Congress. Those changes are usually viewed separately and not as a whole government and thus give the impression of usurpation and rivalry. A composite picture over time tells of more cooperative adjustment to new circumstances. Seen not separately but in terms of functional efficiency, the changed division of labor reflects a continuation and strengthening of the original constitutional design where no one branch has an undue concentration of power. Law and policy still reflect the wishes of the diversity of the community. The evolutionary change maintains stability, separation of powers, and checks and balances.

Fusion Or Separation: Which Is Better?

The British form of government differs from that of the United States. Fusion of legislative, executive, and judicial powers means there is no question about who is lawmaker, who initiates policy, or who can or cannot veto legislation. The Prime Minister and the party hierarchy are responsible for policy leadership. There is no question about the role of the Commons or any other body. If the public is dissatisfied, the party in power is replaced at the next election. There is one thing, however, that the parliamentary system lacks. It lacks an institutional base for a review function.

By definition no distribution of legislative, executive, and judicial roles into separate institutions exists in the parliamentary system. Parliament has only one electoral contact point with the public. More contact would give legitimacy, or legal standing, to one part of the government independently checking on another. Because this is lacking there is no formal means for reviewing the acts of the government except through general elections. Haphazard questioning by the minority party and occasional pesky hesitation by the House of Lords is not a substitute for formal review. The House of Lords is, for the most part, impotent and has been made increasingly so by recent reforms. Minority party challenges have the weakness of being discounted as partisan. Elections as a basis for review have all the merits and limitations of democracy in general. They constitute only the broadest form of public commentary.

Thus, the presidential system has an advantage in the comparison of the two systems. In England a scandal may bring about a resignation and eventually a report. A challenged foreign policy may bring about much political carping. In neither case will there be a formal and systematic review by a legally independent body free of partisan determinations. Non-independent reviews, from the minority party or the majority party, are never free of such suspicions. Ironically, while an independent review board on a particular issue may undertake and accomplish a completely objective study, the lack of a partisan sting will almost ensure only a long delayed effectiveness.

In contrast, it is political considerations that can keep the legally independent review from becoming partisan in the United States. An investigation by one branch of any other branch can backfire politically if not conducted in an objective and unbiased manner. The Watergate hearings had that burden and succeeded because of the painstaking efforts to be politically neutral while emphasizing legality. From the break-in to the ultimate Nixon resignation, almost twenty-six months elapsed. Much of those twenty-six months were spent in making sure that all individuals involved were accorded due process of law, whether before the courts or in the congressional hearings. More recently, the impeachment proceedings against President Clinton were so tinged with partisanship, whether rightly or wrongly, that the Senate trial failed to come close to the two-thirds vote required for conviction.

In England no impeachment proceeding can ever occur. If ever there were a Watergate-type episode, an almost immediate resignation would come about. Eventually there would be a "white paper" or even a "blue book" report by a special panel giving the details of who did what to whom for what purpose. The resignation would come so quickly, however, and the report would be completed so much later that there is no assurance either that the report would be widely read or that due process would be served in the first instance.

Israel is an example of a parliamentary form where the generalization about the lack an effective independent review does not apply. There have been a number of occasions where independent commissions have been established to investigate an incident and the government has agreed to abide by the findings of the review. In these instances the investigation and report follow within months and the government acts swiftly. Rather than a breakthrough that could serve as an example for other parliamentary systems the Israeli experience with the independent commission appears to be an exception flowing from the tremendous political pressures related to Israel's special domestic and international circumstances. Similar conditions do not prevail in other parliamentary systems where an independent review might seem appropriate and consequently the likelihood of the government agreeing to such terms is highly unlikely. The presidential system, therefore, formally retains the advantage over the parliamentary system of having an institutionalized base for the review function. The merit of the presidential system is that it provides an institutional answer to the classical question, *Quis custodiet ipsos custodes*? (Who guards the guardians themselves?)

Another advantage in the presidential system is that the public has more opportunities to actively express its views than the public does in the parliamentary system. In the United States separate elections over varying election periods are held for members of both houses of the Congress and for the presidency itself. Unquestionably it is difficult to interpret the results of the many elections conducted at staggered time periods of two years, six years, and four years. The staggered elections may explain why policy directions and preferences are so mixed. That diversity, however, is in step with the pluralism of the country. The diversity remains even when the same political party dominates the three branches, because the timing of elections and appointments ensures that different expressions of public sentiment are registered regularly. In contrast, the parliamentary system is more a blunt instrument of public views. The options are yes or no on a timetable of about every five years or at the government's determination. The public's voice is clear at the election but subsequent preferences are more indistinct.

Is One System Better than Another?

Despite the initial theoretical advantages in the British system, the American system has advantages of the review function and more frequent elections. Nonetheless there is no greater success in one country over the other. The final conclusion, then, about the better form must be country-specific and only marginally form-specific. In other words, the best form is the one that best suits the needs and experience of the particular country. It may be possible to make valid generalizations about governmental forms, but only to the extent of considering their applicability within a particular country, not cross-nationally. The applicability, or more likely the inapplicability, of the presidential form within England or the parliamentary form within the United States can be discussed as generalized forms, but the universal advantage of one form over the other is a topic of limited practical value. There may indeed be few generalized forms—two or three—but even at that the country-specific qualities make hazardous any attempt at final conclusions about a theoretically "best" form. The case of France and its "mixed form" clearly illustrates this point.

The Mixed Form: France

The mixed form combines elements of the parliamentary and the presidential systems. The principal example is the French government under the Fifth Republic, the constitutional reform instituted by Charles de Gaulle in 1958. (President Marcos attempted a similar adjustment to the Philippine constitution during his reign. It was scuttled quickly at his demise. The Philippine's latest effort at structural reform of a mixed nature is still unsettled.) In the mixed form there is a separately elected, fixed-term, strong president and there is at the same time a separately elected parliamentary body which elects a prime minister or premier. The president nominates and, in effect, appoints the prime minister and the cabinet, which thereby suggests great concentration of power in the executive, but it also suggests potential problems.

Even though selected at elections a month apart, the French president and the majority of the National Assembly were initially of the same political party and so the structural tension seemingly built into the system was untested. In time the theoretical political split between the President and the National Assembly occurred. Sometimes there was a conservative (Gaullist) president and a liberal (Socialist) Assembly and at other times the other way around. The French called this "cohabitation." The French presidency has a seven-year term, longer than any other democratic Western nation, and may stand for reelection. Even when the political split occurs cooperation between the two institutions remain. No one side wants to take full responsibility for a breakdown even though there is the usual maneuvering and finger pointing for political advantage.

The mixed form's strong presidency seems to have eradicated the fundamental weakness of the previous Fourth Republic with its parliamentary, multiparty system. The earlier form was a primary example, as was Italy, of the weak parliamentary form with frequent changes of coalition governments. A chief contribution of the strong presidency and the mixed form has been the polarization of issues and candidates, so that France is now for the most part a two-party system. (As in all two-party systems, even the United States, there are third and minor party efforts that occasionally stir multiparty turbulence.) The five-year gap between the presidential election and the next required Assembly election and then two years until the beginning of the next presidential round appears to contribute to the two-party polarization rather than the revival of multiparty factions.

The mixed form with its strong long-term presidency and multi-member parliamentary Assembly may have an appeal, which the other two forms lack. With the strong executive and the legitimizing character of the Assembly, the French form may serve as a model for developing countries that are in need of both qualities. As even the French experience has shown, however, it takes decades of experience to see the full workings of the form. The design may have theoretical value yet its effectiveness may only be the result of practicalities of the French political culture. It may be easy to observe and tabulate political phenomena but the full implications of the political culture and its interaction with the political structure are much more difficult to comprehend.

Conclusive judgments on the mixed form will require more experience. Special note was made earlier on the unique role of the review function in the presidential system and its lack in the parliamentary form. Experience has not shown a review role to be easily adapted in the mixed form. Review evolved in the American form through two centuries of experience. It may be that the unique political relationship between the executive and the Assembly in France precludes a strong review role. As in the parliamentary system there may be a limitation on effective review because of concerns with the perception of partisanship. Nonetheless the French form may have sufficient durability to merit use elsewhere.

Chapter 15 Political Change

POLITICAL SCIENCE, CHANGE, AND THREE EARLIER VIEWS

Change is intrinsic to politics. Study of the political world, as mentioned in the Introduction, differs from study of the physical world in the nature of the types of change examined. In the physical world, trees lose their leaves, volcanoes erupt, atoms split, rivers overflow. Changes in the physical world usually follow patterns that eventually enable scientists to observe and explain them. In the physical world patterns are such that scientists can produce change, like cloning or developing a hybrid plant, which makes further change and understanding possible. Change in the political world is entirely different.

Accomplishments, if they are such, in the physical sciences have made outer space weapons possible. There are no equally available political insights to make the use of new weapons predictable or controllable. That there is a discoverable fixed pattern to human behavior is an assumption made by social scientists. Yet human behavior is subject to variations. How an individual voter will behave may be predictable but insignificant, how one ruler will behave is unpredictable and significant. That is a salient point about the "science" of human behavior.

We call political science a science to distinguish it from haphazard, unsystematic, random, and purely emotional explanations of political activity. Common sense, which hopefully all persons enjoy, needs to be informed with alternatives, underlying motivators, long-range goals, short-term irritants, and personal predilections that influence social and political events. The consideration of all these factors distinguishes the scientific effort at politics from common sense. If common sense is careful, however, it is no different from what goes by the name of political science. These remarks may disenchant many who want to see political scientists contribute to control of the political world, to avoid wars, to stabilize the economy, to eradicate poverty, to eliminate crime, and to establish justice. If human beings can succeed in all the marvelous technical advances with which the twenty-first century is familiar, can they not look to the same success in the social and political world? The answer to that question is found in all the previous chapters. Depending on the principles that one finds most appropriate, the possibility and desirability of controlling change will vary.

Three basic approaches to change were contained in the chapters on the state (Chapters Four through Seven). Accordingly, change is either completely beyond human control, completely subject to human control, or only partially subject to human control. The proposition that change is beyond human control maintains that some physical or mystical force determines human behavior. As a result of this determined behavior, all that human knowledge can do is discover the underlying forces and be subjectively reconciled to them. The perspectives that human behavior is determined economically, biologically, racially, spiritually, psychologically, astrologically, sexually, or in some other way reflect that proposition.

Alternately, the idea that political change is completely subject to human control is not greatly different from its verbal opposite. If behavior is merely a function of personal and collective choice, then the consequences can be as totalitarian as under the determinative aegis. If by definition there is nothing that ought not and cannot be subject to human control, then the principle by which the control is exercised is potentially as determinative, though more flattering, than the overtly authoritarian positions. Looked at in this way, democracy is viewed as an ideology of complete human control.

Democracy is not an ideology if it holds to the proposition that it is but a form under a constitutional standard of fixed principles. If there are certain unchanging values not totally subject to human manipulation, though subject to understanding and debate, then democracy presents itself as approximating what is best instead of the determinant of what is good. In approximating what is best, allowance is made for being wrong, which allowance is precisely the place of rights, constitutional procedures, and minority privileges in non-ideological, democratic systems. This non-ideological view accepts change as being only partially subject to human control.

The raw data about political change gives conflicting impressions about what describes the political world. As constitutional change is observed, the impressions of partial, complete, and uncontrolled change are all confirmed. Public referenda on constitutional amendments, seemingly spontaneous revolutions, coups d'etat, guerrilla warfare, and sociologically determined structural alterations are all forms of broad constitutional change. Some forms suggest the stable growth of partial change, some suggest complete radical change, and others suggest uncontrolled change.

Appearance And Reality Of Change

Revolutionary Change

Appearances of complete and uncontrolled change are deceptive. Revolutions give the impression of such change, however, they are usually neither complete nor uncontrolled. The Russian revolution of 1917 appeared to be a sharply radical break with the past and to be under the direction of one leadership group. In actuality the leadership took advantage of forces of change already in motion and succeeded only by reestablishing an authoritarian practice under a new name. The new leaders went on to direct other changes but only with much struggle over a long period of time. Purges, great loss of life, shifts in general policy, and contradictory alliances marked the first fifty years of the Russian revolution. The Soviet Union, which was set up as a result of the Russian revolution, collapsed in 1991 although by that time many of the early alterations in government and society had become more permanent.

Many commentators have a romantic notion of the sweeping changes and the idiosyncratic nature of particular revolutions. Yet, revolutions are all alike. Whether occurring in the United States, China, Cuba, France, Nicaragua, or Russia, the appearance of great change combines with a reality of slow growth. As subsidiarity and the relationship between political structure and political culture show, the substratum of society and its institutional arrangements change only incrementally. Attempts at more than incremental change put strain on the overall system and slow down change despite initial appearances. The "cultural revolution" of the 1960s in China and during the same period in the United States are examples of that truth. The late 1970s and early 1980s in both countries saw a shift back in the direction of the original pre-revolutionary position.

The French revolution had its "restoration" beginning not with the abdication of Napoleon but with his arrival. In England the revolution of the "Commonwealth" under Cromwell had its own restoration, and radical historians interpret the American Revolution in the same way. The phenomenon of restoration has led to the generalization that "revolutions restore the tyranny which they replace." It is fairly easy to survey most revolutions and find this truth.

Change in the Developing World

In so-called "developing world" nations of Africa, Asia, Latin America and the Middle East, a restrained rate for change is evident. A look below the surface of most "great" changes shows traditional folkways, superstitions, festivals, primitive health and hygiene practices, rural centered life, and centuries old belief systems that continue and restrain change. That does not mean to imply that developed or "advanced" countries are superior to or better than those that are developing or "primitive." Better or worse, good or bad, do not apply in this context, as was also the case earlier in comparing political structures and political cultures. Development should be recognize for what it often is – visual rhetoric. Neon signs, traffic congestion, and urban crowding in a capital city of a developing nation give an impression of change that deeper examination belies.

Electoral Change

Even in dramatic election changes, the contrast of appearance and reality obtains. In France and Spain in the early 1980s with new socialist governments substantial changes were expected and yet the results were less dramatic than the rhetoric of the election. In the United States it was the conservative, anticommunist, Richard Nixon who opened relations with China and entered into detente with the Soviet Union. When the presidency changes from an incumbent Republican to Democratic the style changes, the language of concern changes, the promises for the future change, but concrete policies change only slowly. Governments are on "iron rails" where the tracks are laid out hundreds of miles ahead such that deviation from the established path can only occur after extensive planning and preparation. Train wrecks help no one. Media prediction of great change with the rise of a challenger to high office creates an audience, but is an unreliable forecast.

DEMOCRACY, CHANGE, AND SCRUTINY

Change is least likely in revolutionary regimes and more likely in stable ones because stable democracies can tolerate change. Revolutionary and authoritarian regimes, whether in Europe, Africa, Asia, Latin America, or the Middle East, are always on the brink. They see any unsanctioned change as threatening their position and so they become intolerant.

When the United Nations was founded in 1945, two thirds of its fifty-one members were democracies. Today the total membership has almost quadrupled to 192, while the percentage of democracies has decreased. The United Nations has gradually changed as an institution and yet within the member states less change occurs. If democracy reflects freedom within a country there is both more of it now than in 1945 and there is less of it. It is undesirable to make a science of political change because the patterns are unreliable. It is likewise unreliable to speak of exact "degrees of freedom," of tolerating change within countries. Still, one group, Freedom House of New York, has attempted to rank countries in a "Comparative Survey of Freedom."

Surveys by Freedom House from 1972 until 2002 show a remarkable degree of stability. Countries are ranked as free, partly free, and not free by a score on a survey of liberties and freedoms as practiced in the respective countries. While the measurement and judgment of the criteria of freedom are open to question, the constancy of oppression or freedom belies more repeated bombardment from other sources of change for the better. Amnesty International makes similar surveys of oppression and degrees of oppression in the world. While Amnesty International's and Freedom House's reports do not match, what is striking is that these entirely different groups agree on the importance of freedom within countries. It is degrees of freedom that tolerate or repress change.

The greatest challenge to freedom and change in any country is internal, instead of external. Enemies attacking from the outside are identifiable, responses can be mounted, rebuttals prepared. Challenges from the inside use freedom to undermine it. That was the concern in the *Schenck*, *Dennis*, *Yates*, and other freedom of expression cases mentioned in Chapter Ten. The threat to undermine freedom on a larger scale and with more imminent dangers occurred in many countries in the last half of the twentieth century in the liberation movements. In the twenty-first century similar movements have become terrorists. The routine remains the same, however, with opposition groups taking advantage of what freedoms currently exist so that a free or partly free regime is overthrown and replaced with one that soon becomes "not free." "Liberationists," particularly the followers, promise freedom but upon success they find that circumstances cannot permit implementation. As in Cuba, with no elections in more than forty years, and in other countries with fleeting experiences of freedom and openness, the day of liberation comes slowly or not at all.

The United States and other stable democracies manage to tolerate such internal challenges. Campus disruptions and protests of the late 1960s and early 1970s in the United States, France, West Germany, and elsewhere have gone the way of other anomic and nonassociational interest groups (as discussed in relation to group dynamics in Chapter Eleven). The multiplier of time eroded the initial popularity of these media-highlighted glamour groups of disruption. With time their membership either faded from sight or became part of diverse established institutions. The change that these groups paraded either proved ephemeral or, perhaps surprisingly, became incorporated into policy and public life (as pointed out with respect to SDS in Chapter One). Today's threats of change from hidden terrorist groups are not handled with equanimity because both the members and goals are unknown. On the basis of past experience the threat will fade, but the toll taken cannot yet be fully fathomed.

Scrutiny

In unstable countries, before time can erode a "liberation" effort or terrorist movement's strength, a regime is overthrown or the military steps in for fear of weakness. Nineteenth and twentieth century history shows that neither liberationist nor military action produces real change. The name of the regime might change and external alliances may be altered, but the internal consequences remain a problem. In Cuba change has indeed occurred, social services, health, and education have allegedly improved, but these improvements alone cannot be the sole test. The "costs" as well as "benefits" have to be weighed and cost data is never available. Concealing costs became a lesson new tyrants learned from the Hitler experience where the atrocities became known and the conclusions of history could be drawn. Consequently no latter-day Hitler will allow the records to be opened for public scrutiny. Refugees and the dead may be approximated. Those who vanish, and the stifled cannot be numbered. Stable regimes are scrutinized all the time. They change as a result of the scrutiny. The Watergate experience in the United States is an example of scrutiny that produced stable change. Scandals, embarrassments, failed policies, unfulfilled promises, and credibility gaps here and elsewhere have defeated incumbents and changed governments. Lessons are learned from such experiences, policies change, and new scrutiny occurs. Stable regimes accept their fallibility and as a result change is a manifestation of strength. Authoritarian and unstable regimes accept neither fallibility nor change and become obsessed with their own weakness.

Slowness Of Change

Although change has an acceptable place in stable systems it does not always come easily or quickly, as the discussion of formal constitutional growth showed. Failure to amend the national Constitution does not preclude lesser change in the states on in ordinary legislation accomplishing the same objective. Change is therefore frequently a matter of many opportunities instead of a single option that becomes accepted or fails. Often change is a matter of perception as in whether the glass is half full or half empty.

In open and stable systems change is dynamic and multifaceted, constitutional growth is both formal and informal and yet remains true to the original spirit of constitutionalism. In unstable and authoritarian regimes change is static and as controlled as possible. The United States Constitution has several provisions on presidential selection, inauguration, limit on terms, succession, and disability, yet the political parties, which are not even mentioned, manage the basic selection process. The subtleties of growth processes work differently according to the circumstances.

Change Without Success

There have been numerous proposals for changing the United States Constitution that have not reached a formal stage. The failed proposals are as much an expression of change as the successful ones. Unsuccessful efforts confirm that the system is dynamic. Attempted but unrealized change often produces better understanding. In contrast to static systems, those open to peaceful change have less need for repressive measures. There may be frustration for many individuals who have worked for years on a proposal that is never accepted, but the frustration cannot compare to reform seekers in repressive regimes who are precluded from even making a proposal.

For many years some individuals seriously proposed amending the Constitution to eliminate the Electoral College in the presidential election process and replacing it with direct popular election. Occasionally that proposal gets to the stage of being introduced in Congress, yet it has never reached the point of passing even one house. There are many convincing arguments against the Electoral College and in favor of popular election. The arguments appear persuasive but not compelling. There are many uncertainties about the proposal, uncertainties relating to the conduct of presidential campaigns, the impact on the President's relationship with Congress, the insulation of the President from the dynamics of group competition, whether the length of the term of the President should be altered at the same time, and whether the President should be limited to one term in office. These uncertainties contribute to the inertia that controls current practice. Nonetheless, every discussion generates new understandings of current practice, which is a benefit from the effort, even if only a byproduct.

Change After Crisis

Because of the questions about the ramifications of change in the presidential electoral process, the proposal for eliminating the Electoral College is not likely to get any further unless there is a crisis. The Bush/Gore fiasco in Florida in the 2000 election had the potential for being a crisis yet it produced little immediate concrete change in the balloting system. Six years later the country still struggles with finding a foolproof ballot. The prospect of crisis in itself tells much about the process of change. We like to think of change as planned and rational, especially in stable democratic systems, yet in a certain respect stable systems are no different from unstable and authoritarian ones because necessary change is usually a response to a crisis instead of the product of calm foresight. The main difference, however, is that in the stable systems the changes are often anticipated and discussed openly in the society years before the crisis. The earlier discussions prepare society for the changes when crisis occur. It is similar to talking about a new roof several years prior to the midwinter leak and then calmly responding to the crisis when it occurs.

New Understanding

The discussion of change focuses on a "shift" in existing practices. Equal attention should be given to the "existing practices." Often a change is celebrated or advocated when the existing procedures are not fully understood. That is the case even for revolutions since it is easy to tear down and more difficult to build. The lack of full understanding does not apply just to the large issues for society. There are longstanding institutional arrangements that are not fully understood. A consideration of these gaps points out what can be done about change and how this reflection on change is related to the earlier discussion of "principles of politics." The discussion of the parliamentary and presidential forms of government showed the gap in knowledge about institutional arrangements. An understanding of the principles of government and of the state can help to ameliorate concerns.

The discussion of forms can be usefully employed to analyze intermediate and local forms of government. In the United States the state level of government utilizes only the presidential form as seen in their separately elected governor, legislature, and independent court system. At the more local level in the United States the presidential and parliamentary forms are seen respectively in the mayor-council and the council-manager systems as well as in the school board and superintendent relationships. In Canada the parliamentary form predominates at the intermediate, or provincial, level with no more justification for it than the opposite domination at the state level in the United States. In many countries outside of the United States, the strong mayor, similar to the French presidency, predominates as the local form. Why the pattern of intermediate and local forms exists has no clear explanation except imitation. Why within countries there is so little variety and change where there is no compulsion is not clear. Institutional traditions have as solid a grip on local government forms as folkways in more primitive cultures. Change and the lack of change are equally inexplicable.

Where Principles Fit

Practical principles of fusion and separation and theoretical principles of the necessity of rule are involved in the forms of government. Common forces are at work at all levels of government in all countries. Choices are made about the best means to accomplish effective rule. Change or the lack of change can be considered as the response to principles in sustaining a particular course of action. Support or resistance to change is not separate from the principles for which change is advocated. Change can be neither accepted nor rejected on its own account. Change for the sake of change is no more justified than unreasoned resistance. The reflective consideration of change is the place for principles in political science. Principles give an accurate and workable understanding of the functioning of government and the changes that are constantly occurring.

In the Introduction it was pointed out that there is a parallel contrast between the scientific and popular or "poetic" explanations of the physical and political worlds. The argument is that scientific explanations are more accurate and valuable that poetic ones. The astronaut may poetically speak of the sunrise even though scientifically the astronaut knows that the earth rotates, which give the illusion of sunrise. In that context the scientific and poetic explanations do not interfere with each other. In the political world the "scientific" and poetic were posited to be in conflict and that contrast does make a difference. It is now possible to point out that the consequences of the contrast in the political realm are at the same time both more important and less important than originally suggested.

That, contrary to the poetic understanding, democracy (in Chapter One) is not "popular control" is not so much a scientific explanation as an elaboration of what popular control means and what alternate views on democracy are. "Federalism is a fiction" (Chapter Thirteen) is not so much a scientific wonder as an explication of the fundamental subsidiarity character of federalism, which everyone has an original intuitive grasp of anyway. That separation of powers (Chapter Fourteen) does not work exactly as imagined does not greatly disturb anyone since the system still works and voters do not debate such technical issues. The most important consequence of examining these conflicting views is that a better understanding of politics is gained in the process. This improvement is illustrative of the potential for personal growth that is an important ingredient in the popular selection view of democracy. The simple poetic positions are not so much rejected as improved upon and deepened.

What is found while examining democracy, federalism, separation of powers, rights, and group interaction is that there are certain basic principles of politics that affect all aspects of political life. The nature and end of the state, the origin and justification of political authority, the nature and place of justice, and the concept of subsidiarity and constitutionalism, all have a profound effect on particular political activities. It is on these principles that change and variation in political activities can be evaluated. It is imperative to remember, however, that all the principles come with alternatives. Popular control is seen as a myth and as replaceable with popular selection. Collectivism is opposed to Individualism, and both are opposed by the Common Good. In other words there are principles and there are also choices about principles.

That there are good and bad principles, acceptable and unacceptable principles, is not to be denied. What is good or unacceptable is what study, reflection, reading, and inquiry help discern. There are no ready-made answers in the back of the political science book. Right choice is still the order of political inquiry. Knowledge of the facts is pursued so that understanding of the application of principles is accurate. Unorganized facts alone accomplish nothing and there is always the concern that they will be organized by default according to an unarticulated principle.

CONCLUSION: GOVERNMENT WORKS

There should be no great disappointment if this book is completed without a definitive knowledge of a number of aspects of the political world. After years of study that complete knowledge will still be elusive since the political and social world is like so much unencumbered quicksilver, shiny, alluring, and difficult to grasp. It seems appropriate to recall the observation by Einstein that "politics is infinitely more complex than physics and relativity." Einstein was using the word "infinitely" with a well-informed sense of its implications.

With Einstein's proposition as a backdrop, to come away with knowledge of some principles that offer a coherent explanation of the political world is no slight accomplishment. The principles may be in the form of not entirely resolved competing theories, but if the world is looked at in those terms there is a greater chance of understanding what is going on than if the world is approached from a single perspective. The experiences of the Western and the non-Western world support the broader approach of competing theories.

What can be concluded from this principle approach to politics outlined in this book is that government does make sense, even though there is much disagreement on what approach to understanding makes the most sense. Different individuals and different groups of people have widely divergent views on the nature and end of the state and the origin and justification of political authority. That those views can be grouped into three general perspectives should help immensely in coming to an appreciation of politics. Knowing the principles that separate people does not automatically or quickly lead to reconciliation. The principles are too divergent and deeply held to be reconciled easily. This knowledge, however, will lead to respect for the differences. From respect comes tolerance and tolerance is the beginning of civility, the first virtue of politics. With the realization of civility, political prudence, the virtue by which all principles are implemented, has a chance to be effective.

Appendix

APPENDIX "A"

Simple System:

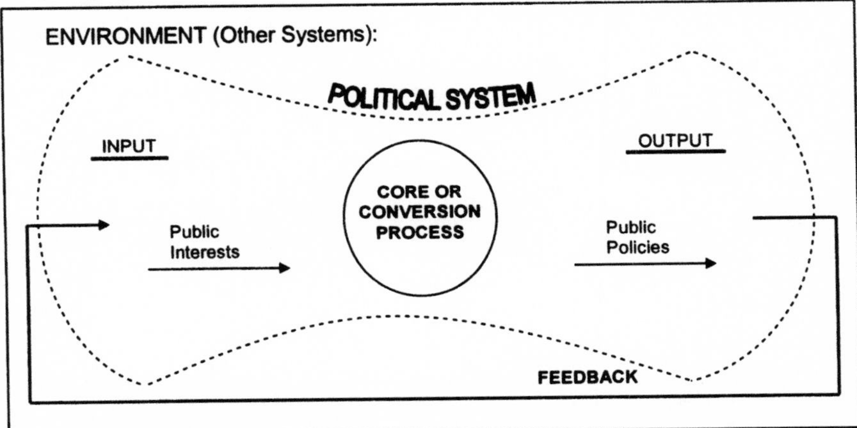

More Detailed System:

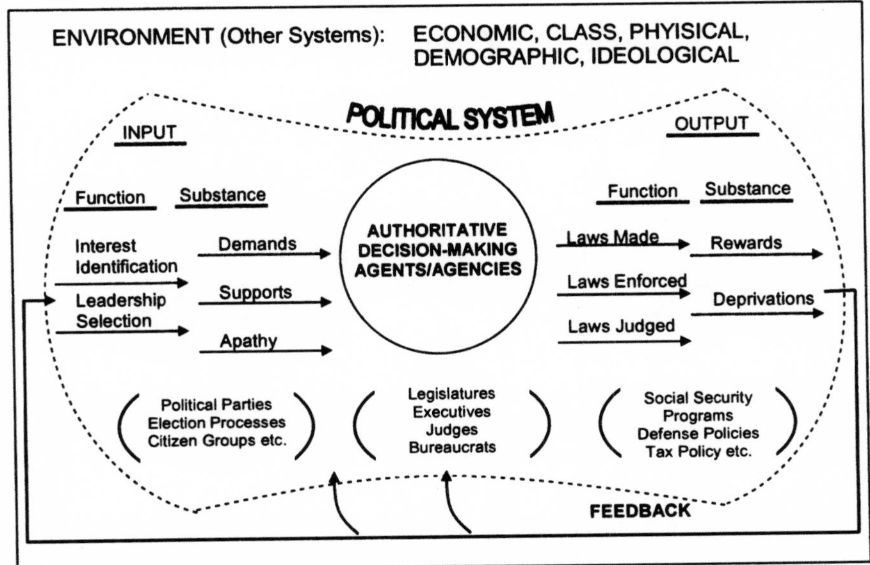

APPENDIX "B"

	A	B	C
Hobbes	warlike	a function of will or desire	Absolute government
Locke	~~"peaceful"~~ warlike "inconvenient"	a function of reason or awareness	"Limited government"
Rousseau	peaceful	a function of accidents/ general will	Enslavement/ Chains

Historical or Story Version: (A → B → C)

(A) Original state of nature →	(B) Contract or agreement to set up →	(C) State or condition following the contract

Philosophical Intention of the Above "Story" Line: (A ← B ← C)

(A) To avoid (or approximate for Rousseau) the state of nature	← (B) Which humans agree to, at least implicitly or tacitly	← (C) To describe or be reconciled to the existing condition

APPENDIX "C"

THE PURPOSE OF THE STATE IN SYMBOLS

Anarchism

$W=0$
(The state should not exist.)

COLLECTIVISM

$W > P1 + P2 + \ldots + Pn > Pi$
(The whole is greater than the sum of the parts <u>and</u> it is greater than any individual part.)

(That is, parts are subordinated to the whole.)

INDIVIDUALISM

$W = P1 + P2 + \ldots + Pn$
(The whole is equal to the sum of the parts.)

(Only the parts are real.)

COMMON GOOD

$W > P1 + PS + \ldots + Pn \ngtr Pi$
(The whole is greater than the sum of the parts but not greater than any individual part.)

(Parts are not subordinated to the whole.)

APPENDIX "D"

PRINCIPLE APPROACH TO RIGHTS

RIGHT	PRINCIPLE - assume the integrity of:	COROLLARY – circumstances which limit the right, i.e., the principle applies unless
1. Life	1. Murderer's life	1. Inability to protect society from future harm
2. Speech	2. Whatever is said	2. "Clear and present danger" (Schenck Case) or "Grave and probable danger" (Dennis Case)
3. Press	3. Whatever is printed or produced	3. Libel (after the fact) Obscenity (after the fact)
4. Privacy	4. Personal possessions and surroundings	4. National security is threatened
5. Criminal procedure	5. Innocent person	5. Proven guilty
6. Property ownership	6. Individual ownership	6. Necessary task is not performed adequately

APPENDIX "E"

I. The church is no different from other voluntary associations

State

Voluntary Associations

=

Church

II. There is a wall of Separation between church and state

State

WALL OF SEPARATION

Church

(Relegates religion to the refuse heap of arbitrary private whim)

III. The church is higher than the state

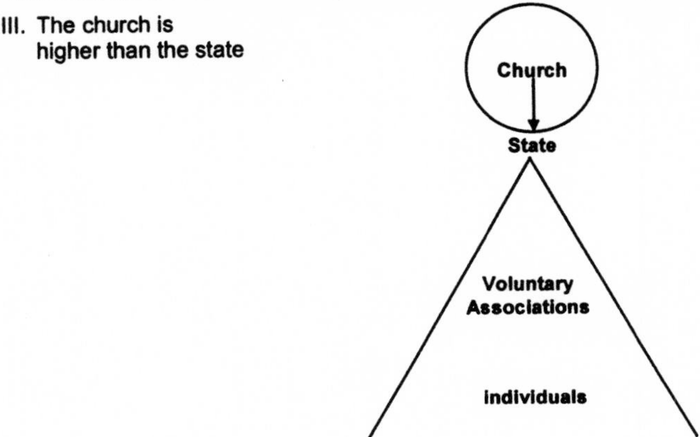

APPENDIX "F"

A. Direct Sun/Moon
The church should
rule the state

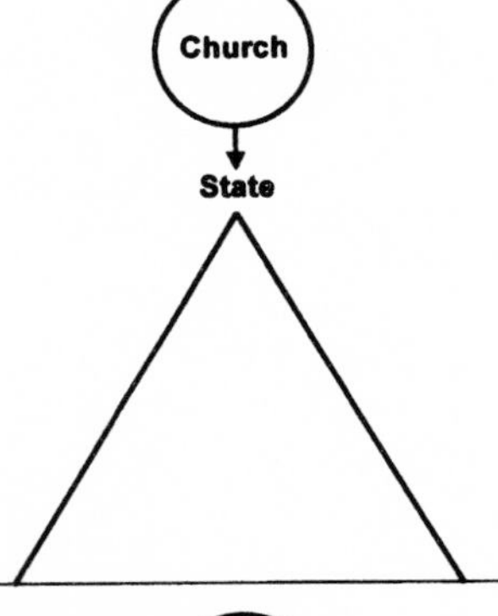

B. Disjunctive: The
church should rule the
state but only if it is
in the majority

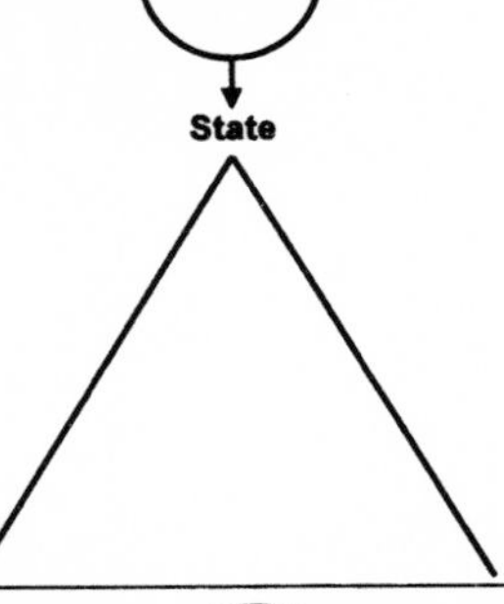

C. "Indirect"/Unitary: The
church rules its individual
members, who in turn
tell the state what to do

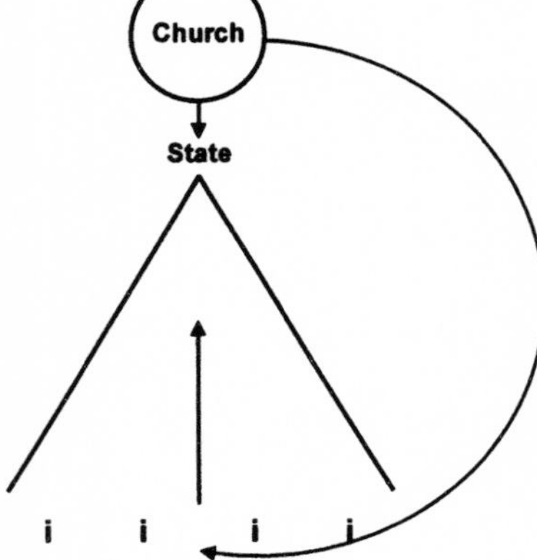

APPENDIX "G"

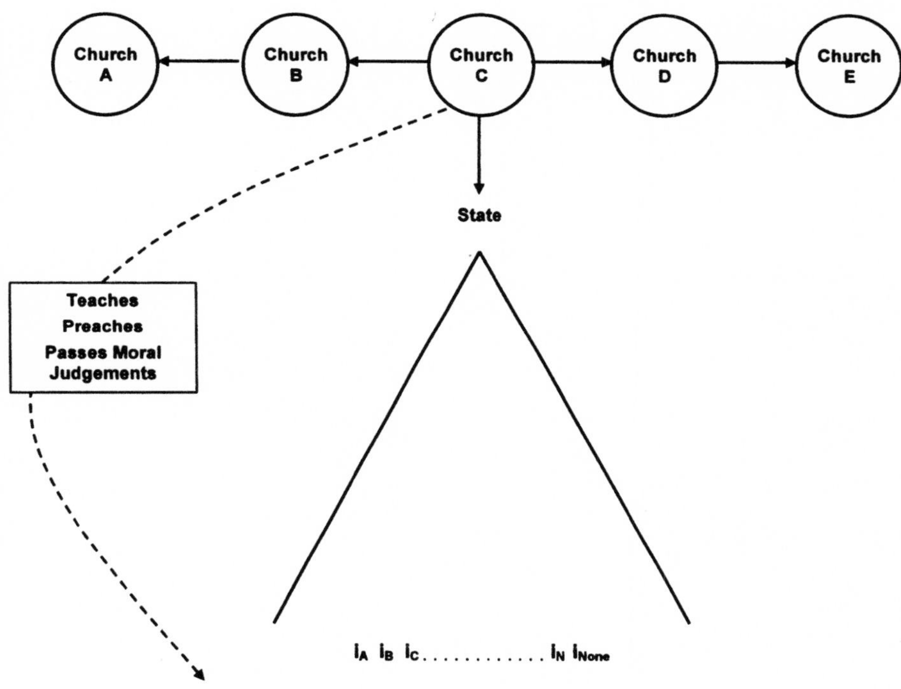

Church C respects Church A, B, D, . . . N and individuals A, B, C, D, . . . N and None.

Church C teaches, preaches, and passes moral judgment and attempts to reach individuals in this way. It does not by law impose its beliefs on other churches or other individuals. Church C has much to do.

APPENDIX "H"

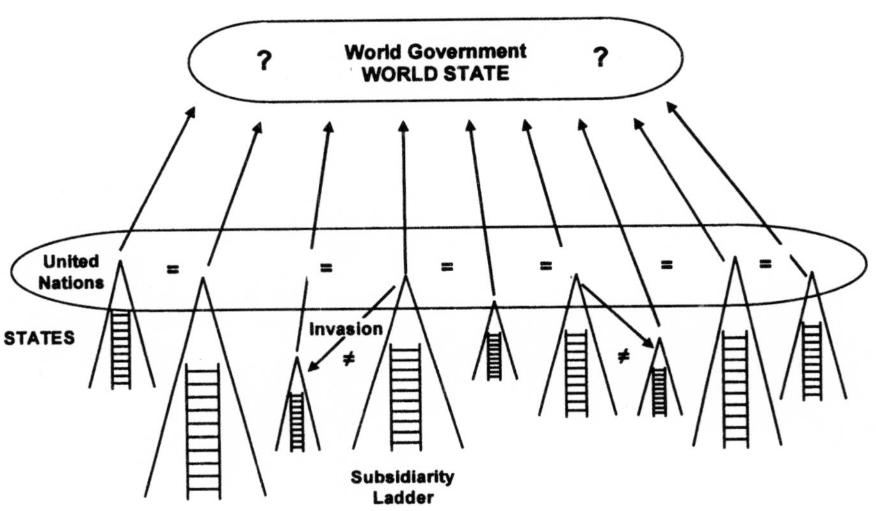
? ? ? ? ? ? ? ?
?
World Government
WORLD STATE
?
United
Nations
=
=
=
=
=
=
STATES
Invasion
≠
≠
Subsidiarity
Ladder

APPENDIX "I"

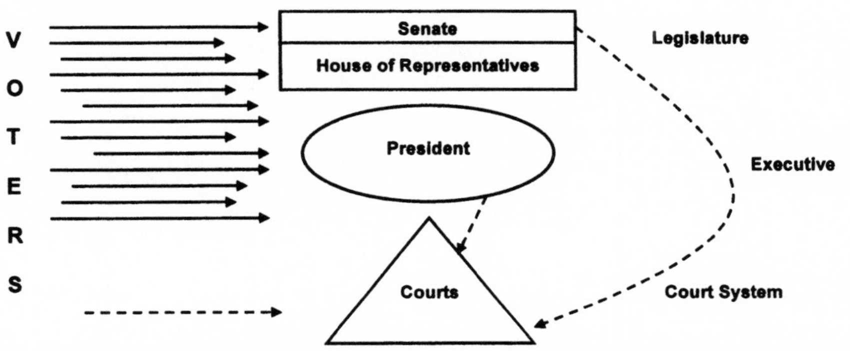
PRESIDENTIAL SYSTEM
V
O
T
E
R
S
Senate
House of Representatives
Legislature
President
Executive
Courts
Court System

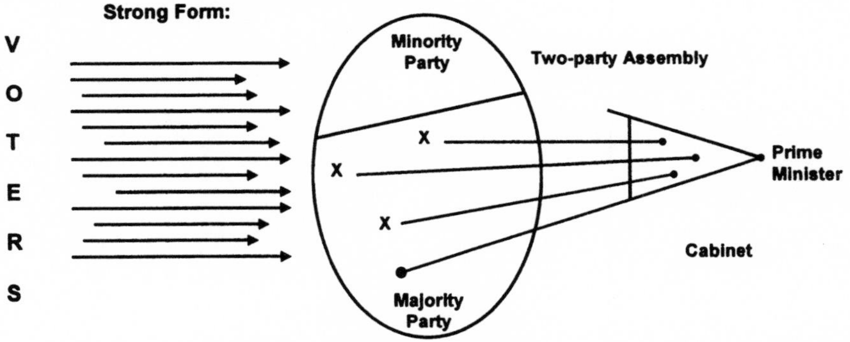
PARLIAMENTARY/CABINET SYSTEM
Strong Form:
V
O
T
E
R
S
Minority Party
Two-party Assembly
X
X
X
Prime Minister
Cabinet
Majority Party

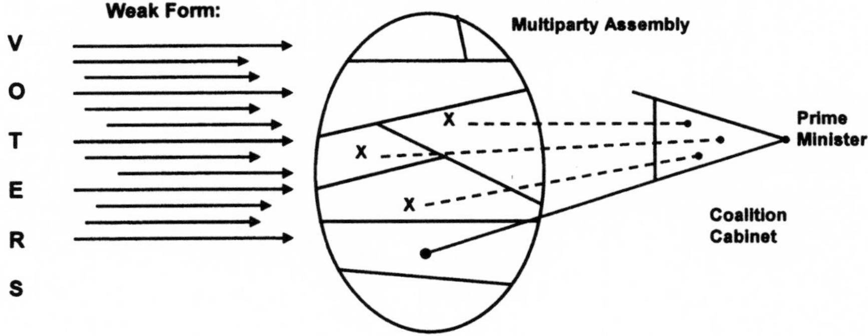
Weak Form:
V
O
T
E
R
S
Multiparty Assembly
X
X
X
Prime Minister
Coalition Cabinet

Bibliography

Almond, Gabriel and G Bingham Powell, Jr., *Comparative Politics* (Boston: Little Brown, 1966)

Ardrey, Robert, *The Social Contract* (New York: Atheneum, 1970)

Aristotle, *Ethics* (Great Books of the Western World, Volume 9, Chicago: Encyclopaedia Britannica, Inc., 1952)

_______ *Politics* (Great Books of the Western World, Volume 9, Chicago: Encyclopaedia Britannica, Inc., 1952)

Baradat, Leon, *Political Ideologies: Their Origin and Impact* (Upper Saddle River, N.J.: Prentice-Hall Inc, 2005)

Beard, Charles, *An Economic Interpretation of the Constitution of the United States* (Union, N.J.: Lawbook Exchange, 2001)

Belloc, Hilaire and Cecil Chesterton, *The Party System* (London: S. Swift Co., 1911)

Brecht, Arnold, *Political Theory; The Foundation of Twentieth Century Political Thought* (Princeton: Princeton University Press, 1959)

Brown, Robert, *Charles Beard and the Constitution* (Westport, Conn.: Greenwood Press, 1979)

Burke, Edmund, "Speech to the Electors of Bristol," November 3, 1774, *The Works of Edmund Burke* (London)

Coles, Robert, *The Secular Mind* (Princeton: Princeton University Press, 1999)

Connerly, Ward, *Creating Equal: My fight Against Race Preferences* (San Francisco: Encounter Books, 2000)

Dahl, Robert, *Who Governs?* (New Haven: Yale University Press, 2005) see also *Dilemmas of Pluralist Democracy: Autonomy versus Control* (New Haven: Yale University Press, 1982)

Dante, *De Monarchia* (Great Books of the Western World, Volume 9, Chicago: Encyclopaedia Britannica, Inc., 1952)

Dworkin, Ronald, *Taking Rights Seriously* (Cambridge: Harvard University Press, 1977)

Easton, David, *The Political System* (Chicago: University of Chicago Press, 1981)

Ebenstein, William, *Great Political Thinkers* (Fort Worth: Harcourt College Publishers, 2000)

Ellul, Jacques, *The Political Illusion* (New York: Vintage Books, 1972)

Fuller, R. Buckminister, *Utopia or Oblivion* (New York: Overlook Press, 1972)

Galbraith, John Kenneth, *The New Industrial State* (Boston: Houghton Mifflin, 1985)

Hamburger, Philip, *Separation of Church and State* (Cambridge: Harvard University Press, 2002)

Hayden, Tom, "Port Huron Statement," see Kenneth M Dolbeare, *Directions in American Political Thought* (New York: John Wiley, 1969) see also by Hayden *The American Future* (Boston: South End Press, 1980)

Hegel, *The Philosophy of Law* (Great Books of the Western World, Volume 46, Chicago: Encyclopaedia Britannica, Inc., 1952)

Hobbes, Thomas, *Leviathan* (Great Books of the Western World, Volume 23, Chicago: Encyclopaedia Britannica, Inc., 1952)

Irish, Marian D, James Prothro, and Richard Richardson, *Politics of American Democracy* (Upper Saddle River, N.J.: Pearson Education, Inc. 1981)

Isaak, Alan, *Scope and Methods in Political Science* (Homewood, IL: Dorsey Press, 1985)

Jaffa, Harry V, *Equality and Liberty* (New York: Oxford University Press, 1985)

Levy, Guenther, *The Catholic Church and Nazi Germany* (Boulder, Colorado: De Capo Press, 2000)

Lindblom, Charles E, *Politics and Markets* (New York: Basic Books, 1977)

Locke, John, *Second Treatise on Government* (Numerous editions)

Machiavelli, *The Prince* (Great Books of the Western World, Volume 23, Chicago: Encyclopaedia Britannica, Inc., 1952)

Malraux, Andre, *La Condition Humaine* (London: University of London Press, 1968) as *Man's* Fate (Franklin Center, PA: Franklin Library, 1980)

McCoy, Charles A. and John Playford, *Apolitical Politics* (New York: Thomas Y Crowell, 1967)

Mill, John Stuart, *On Liberty* (Great Books of the Western World, Volume 43, Chicago: Encyclopaedia Britannica, Inc., 1952)

Morgenthau, Hans, *Politics Among Nations* (Boston: McGraw-Hill Higher Education, 2006)

Morris, Desmond, *The Human Zoo* (New York: A Dell Book, 1969) also *The Naked Ape* (New York: McGraw-Hill, 1967)

Paine, Thomas, "Common Sense," *Life and Works of Thomas Paine*

Plato, *The Republic* (Great Books of the Western World, Volume 7, Chicago: Encyclopaedia Britannica, Inc., 1952)

Rawls, John, *A Theory of Justice* (Cambridge: Harvard University Press, 2005)

Riker, William H, "Six Books in Search of a Subject or Does Federalism Exist and Does It Matter?" *Comparative Politics* , October 1969)

Roche, John P, "The Founding Fathers: A Reform Caucus In Action," *American Political Science Review*, March 1962

Rousseau, *Discourses on the Origin of Inequality* (Great Books of the Western World, Volume 38, Chicago: Encyclopaedia Britannica, Inc., 1952)

_______ *On the Origin and Foundations of the Inequality of Mankind* (Great Books of the Western World, Volume 38, Chicago: Encyclopaedia Britannica, Inc., 1952)

_______ *Social Contract* (Great Books of the Western World, Volume 38, Chicago: Encyclopaedia Britannica, Inc., 1952)

Samuelson, Paul, *Economics* (New York: McGraw-Hill, 1997)

Schmandt, Henry J and Paul G Steinbicker, *Fundamentals of Government* (Milwaukee: Bruce Publishing, 1963)

Schumacher, E F, *Small Is Beautiful* (New York: HarperPerennial, 1989)

Skinner, B F, *Beyond Freedom and Dignity* (Indianapolis: Hackett Publishers, Chapter 34, 2002)

_______ *Walden Two* (New York: Macmillian, 1976)

Somit, Albert and Joseph Tanenhaus, *The Development of American Political Science* (New York: Irvington Publishers 1982)

Spencer, Herbert, *Social Statics* ,See: Ebenstein, William, Great Political Thinker (Fort Worth: Harcourt College Publishers, 2000)

Taft, William Howard, *Our Chief Magistrate and His Powers* (Durham, N.C., Carolina Academic Press, 2002)

Index